EVERY NIGHT &
EVERY MORN

Portraits of Asian, Hispanic, Jewish, African-American,

and Native-American Recipients

of the Congressional Medal of Honor

John L. Johnson (ed.)

Thanks

John John 13 OCT 10

EVERY NIGHT & EVERY MORN

Portraits of Asian, Hispanic, Jewish, African-American,
and Native-American Recipients
of the Congressional Medal of Honor

Tristan Press
Winston-Salem, North Carolina

Published by:
TRISTAN PRESS
1937 Gaston Street
Winston-Salem, North Carolina 27103

While the author has made every effort to provide accurate telephone numbers and Internet addresses at the time of publication, neither the publisher nor the author assumes any responsibility for errors, or for changes that occur after publication.

EVERY NIGHT & EVERY MORN

Interior photos courtesy of www.homeofheroes.com
Book design by Sigrid Hall
Printed by Keiger Printing

This book is an original publication of TRISTAN PRESS.

First Edition: October, 2007

ISBN: 0-9799572-0-6
ISBN: 978-0-9799572-0-8

An application to register this book for cataloging has been submitted to the Library of Congress.

PRINTED IN THE UNITED STATES OF AMERICA

10 9 8 7 6 5 4 3 2 1

Every Night & every Morn
Some to Misery are Born
Every Night & every Morn
Some are Born to sweet delight
Some are Born to sweet delight
Some are Born to Endless Night
God Appears and God is Light

(William Blake)

To my wife, Francine, and son, Tristan

TABLE OF CONTENTS

ACKNOWLEDGMENTS

Without the support, encouragement, and assistance of a number of individuals and organizations, this book would not have been completed. First, I wish to thank the National Council of La Raza and the Cherokee Nation for their financial support. When solicited for financial help to begin this book, these two organizations quickly and generously stepped forward when others did not.

I also wish to thank the Congressional Medal of Honor Society and especially Victoria Kueck, Caro Cepregi, Laurie Jowdy, and Timothy Frank for their advice and help and especially for making available the Society's invaluable archives.

I gratefully acknowledge those who read and provided advice valuable technical assistance in the development of the book, including Dr. Julie Edelson, for her excellent editorial guidance and assistance, Ms. Sigrid Hall for design and layout, Mr. Rudy Anderson for media relations, and Scott Crockett of Keiger Printing. All of these friends and colleagues gave generously of their time and knowledge to my work. I wish to thank homeofheroes.com for giving permission to use some of their photographs of Medal of Honor recipients.

And a very special thanks to Dr. Peggy Valentine, dean, School of Health Sciences at Winston-Salem State University for her *most persistent* and ever present encouragement, as well as, giving me the necessary time and space to complete this book.

Last, I wish to thank my colleagues Ms. Julia Simmons and Floyd Davis at Dr. J's House of Soul Food for their encouragement and support.

37TH CONGRESS,
2D SESSION.

S. R. 82.

IN THE SENATE OF THE UNITED STATES.

MAY 13, 1862.

Mr. WILSON, of Massachusetts, from the Committee on Military Affairs and the Militia, reported the following joint resolution; which was read and passed to a second reading.

JOINT RESOLUTION

To provide for the presentation of "medals of honor" to the enlisted men of the army and volunteer forces who have or who may distinguish themselves in battle during the present rebellion.

1   *Resolved by the Senate and House of Representatives*
2   *of the United States of America in Congress assembled,*
3   That the President of the United State be, and he is hereby,
4   authorized to cause two thousand "medals of honor" to be
5   prepared with suitable emblematic devices, and to direct that
6   the same be presented, in the name of Congress, to such non-
7   commissioned officers and privates as shall most distinguish
8   themselves by their gallantry in action, and other soldier-like
9   qualities, during the present insurrection. And that the sum
10   of ten thousand dollars be, and the same is hereby, appropri-
11   ated out of any money in the treasury not otherwise appro-
12   priated, for the purpose of carrying this resolution into effect.

MEDAL OF HONOR FACTS

The first Medal of Honor (MOH) was awarded March 25, 1863, to Private Jacob Parrott and five others. Since then, there have been:

- 3,463 Medals of Honor awarded

- for 3,458 separate acts of heroism

- performed by 3,444 individuals (including 9 "Unknowns").

- 111 Medal of Honor recipients are living.

- 45% of the living recipients earned their medals more than 50 years ago, while serving in WWII (35) or Korea (15).

- 61 living recipients performed actions in Vietnam.

- Both Persian Gulf Wars produced 4 recipients, awarded posthumously.

The current youngest living recipient is Gordon R. Roberts, aged 56, born June 14, 1950.

Among America's ethnic and religious minorities to receive the medal are:

- 87 African Americans [1],

- 40 Hispanic Americans,

- 32 Asian/Pacific Islanders,

- 22 Native Americans [2],

- 18 Jewish Americans [3], and

- 1 female

CHAPTER 1

INTRODUCTION

Why This Book?

One day in 2001, while standing on a corner in downtown Atlanta waiting for the street light to change, I overhead several high school students having a conversation about career opportunities in the military. It was soon apparent they had little knowledge about the military, as their discussion was full of misconceptions and outright errors. The most prominent emerged when one of the students expressed serious doubts about whether any African American had ever received the Congressional Medal of Honor, the country's highest award for military valor. The student's misstatement was quickly accepted as fact by his friends as they boarded the bus. I wanted to intervene and tell them they were wrong; that African Americans have served proudly in all branches of the armed services and in all of the country's wars, even before the Revolutionary War, before the United States became a country, and *many* were awarded the Medal of Honor, but it was too late—the bus pulled away.

Watching it leave, I wondered how many other young men and women were ignorant of the fact that more than 87 African Americans have received the Medal of Honor dating back to the Civil War. Later, I wondered whether students of other ethnic and religious minorities knew about their histories and the role members of their communities had played in the military history of the United States: 40 Hispanic Americans, 32 Asian Americans, 20 Native Americans, 18 Jewish Americans, and one female have received the Medal of Honor.

In the following days, I asked every high school and college student I met what they knew about the Medal of Honor and its recipients. I was disappointed to learn most knew little or nothing at all about the award. A large number had never heard of the Medal of Honor or knew what it represented. That was the day I received my *calling* to prepare this book.

This book attempts to identify and to profile all known African Americans, Hispanic Americans, Asian Americans, Pacific Islanders, Jewish Americans, Native Americans, and the one female who were awarded the Medal of Honor since 1863, when it was first established by Congress during the American Civil War. My hope is that the book fulfills three main goals. First, it should serve as a reliable educational tool and resource guide that delineates the roles, deeds, and sacrifices Americans of various ethnic and religious minority groups have made in service to their country during time of war. Second, by learning about the actions that resulted in the award of the Medal, I hope that we come to honor their bravery and valor individually for the sacrifices made in the defense of their country. Last, I want to put a human face on these individuals, many of whom are like us—simple, ordinary people who found themselves in extraordinary and unimaginable circumstances, which, in turn, resulted in extraordinary and unimaginably heroic actions.

The main body of this book presents portraits of each Medal recipient. Each includes a photograph, if available; surprisingly, photos were available for most, including recipients from the Civil War period. As anticipated, photos of earlier periods are usually of poorer quality. When photos were not available, the seal or the coat of arms of the armed service in which the recipient served —Army, Navy, Air Force, Marine Corps, Coast Guard—was used in its place.

Each profile also contains basic biographical and military service information: generally, the recipient's military rank and organization or unit, branch of service, date and place of the action where the Medal was earned, and date and place the recipient entered the service . Each profile also contains the *Citation*, which describes in detail the actions and circumstances for which the Medal was awarded[5]. A surprise finding is that some files are full of errors, in most cases, created by the military. In more than one instance, names are misspelled, dates inaccurate, and the photographs wrong. However, because these are the *official records* of the Department of Defense, I did not correct or update them but rather notified the Department of Defense of the discrepancies.

The last component of the profile, the epilogue, summarizes what is known about recipients and their lives prior to, during, and after receiving the Medal. Some of these narratives are extensive, while for others, we know nothing or next to nothing. For example, as expected, information was very limited or nonexistent for recipients from the Civil War period, as most were slaves prior to the war, with little documentation about their lives. During the war, the military had only the most essential information for these men, including enlistment and medical records. After the war, recipients melted back into a highly segregated society, and most became "lost to history." I elaborate on the problems of lack of information in the section called *Limitation*.

Method

In preparing this book, I had very few resources, which presented several major obstacles. I could not travel to military and government archives, military bases, federal and state court houses, libraries, cemeteries, schools, museums, or presidential libraries to review documents and records. Nor could I interview recipients, relatives, friends, and associates to collect information.

Instead, I relied on a single source: the archives and files of the Congressional Medal of Honor Society (CMOHS). The CMOHS is located on a historic decommissioned navy aircraft carrier, the USS Yorktown, moored in the harbor of Charleston, South Carolina. A nonprofit organization that receives no government financial support, one of its primary missions is to serve as a repository of information on each Medal of Honor recipient.

These archives proved an invaluable resource, although the amount of information for each recipient varies widely. Most files contained a wealth of information, including copies of enlistment records (see APPENDIX A), Medal of Honor recommendation forms (see APPENDIX B), enlistment records, court documents (see AAPENDIX C), bonus applications, medical records, notes on scraps of paper, newspaper clippings, letters from recipients and/or their families, friends, and associates, and research notes prepared by historians, researchers, and authors. Other recipient files, however, had minimal information and, in most cases, just a single form (Recipient Data Form), indicating that the individual had received the Medal.

Not only does the quantity of information vary considerably, the physical quality is also inconsistent, usually related to the quality of the photocopier used, illegible handwriting, and missing information, such as magazine articles and newspaper clippings.

The contents of each recipient's file were photocopied and analyzed, and the result of the analysis used to prepare this book.

Summary and Findings

Review and analysis of recipient files produced a number of both expected and unanticipated results. Documents revealed persistent and longstanding institutional bigotry and racism in the US military, particularly as it relates to awarding the Medal of Honor. For example, after a heroic deed deserving of the Medal, commanders would instead recommend a lower award. In other cases, evidence shows that commanders blatantly overturned recommendation for the Medal because of the nominee's color or race or religious affiliation. In still other cases, recommendations would become conveniently *lost* or *misplaced*. In most of these cases, the Medal would eventually be awarded after appeals and efforts by relatives, usually in conjunction with public officials, and after many years, or when the recipient had died.

Reviewing each recipient's file was like taking a journey back in time. Documents reveal that most Medal recipients were ordinary Americans from small towns and traditional families, who entered the military to serve their country and to seek better opportunities for themselves and their families. Some were slaves, and others, recent immigrants from Mexico and Europe. Others, mainly Asians and Native Americans, were born American citizens but treated as second-class citizens. All had one thing in common—a desire to demonstrate to the rest of America their loyalty and patriotism and their earned right to be considered and treated as equal citizens.

Before receiving the Medal, some recipients were rascals and scoundrels, with unimpressive military records and numerous court martials; some even deserted and were imprisoned. For some, there were no happy endings after receiving the Medal. Because of their race, society outside of the military did not or could not give them the recognition they deserved, and they seemed to encounter one humiliation after another.

In several cases, recipients hid their true ethnic identity while in the service, only to have it revealed after their death, when relatives and friends came forward. The concept of *passing* for another or, usually, the majority race has always been prevalent, especially in a society where racial identity opens or closes doors for opportunity and advancement. Consequently, the exact number of recipients who were Black, Indian, Asian, Hispanic, or Jewish may never be known.

The most significant and moving aspect of reviewing the files was to

10

read the first-hand accounts of extraordinary and selfless acts of heroism that would eventually lead these men and one female to receive the Medal of Honor.

Limitations

This book has several limitations. First, the information used to develop the portraits is derived from primarily one source, the archives of the Congressional Medal of Honor Society. It is always preferable to have as many primary sources as possible when conducting research. However, lack of resources prevented conducting interviews or access to other data sources, such as the National Archives; Department of Defense Archives; National Military Personnel Center; cemetery, court, school, and church records.

Second, while some recipient files contain a wealth of information, most do not. Consequently, the depth and breadth of the narratives for some recipients cannot meet my original goal of presenting full descriptions for all.

Third, the numerous errors found in the source documents and their poor quality could not be changed, as they constitute the *official record*, which, by definition, cannot be corrected or updated. The poor quality of some documents, caused by age, defective photocopy machines, and/or illegible handwriting made information hard to discern and sometimes impossible to report. Last, there were many instances in recipient files when newspaper clippings, magazine articles, and other publications lacked proper citations; for example, copies of newspaper articles were missing authors, dates, and sources.

I hope to address these and other limitations of the book in future by enlisting the help of you, the reader.

A Lifelong Project & Legacy

My chief goal when I began this book was to prepare highly detailed, descriptive, and informative narratives for each Medal of Honor recipient. Unfortunately, this goal could not be realized for the reasons noted above and the lack of financial resources to collect information from sources that are widely dispersed throughout the world. To address this problem, I hope to publish future editions with updated portraits for each Medal recipient with information received from you!

I want to enlist each and every one of you who read this book to contribute to future editions. Conduct research on the life of a Medal recipient and submit your findings to me for inclusion in the next edition. You may choose to investigate a recipient who hails from your hometown or state or attended the same school. You may write about a recipient who served in the same military unit as you did. You may also consider making your submission a group project by asking friends, your class, or organization to collaborate with you.

What should your submission or narrative contain? Any personal information about the recipient will be helpful: details about birthplace and date; parents' names and occupations; schools (elementary through college); employment (positions/titles, dates); military service; spouses' names and occupation; children (gender, ages); activities (sports, volunteering, hobbies); and memorable quotes. Possible sources of information might include newspaper articles, report cards, interviews of recipients and their families, friends and associates. No information is unimportant.

You do not have to be a professional writer. You can submit short notes, outlines, or full articles. Particularly important would be photos of recipients and their families. When you are ready, forward your submission to:

John Johnson
4496 Peachtree Rd.
Atlanta, GA 30338
Email: jjfjtj@tristanpress.com

I hope to publish the next edition by March 5, 2012.

CHAPTER 2

HISTORY OF THE
MEDAL OF HONOR
(Source: U.S. Department of Defense)

The Medal of Honor is the highest military decoration awarded by the United States. It is often referred to as the *Congressional Medal of Honor* because the President awards it in the name of the Congress. It is bestowed on members of the United States armed forces who conspicuously distinguish themselves by gallantry and intrepidity at the risk of their lives, above and beyond the call of duty, while engaged in action against an enemy of the United States.

All branches of the US military are eligible to receive the Medal, and each service has a unique design, with the exception of the Marine Corps and Coast Guard, which both use the Navy's medal. The Medal of Honor is often presented personally to the recipient or, in the case of posthumous awards, to survivors, by the President of the United States. Due to its high status, the medal has special protection under US law.

The first formal system for rewarding acts of individual gallantry by American soldiers was established by George Washington on August 7, 1782, when he created the Badge of Military Merit, designed to recognize "any singularly meritorious action." This decoration is America's first combat award and the second oldest American military decoration of any type, after the Fidelity Medallion, which was awarded only once and is viewed as commemorative.

Although the Badge of Military Merit fell into disuse after the

Revolutionary War, the concept of a military award for bravery had been established. In 1847, after the outbreak of the Mexican-American War, a Certificate of Merit was established for soldiers who distinguished themselves in action. The certificate was later granted medal status as the Certificate of Merit Medal.

Early in the Civil War, a medal for individual valor was proposed to Winfield Scott, the commanding general of the United States Army. He did not approve the proposal, but the medal did come into use by the Navy. Public Resolution 82, containing a provision for a Navy Medal of Valor, was signed into law by President Abraham Lincoln on December 21, 1861. The medal was to be bestowed upon petty officers, seamen, landsmen, and Marines who "most distinguish[ed] themselves by their gallantry and other seamanlike qualities during the present war." Secretary of the Navy Gideon Welles directed the Philadelphia Mint to design the new decoration. Shortly afterward, a resolution of similar wording was introduced on behalf of the Army and signed into law on July 12, 1862. This measure provided for awarding a Medal of Honor, as the Navy version also came to be called: "to such noncommissioned officers and privates as shall most distinguish themselves by their gallantry in action, and other soldier-like qualities, during the present insurrection."

Appearance

The appearance of the Medal of Honor has evolved since its creation in 1862. The present Army medal consists of a gold star surrounded by a wreath, topped by an eagle on a bar inscribed with the word "Valor." The medal is attached by a hook to a light blue, moiré silk neckband that is 1 3/16 inches wide and 21? inches long.

There is a version of the medal for each branch of the US armed services: the Army, Navy, and Air Force. Since the US Marine Corps is administratively a part of the Navy, Marines receive the Navy medal. Before 1965, when the US Air Force design was adopted, members of the US Army Air Corps, US Army Air Forces, and Air Force received the Army version of the medal.

The Coast Guard Medal of Honor, which was distinguished from the Navy medal in 1963, has never been awarded, partly because the US Coast Guard is subsumed into the US Navy when war is declared. No design yet exists for it. Only one member of the Coast Guard has ever received a Medal of Honor: Signalman 1st Class Douglas Munro, who was awarded the Navy version of the medal for action during the Battle of

Guadalcanal.

In the 19 cases where a service member has been awarded more than one Medal of Honor, current regulations specify that an appropriate device be centered on the Medal and ribbon. The Army and Air Force bestow an oak leaf cluster, while the Navy Medal of Honor is worn with a gold star.

A ribbon that is the same shade of light blue as the neckband and includes five white stars, pointed upward, in the shape of an "M" is worn for situations other than full dress uniform. When the ribbon is worn, it is placed alone, ? inch above the center of the other ribbons. For wear with civilian clothing, a rosette is issued, instead of a miniature lapel pin that usually shows the ribbon bar. The rosette is the same shade of blue as the neck ribbon and includes white stars. The ribbon and rosette are presented at the same time as the Medal.

The Medal of Honor can be awarded in one of two ways. The first and most common is nomination by a service member in the chain of command, followed by approval at each level of command. The other is nomination by a member of Congress, generally at the request of a constituent, and approval by a special act of Congress. In either case, the Medal of Honor is presented by the President on behalf of the Congress. Although commonplace, the term "Congressional Medal of Honor" is not correct. The Congressional Medal of Honor Society was named by an act of Congress, signed into law by President Eisenhower on August 5, 1958, as 36 U.S.C. Section 33.

Evolution of Criteria

A year after President Abraham Lincoln signed Public Resolution 82 into law on December 21, 1861, a similar resolution for the Army was passed. Six Union soldiers who hijacked a Confederate locomotive were the first recipients. Raid leader James J. Andrews, a civilian hanged as a Union spy, did not receive the medal because it was originally awarded only to enlisted men. Army officers first received them in 1891 and Navy officers in 1915. Many Medals of Honor awarded in the nineteenth century were associated with saving the flag, not just for patriotic reasons, but because it was a primary means of battlefield communication.

During the Civil War, no other military award was authorized, which explains some of the less notable actions that were recognized by the Medal of Honor. Secretary of War Edwin Stanton promised a Medal of Honor to every man in the 27th Maine Regiment who extended his enlistment beyond the agreed upon date. Many stayed four days extra and were then discharged. Due to confusion, Stanton awarded a Medal of Honor to all 864 men in the regiment.

The criteria for award tightened after World War I. In 1916, a board of five Army generals convened by law to review every Army Medal of Honor awarded. The commission, led by Nelson Miles, recommended that the Army rescind 911 medals, including the 864 to members of the 27th Maine; 29 to Abraham Lincoln's funeral guard; six civilians, including Dr. Mary Edwards Walker, the only female to have been awarded the Medal, and Buffalo Bill Cody, and 12 others whose awards were judged frivolous. Dr. Walker's medal was restored posthumously by President Jimmy Carter in 1977. Cody's award was restored in 1989.

Early in the twentieth century, the Navy awarded many Medals of Honor for peacetime bravery. For instance, seven sailors aboard the USS Iowa received the Medal when a boiler exploded on January 25, 1904. Aboard the USS Chicago in 1901, John Henry Helms received the medal for saving Ishi Tomizi, the ship's cook, from drowning. Even after World War I, Richard Byrd and Floyd Bennett received the medal for exploration of the North Pole. Thomas John Ryan received it for saving a female from the burning Grand Hotel in Yokohama, Japan, following the 1923 Great Kantÿ earthquake.

Since the beginning of World War II, the medal has been awarded for extreme bravery beyond the call of duty while engaged in action against an enemy. Arising from these criteria, approximately 60 percent of the medals earned during and after World War II have been awarded posthumously. Captain William McGonagle is an exception to the enemy-action rule, earning his medal during the USS *Liberty* incident, which the Israeli government claimed was friendly fire. In the post-World War II era, many eligible recipients might instead have been awarded a Silver Star, Navy Cross, or similar award.

Controversies

A 1993 study commissioned by the Army described systematic racial discrimination in the criteria for awarding medals during World War II. At the time, no Medals of Honor had been awarded to black soldiers. After an exhaustive review of files, the study recommended that several black Distinguished Service Cross recipients be upgraded to the Medal of Honor. On January 13, 1997, President Bill Clinton awarded the medal to seven

African American World War II veterans. Of these, only Vernon Baker was still alive. A similar study of Asian Americans in 1998 resulted in President Clinton awarding 21 new Medals of Honor in 2000, including 20 to Japanese-American members of the 442nd Regimental Combat Team; one of them was Senator Daniel Inouye. In 2005, President George W. Bush awarded the Medal of Honor to Jewish veteran and Holocaust survivor Tibor Rubin, who many believed to have been previously overlooked because of his religious beliefs.

Privileges

The Medal of Honor confers special privileges on its recipients, both by tradition and law. By tradition, all other soldiers, sailors, Marines, and airmen—even higher ranking officers up to the President of the United States—initiate the salute. In the event of an officer encountering an enlisted member of the military who has been awarded the Medal of Honor, officers salute, not the person, but the medal itself, attempting to time their salute to coincide with the enlisted members'. By law, recipients have several benefits:

- All Medal recipients are entitled to be entered on the Medal of Honor Roll. As a result, each Recipient is entitled to receive a special pension of $1,027 per month.

- Enlisted recipients are entitled to receive a supplemental uniform allowance.

- Recipients are entitled to travel on military aircraft when space is available.

- Recipients are entitled access to commissary and exchange privileges.

- Children of recipients are eligible for admission to service academies without regard to quotas.

- Recipients after 2002 are entitled to receive the Medal of Honor Flag.

- Recipients are entitled to wear the Medal with appropriate civilian clothes.

17

Legal Protection

Until late 2006, the Medal of Honor was the only service decoration singled-out for federal legislative protection under the Stolen Valor Act of 2005. Now, any false verbal, written, or physical claim to an award or decoration authorized for wear by military members or veterans is a federal felony.

All Medals of Honor are issued in the original only by the Department of Defense to a recipient. Misuse of the medal, including unauthorized manufacture or wear, is punishable by fine and imprisonment, and a harsher penalty is prescribed than for violations concerning other medals. After the Army redesigned its medal in 1903, a patent was issued to legally prevent others from making it. When the patent expired, the federal government enacted a law making it illegal to produce, wear, or distribute the Medal of Honor without proper authority. Violators of this law have been prosecuted. In 2003, Edward Fedora and Gisela Fedora were charged with Unlawful Sale of a Medal of Honor. They sold medals awarded to US Navy Seaman Robert Blume for action during the Spanish-American War and US Army First Sergeant George Washington Roosevelt for action during the Civil War to an FBI agent. Edward Fedora, a Canadian businessman, pleaded guilty and was sentenced to prison; Gisela Fedora's status is unknown.

While it is illegal to wear the Medal of Honor without authorization, someone can still legally claim to be a recipient unless the claim is made with the intent of securing veteran benefits. A number of veterans' organizations and private companies devote themselves to exposing those who falsely claim to have received the Medal of Honor. Imposters are said to outnumber true recipients.

Recipients

In total, 3,463 medals have been awarded to 3,444 different people. Nineteen men received a second award; 14 of these received two separate Medals for two separate actions, and five received both the Navy and the Army Medals of Honor for the same action. Since the beginning of World War II, 852 Medals of Honor have been awarded, 526 posthumously. In total, 616 had their Medals presented posthumously.

The Army Medal of Honor was first awarded to Private Jacob Parrott during the American Civil War for his role in the Andrews Raid; the most recent medal was awarded on February 26, 2007 to retired US Army pilot

Lieutenant Colonel Bruce P. Crandall, an upgrade of the Distinguished Service Cross he received for heroism during the Battle of Ia Drang in Vietnam on November 14, 1965. Crandall's actions at Ia Drang were depicted in the 2002 movie *We Were Soldiers*.

While current regulations, beginning in 1918, explicitly state that recipients must be serving in the US Armed Forces at the time of performing a valorous act that warrants the award of the Medal of Honor, exceptions have been made. For example, Mary Walker worked as a military contractor, and Charles Lindbergh, while a reserve member of the US Army Air Corps, received his Medal of Honor as a civilian pilot. In addition, the Medal of Honor was presented to the British Unknown Warrior by General Pershing on October 17, 1921; later the US Unknown Soldier was reciprocally awarded the Victoria Cross, Britain's highest award for gallantry, on November 11, 1921. Apart from these few exceptions, Medals of Honor can only be awarded to members of the US Armed Forces, although being a US citizen is *not* a prerequisite. Sixty-one Canadians serving in the US Armed Forces have been awarded the Medal of Honor, most for actions in the Civil War. Since 1900, only four have been awarded to Canadians. In the Vietnam War, Peter C. Lemon was the only Canadian recipient of the Medal of Honor.

The Medal of Honor has been awarded only four times, all of them posthumously, for actions occurring since the withdrawal of US forces from Vietnam in 1973. The first two were earned by Sergeant First-Class Randy Shughart and Master Sergeant Gary Gordon, who were defending downed Black Hawk helicopter pilot Chief Warrant Officer Michael Durant and his crew during the Battle of Mogadishu in 1993. The others were awarded during the Iraq Campaign. In 2005, a posthumous Medal of Honor awarded to Sergeant First-Class Paul R. Smith for actions in Operation Iraqi Freedom was presented to his survivors. In April 2003, Smith killed over 50 Iraqis near Baghdad International Airport, while providing cover for an aid station full of wounded Americans to evacuate. On January 11, 2007, President George W. Bush awarded Marine Corporal Jason Dunham of Scio, New York, the Medal of Honor posthumously for his bravery in Iraq; he threw himself on a grenade to save his fellow Marines during an action near the Syrian border in April 2004.

Figure 1: Medal of Honor Statistics: Aggregate Distribution

War	Total Awards	Army	Navy	Marines	Air Force	Coast Guard	Posthumous	Posthumous Percentage	Civilian	Air Corps
Civil War	1522	1198	307	17			32	2%	(2) Navy (2) Army	
Indian Campaigns	426	426					13	3%	(4) Army	
Korea 1871	15		9	6				0		
Spanish American	110	31	64	15			1	1%		
Samoa	4		1	3				0		
Philippine Insurrection	80	69	5	6			4	7%		
Philippine Outlaws	6	1	5					0		
Boxer Rebellion	59	4	22	33			1	2%		
Mexican Campaign	56	1	46	9				0		
Haiti	6			6				0		
Dominican Republic	3			3				0		
World War I	124	95	21	8			33	26%		Army (4)
Haiti 1919-1920	2			2				0		
Nicaraguan Campaign	2			2				0		
World War II	464	324	57	82		1	266	57%		Army (37)
Korean War	132	79	7	42	4		94	71%		
Vietnam	246	160	16	57	13		154	62%		
Somalia	2	2					2	100%		
War on Terror (Iraq)	2	1		1			2	100%		
Non-Combat	193	3	185	5			5	2%		Army (1)
Unknowns	9	9					9	100%		
Totals	3463	2402	745	297	17	1	616	18%		

Figure 2: Medal of Honor Statistics: Medal Distribution by Ethnicity and Gender

War	Total Awards	Female	African	Asian/Pacific Islanders	Native Americans	Hispanic American	Jewish American
Civil War	35	1	25			3	6
Indian Campaigns Korea 1871	31		18		15		3
Spanish American	0						
Samoa	6		6				
Philippine Insurrection	0						
Philippine	0						
Outlaws	0						
Boxer Rebellion	0						
Mexican Campaign/ Haiti	1					1	
Dominican Republic	0						
World War I	5		1			1	3
Haiti 1919-1920	0						
Nicaraguan Campaign	1		1				
World War II	51		7	25	4	12	3
Korean War	16		2	2	3	8	1
Vietnam	41		20	4		15	2
Somalia	0						
War on Terror (Iraq)	0						
Non-Combat	8		7	1			
Unknowns	0						
Totals	195	1	87	32	22	40	17

CHAPTER 3

PORTRAITS OF
MEDAL OF HONOR
RECIPIENTS

FEMALE RECIPIENT
OF THE MEDAL OF HONOR

WALKER, MARY
US Army
American Civil War

Rank and organization: Contract Acting Assistant Surgeon (civilian), US Army. Places and dates: Battle of Bull Run, July 21, 1861; Patent Office Hospital, Washington, DC, October 1861; Chattanooga, Tenn., following Battle of Chickamauga, September 1863; Prisoner of War, April 10, 1864-August 12, 1864, Richmond, Va.; Battle of Atlanta, September 1864. Entered service at: Louisville, Ky. Born: 26 November 1832, Oswego County, N.Y.

Citation: Whereas it appears from official reports that Dr. Mary E. Walker, a graduate of medicine, "has rendered valuable service to the Government, and her efforts have been earnest and untiring in a variety of ways," and that she was assigned to duty and served as an assistant surgeon in charge of female prisoners at Louisville, Ky., upon the recommendation of Major-Generals Sherman and Thomas, and faithfully served as contract surgeon in the service of the United States, and has devoted herself with much patriotic zeal to the sick and wounded soldiers, both in the field and hospitals, to the detriment of her own health, and has also endured hardships as a prisoner of war four months in a Southern prison while acting as contract surgeon; and Whereas by reason of her not being a commissioned officer in the military service, a brevet or honorary rank cannot, under existing laws, be conferred upon her; and Whereas in the opinion of the President an honorable recognition of her services and sufferings should be made: It is ordered, That a testimonial thereof shall be hereby made and given to the said Dr. Mary E. Walker, and that the usual medal of honor for meritorious services be given her. Given under my hand in the city of Washington, D.C., this 11th day of November, A.D. 1865.

Epilogue: Walker, one of the nation's 1.8 million female veterans, is the only one to earn the Congressional Medal of Honor She and the others were honored in October 1997 by the newly dedicated Women in Military Service for America Memorial.

Controversy surrounded Walker throughout her life. She was born into an abolitionist family in the Town of Oswego, New York, on November 26, 1832. Her birthplace on the Bunker Hill Road is noted by a historical marker. Her father, a country doctor, was a free-thinking participant in many of the reform movements that thrived in upstate New York in the mid-1800s. He had one son, Alvah, and believed strongly in education and equality for his five daughters Mary, Aurora, Luna, Vesta, and Cynthia. He also believed they were hampered by the tight-fitting women's clothing of the day.

Mary Walker became an early enthusiast for Women's Rights and passionately espoused dress reform. The most famous proponent of dress reform was Amelia Bloomer, a native of Homer, New York, who defended a colleague's right to wear "Turkish pantaloons" in her Ladies' Temperance newspaper, *The Lily*. "Bloomers," as they became known, did achieve some popular acceptance toward the end of the nineteenth century as women took up the new sport of bicycling. Mary Edwards Walker discarded the restrictive women's clothing of the day and donned full men's evening dress to lecture on Women's Rights.

In June 1855, Walker, the only female in her class, joined the tiny number of female doctors in the nation when she graduated from the eclectic Syracuse Medical College, the nation's first medical school that accepted women and men on an equal basis. She graduated at age 21, after three 13-week semesters of medical training for which she paid $55 each.

In 1856, wearing trousers and a man's coat, she married another physician, Albert Miller, and kept her own name. Together, they set up a medical practice in Rome, NY, but the public was not ready to accept a female physician, and it floundered. They were divorced 13 years later.

When war broke out, she came to Washington and tried to join the Union Army. Denied a commission as a medical officer, she volunteered anyway, serving as an acting assistant surgeon, the first female surgeon in the US Army. As an unpaid volunteer, she worked in the US Patent Office Hospital in Washington. Later, she worked as a field surgeon near the Union front lines, including Fredericksburg, and in Chattanooga after the Battle of Chickamauga, for almost two years.

In September 1863, Walker was finally appointed assistant surgeon in the Army of the Cumberland. She made herself a slightly modified officer's uniform, in response to the demands of traveling with the soldiers and working in field hospitals. She was then appointed assistant surgeon of the 52nd Ohio Infantry. During this assignment, it is generally accepted that she also served as a spy. She continually crossed Confederate lines to treat civilians. She was taken prisoner in 1864 by Confederate troops and imprisoned in Richmond for four months until she was exchanged, with two dozen other Union doctors, for 17 Confederate surgeons.

She was released back to the 52nd Ohio as a contract surgeon but spent the rest of the war practicing at a Louisville women's prison and an orphan asylum in Tennessee. She was paid $766.16 for her wartime service. Afterward, she got a monthly pension of $8.50, later raised to $20, but still less than some widows' pensions.

On November 11, 1865, President Andrew Johnson signed a bill to present Walker with the Congressional Medal of Honor for Meritorious Service, in order to recognize her contributions to the war effort without awarding her an army commission. She is the only female ever to receive the Medal of Honor, her country's highest military award.

In 1917, her Congressional Medal, along with the 910 others, was taken away when Congress revised the Medal of Honor standards to include only "actual combat with an enemy." She refused to give hers back, wearing it every day until her death in 1919. A relative told the *New York Times*: "Dr. Mary lost the medal simply because she was a hundred years ahead of her time and no one could stomach it." An Army board reinstated Walker's medal posthumously in 1977, citing her "distinguished gallantry, self-sacrifice, patriotism, dedication and unflinching loyalty to her country, despite the apparent discrimination because of her sex."

After the war, Walker became a writer and lecturer, touring here and abroad to speak on women's rights, dress reform, health, and temperance. Tobacco, she said, caused paralysis and insanity. Women's clothing, she said, was immodest and inconvenient. She was elected president of the National Dress Reform Association in 1866. Walker prided herself on being arrested numerous times for wearing male dress, including wing collar, bow tie, and top hat. She was also something of an inventor, coming up with the idea of using a return postcard for registered mail. She wrote extensively, including a combination biography and commentary called *Hit* and a second book, *Unmasked, or the Science of Immortality*. She died in the Town of Oswego on February 21, 1919 and is buried in the Rural Cemetery on Cemetery Road.[vi]

AFRICAN-AMERICAN RECIPIENTS
OF THE MEDAL OF HONOR

ANDERSON, BRUCE
US Army — American Civil War

Rank and organization: Private, Company K, 142nd New York Infantry. Place and date: At Fort Fisher, N.C., 15 January 1865. Entered service at: Ephratah, N.Y. Born: Mexico, Oswego County, N.Y., 9 June 1845. Date of issue: 28 December 1914.

Citation: Voluntarily advanced with the head of the column and cut down the palisading.

Epilogue: Anderson was one of a few Blacks to serve in White units during the Civil War. Although the Medal was awarded for actions during the Civil War, Anderson did not receive it until 1914. Records are unclear about the delay. CMOHS files show a petition for the Medal by Anderson, letters indicating that he would, in fact, receive the Medal, and a letter by Anderson indicating he had received the Medal sent to him by the War Department. Anderson died in 1922 and is buried in Green Hill Cemetery, Amsterdam, New York.[7]

BARNES, WILLIAMS H.
US Army — American Civil War

Rank and organization: Private, Company C, 38th US Colored Troops. Place and date: At Chapins Farm, Va., 29 September 1864. Entered service at: -----. Birth: St. Mary's County, Md. Date of issue: 6 April 1865.

Citation: Among the first to enter the enemy's works; although wounded.

Epilogue: Barnes was a slave, as was his wife, Elizabeth, and daughter, Mary, owned by Benjamin McKay of St. Mary's County, Maryland. Barnes died in 1866 at a military hospital in Indianola, Texas, and is buried in San Antonio National Cemetery, Texas.[8]

BEATY, POWHATAN
US Army — American Civil War

Rank and organization: First Sergeant, Company G, 5th US Colored Troops. Place and date: At Chapins Farm, Va., 29 September 1864. Entered service at: Delaware County, Ohio. Birth: Richmond, Va. Date of issue: 6 April 1865.

Citation: Took command of his company, all the officers having been killed or wounded, and gallantly led it.

Epilogue: Beaty died in 1913 and is buried in Union Baptist Cemetery, Cincinnati, Ohio.[9]

BLAKE, ROBERT
US Navy — American Civil War

Rank and organization: Contraband, US Navy. Entered service at: Virginia. G.O. No.: 32, 16 April 1864. Accredited to: Virginia.

Citation: On board the U.S. Steam Gunboat Marblehead off Legareville, Stono River, 25 December 1863, in an engagement with the enemy on John's Island. Serving the rifle gun, Blake, an escaped slave, carried out his duties bravely throughout the engagement which resulted in the enemy's abandonment of positions, leaving a caisson and one gun behind.

Epilogue: The Navy rated its first Black Medal recipient as "contraband". Blake is thought to have been born in Virginia[10] and most likely escaped slavery from a Virginia plantation.[11] However, other research indicates that he was born in South Carolina and returned to Vermont after the Navy, where he may have died. In the end, most historians state that little is known about him, except the actions for which he received the Medal.[12]

BRONSON, JAMES H.
US Army — American Civil War

Rank and organization: First Sergeant, Company D, 5th US Colored Troops. Place and date: At Chapins Farm, Va., 29 September 1864. Entered service at: Delaware County, Ohio. Birth: Indiana County, Pa. Date of issue: 6 April 1865.

Citation: Took command of his company, all the officers having been killed or wounded, and gallantly led it.

Epilogue: Bronson was freed from slavery April 19, 1861.[13] He was classified as a "mulatto" with "grey" eyes and "dark" hair and employed as a "barber" before enlisting in the Army. At his request, he was reduced in rank several times in order to remain with his military unit, the band.[14]

BROWN, WILLIAMS
US Navy — American Civil War

Rank and organization: Landsman, US Navy. Born: 1836, Baltimore, Md. Accredited to: Maryland. G.O. No.: 45, 31 December 1864.

Citation: On board the U.S.S. Brooklyn during successful attacks against Fort Morgan rebel gunboats and the ram Tennessee in Mobile Bay on 5 August 1864. Stationed in the immediate vicinity of the shell whips which were twice cleared of men by bursting shells, Brown remained steadfast at his post and performed his duties in the powder division throughout the furious action which resulted in the surrender of the prize rebel ram Tennessee and in the damaging and destruction of batteries at Fort Morgan.

Epilogue: Brown died in 1896 and is buried in Arlington National Cemetery. [15]

BROWN, WILSON
US Navy — American Civil War

Rank and organization: Landsman, US Navy. Born: 1841, Natchez, Miss. Accredited to: Mississippi. G.O. No.: 45, 31 December 1864.

Citation: On board the flagship U.S.S. Hartford during successful attacks against Fort Morgan, rebel gunboats and the ram Tennessee in Mobile Bay on 5 August 1864. Knocked unconscious into the hold of the ship when an enemy shell burst fatally wounded a man on the ladder above him, Brown, upon regaining consciousness, promptly returned to the shell whip on the berth deck and zealously continued to perform his duties although 4 of the 6 men at this station had been either killed or wounded by the enemy's terrific fire.

Epilogue: Brown died in 1900 and was buried in Natchez National Cemetery.[16] Questions about his ethnicity are evident from the numerous letters in his files at the CMOHS from researchers debating the issue.[17] The matter was settled when the cemetery superintendent confirmed he was a "Negro."

CARNEY, WILLIAM H.
US Army — American Civil War

Rank and organization: Sergeant, Company C, 54th Massachusetts Colored Infantry. Place and date: At Fort Wagner, S.C., 18 July 1863. Entered service at: New Bedford, Mass. Birth: Norfolk, Va. Date of issue: 23 May 1900.

Citation: When the color sergeant was shot down, this soldier grasped the flag, led the way to the parapet, and planted the colors thereon. When the troops fell back he brought off the flag, under a fierce fire in which he was twice severely wounded.

Epilogue: Carney was the first Black to receive the Medal of Honor. He was born in Norfolk, Virginia, in 1840. He and his family were slaves, but he was freed by their owner soon after his birth. From an early age, he was taught to read by his minister, which was illegal, and he wanted to be a minister. Carney and his family left Norfolk in 1850 and settled in New Bedford, Massachusetts, where he enlisted in the newly formed 54th Massachusetts Infantry Regiment, the first unit to recruit to blacks for the Union Army and the first unit of blacks to fight in combat against the Confederates. After the action for which he received the Medal, he was discharged, returned to Massachusetts, married Susanna Williams, and had one child, Clara. Carney was issued the Medal in 1900, some 37 years after the battle, largely due to the efforts of Christian Fleetwood, also a recipient. Carney became a leading citizen of New Bedford and was instrumental in establishing the famous Shaw Monument. Carney died in 1908 after suffering a compound fracture of the leg when he fell down an elevator shaft trying to save a women. He is buried in Oak Grove Cemetery. The location of the Medal is unknown.[18]

DORSEY, DECATUR
US Army — American Civil War

Rank and organization: Sergeant, Company B, 39th US Colored Troops. Place and date: At Petersburg, Va., 30 July 1864. Entered service at: Baltimore County, Md. Birth: Howard County, Md. Date of issue: 8 November 1865.

Citation: Planted his colors on the Confederate works in advance of his regiment, and when the regiment was driven back to the Union works he carried the colors there and bravely rallied the men.

Epilogue: A former slave, at war's end, Dorsey settled in Hoboken, New Jersey, where he and his wife, Mannie Christie, took up residence at 227 Newark Street.[19] After he died at the age of 55 in 1891, his wife secured a military pension that amounted to no more than $12 per month. Dorsey's grave went unnoticed until the late Paul Angelo of the Union County Veterans Affairs office took up the cause of securing a proper headstone indicating that Dorsey had received the Medal of Honor, which was accomplished in 1984. [20]

FLEETWOOD, CHRISTIAN A.
US Army — American Civil War

Rank and organization: Sergeant Major, 4th US Colored Troops, Place and date: At Chapins Farm, Va., 29 September 1864. Entered service at: ------. Birth: Baltimore, Md. Date of issue: 6 April 1865.

Citation: Seized the colors, after 2 color bearers had been shot down, and bore them nobly through the fight.

Epilogue: From many perspectives, Fleetwood led a remarkable and rewarding life. Taught to read by his White slave owners, he traveled to Africa to serve as their business manager and representative. He attended college (now Lincoln University), started a literary journal, served in the Union army as sergeant major of his battalion, and was recommended for a officer's commission that was denied by the Secretary of War. Later, he was commissioned a major in the DC militia, a precursor of the National Guard. After his military service, he held various impressive administrative positions in and out of government. He was a man ahead of his times. Fleetwood died in 1914 and is buried in Harmony Cemetery, Landover, Maryland.[21]

GARDINER, JAMES
US Army — American Civil War

Rank and organization: Private, Company I, 36th US Colored Troops. Place and date: At Chapins Farm, Va., 29 September 1864. Entered service at: ------. Birth: Gloucester, Va. Date of issue: 6 April 1865.

Citation: Rushed in advance of his brigade, shot a rebel officer who was on the parapet rallying his men, and then ran him through with his bayonet.

Epilogue: Little is known about Gardiner before or after receiving the Medal. He died in Clark's Summit, Pennsylvania, and is buried in Calvary Crest Cemetery, Ottumwa, Iowa.[22]

HARRIS, JAMES H.
US Army — American Civil War

Rank and organization: Sergeant, Company B, 38th US Colored Troops. Place and date: At New Market Heights, Va., 29 September 1864. Entered service at: ------. Birth: St. Mary's County, Md. Date of issue: 18 February 1874.

Citation: Gallantry in the assault.

Epilogue: Little is known about Harris before or after the action that led to him receiving the Medal. He died in 1898 and is buried in Arlington National Cemetery.[23]

HAWKINS, THOMAS R.
US Army — American Civil War

Rank and organization: Sergeant Major, 6th US Colored Troops. Place and date: At Chapins Farm, Va., 29 September 1864. Entered service at: Philadelphia, Pa. Birth: Cincinnati, Ohio. Date of issue: 8 February 1870.

Citation: Rescue of regimental colors.

Epilogue: Little is known about Hawkins before and after the actions that led to him receiving the Medal. He died in Washington, DC, in 1870 and is buried in Landover Cemetery, Landover, Maryland, although the site is unknown.[24]

HILTON, ALFRED B.
US Army — American Civil War

Rank and organization: Sergeant, Company H, 4th US Colored Troops. Place and date. At Chapins Farm, Va., 29 September 1864. Entered service at: ------. Birth: Harford County, Md. Date of issue: 6 April 1865.

Citation: When the regimental color bearer fell, this soldier seized the color and carried it forward, together with the national standard, until disabled at the enemy's inner line.

Epilogue: Little is known about Hilton. A public park in Maryland was named after him.[25] He died at Fortress Monroe, Maryland, and is buried in Hampton National Cemetery, Hampton, Virginia.[26]

HOLLAND, MILTON M.
US Army — American Civil War

Rank and organization: Sergeant Major, 5th US Colored Troops. Place and date: At Chapins Farm, Va., 29 September 1864. Entered service at: Athens, Ohio. Born: 1844, Austin, Tex. Date of issue: 6 April 1865.

Citation: Took command of Company C, after all the officers had been killed or wounded, and gallantly led it.

Epilogue: Holland was born and raised in Austin, Texas. He was an 18-year-old shoemaker when he entered the Army, and due to his heroic action at Chapin Farms, he was also promoted to Captain, but the War Department rescinded the promotion because of his race. He was promoted to sergeant major and discharged from the Army in 1865, when he married Virginia Dickey. He lived in Columbus, Ohio, and later, Washington, DC. He worked as an auditor for the Treasury Department and the Post Office. He died in 1910 in Silver Spring, Maryland, and is buried in Arlington National Cemetery.

JAMES, MILES
US Army — American Civil War

Rank and organization: Corporal, Company B, 36th US Colored Troops. Place and date: At Chapins Farm, Va., 30 September 1864. Entered service at: Norfolk, Va. Birth: Princess Anne County, Va. Date of issue: 6 April 1865.

Citation: Having had his arm mutilated, making immediate amputation necessary, he loaded and discharged his piece with one hand and urged his men forward; this within 30 yards of the enemy's works.

Epilogue: James remained in the Army until 1865. He died in Norfolk, Virginia, in 1871. His burial site is unknown. [27]

KELLY, ALEXANDER
US Army — American Civil War

Rank and organization: First Sergeant, Company F, 6th US Colored Troops. Place and date: At Chapins Farm, Va., 29 September 1864. Entered service at: ------. Birth. Pennsylvania. Date of issue: 6 April 1865.

Citation: Gallantly seized the colors, which had fallen near the enemy's lines of abatis, raised them and rallied the men at a time of confusion and in a place of the greatest danger.

Epilogue: Kelly died in 1907 and is buried in St. Peter's Cemetery, Pittsburgh, Pennsylvania.[28]

LAWSON, JOHN
US Navy — American Civil War

Rank and organization: Landsman, US Navy. Born: 1837, Pennsylvania. Accredited to: Pennsylvania. G.O. No.: 45, 31 December 1864.

Citation: On board the flagship U.S.S. Hartford during successful attacks against Fort Morgan, rebel gunboats and the ram Tennessee in Mobile Bay on 5 August 1864. Wounded in the leg and thrown violently against the side of the ship when an enemy shell killed or wounded the 6-man crew as the shell whipped on the berth deck, Lawson, upon regaining his composure, promptly returned to his station and, although urged to go below for treatment, steadfastly continued his duties throughout the remainder of the action.

Epilogue: Lawson would remain in the Navy as a cook for a number of years after receiving the Medal. He died in 1919 in Philadelphia and is buried in Mount Peace Cemetery, Camden, New Jersey.[29]

MIFFLIN, JAMES
US Navy — American Civil War

Rank and organization: Engineer's Cook, US Navy. Born: 1839, Richmond, Va. Accredited to: Virginia. G.O. No.: 45, 31 December 1864.

Citation: On board the U.S.S. Brooklyn during successful attacks against Fort Morgan, rebel gunboats and the ram Tennessee in Mobile Bay, on 5 August 1864. Stationed in the immediate vicinity of the shell whips which were twice cleared of men by bursting shells, Mifflin remained steadfast at his post and performed his duties in the powder division throughout the furious action which resulted in the surrender of the prize rebel ram Tennessee and in the damaging and destruction of batteries at Fort Morgan.

Epilogue: Very little is known about Mifflin before or after he received the Medal. He is *lost to history.*[30]

PEASE, JOACHIM
US Navy — American Civil War

Rank and organization: Seaman, US Navy. Born: Long Island, N.Y. Accredited to: New York. G.O. No.: 45, 31 December 1864.

Citation: Served as seaman on board the U.S.S. Kearsarge when she destroyed the Alabama off Cherbourg, France, 19 June 1864. Acting as loader on the No. 2 gun during this bitter engagement, Pease exhibited marked coolness and good conduct and was highly recommended by the divisional officer for gallantry under fire.

Epilogue: Little is known about Pease before or after he received the Medal. He is *lost to history.*[31]

PINN, ROBERT
US Army — American Civil War

Rank and organization: First Sergeant, Company I, 5th US Colored Troops. Place and date: At Chapins Farm, Va., 29 September 1864. Entered service at: Massillon, Ohio. Born: 1 March 1843, Stark County, Ohio. Date of issue: 6 April 1865.

Citation: Took command of his company after all the officers had been killed or wounded and gallantly led it in battle.

Epilogue: Little is known about Pinn before or after he received the Medal. He is *lost to history.*

RATCLIFF, DAVID
US Army — American Civil War

Rank and organization: First Sergeant, Company C, 38th US Colored Troops. Place and date: At Chapins Farm, Va., 29 September 1864. Entered service at: ------. Birth: James County, Va. Date of issue: 6 April 1865.

Citation: Commanded and gallantly led his company after the commanding officer had been killed; was the first enlisted man to enter the enemy's works.

Epilogue: Little is known about Ratcliff before or after he received the Medal. He died in 1915 near Nelson, Virginia, and is buried in Chescake Cemetery, Lackey, Virginia.[32]

SMITH, ANDREW JACKSON
US Army — American Civil War

Citation: Corporal Andrew Jackson Smith, of Clinton, Illinois, a member of the 55th Massachusetts Voluntary Infantry, distinguished himself on 30 November 1864 by saving his regimental colors, after the color bearer was killed during al bloody charge called the Battle of Honey Hill, South Carolina. In the late afternoon, as the 55th Regiment pursued enemy skirmishers and conducted a running fight, they ran into a swampy area backed by a rise where the Confederate Army awaited. The surrounding woods and thick underbrush impeded infantry movement and artillery support. The 55th and 34th regiments formed columns to advance on the enemy position in a flanking movement. As the Confederates repelled other units, the 55th and 54th regiments continued to move into tanking positions. Forced into a narrow gorge crossing a swamp in the face of the enemy position, the 55th's Color-Sergeant was killed by an exploding shell, and Corporal Smith took the Regimental Colors from his hand and carried them through heavy grape and canister fire. Although half of the officers and a third of the enlisted men engaged in the fight were killed or wounded, Corporal Smith continued to expose himself to enemy fire by carrying the colors throughout the battle.

Through his actions, the Regimental Colors of the 55th Infantry Regiment were not lost to the enemy. Corporal Andrew Jackson Smith's extraordinary valor in the face of deadly enemy fire is in keeping with the highest traditions of military service and reflect great credit upon him, the 55th Regiment, and the United States Army.

Epilogue: Smith received the Medal more than 80 years after he had earned it during the Civil War. His two previous petitions for the award, filed before his death in 1932, were denied. Smith's cause was taken up by a grandnephew, Andrew Bowman, a retired systems engineer from Indianapolis, whose effort finally corrected a wrong. Special Congressional legislation was signed into law by President Clinton, who presented the Medal to Smith's surviving family members at a White House ceremony[33]. Smith was born a slave and was probably fathered by his owner. He became a boatman and ran away at 18, ending up serving a Union colonel at the Battle of Shiloh. He returned to his hometown with the wounded colonel and later joined the 55th Massachusetts Infantry Regiment,[34] the unit he served during the action for which he received the Medal.

SANDERSON, AARON
US Navy — American Civil War

Rank and organization: Landsman, US Navy. Entered service at: Philadelphia, Pa. Birth: North Carolina. G.O. No.: 59, 22 June 1865.

Citation: Served on board the U.S.S. Wyandank during a boat expedition up Mattox Creek, 17 March 1865. Participating with a boat crew in the clearing of Mattox Creek, L/man Anderson carried out his duties courageously in the face of a devastating fire which cut away half the oars, pierced the launch in many places and cut the barrel off a musket being fired at the enemy.

Epilogue: All that is known about Sanderson is that he served in the Navy under the name Anderson. His burial site is unknown, and he is lost to history.

VEAL, CHARLES
US Army — American Civil War

Rank and organization: Private, Company D, 4th US Colored Troops. Place and date: At Chapins Farm, Va., 29 September 1864. Entered service at: Portsmouth, Va. Birth: Portsmouth Va. Date of issue: 6 April 1865.

Citation: Seized the national colors after 2 color bearers had been shot down close to the enemy's works, and bore them through the remainder of the battle.

Epilogue: Upon his death in 1872, Veal was laid to rest in Hampton National Cemetery, Virginia.[35]

BOYNE, THOMAS
US Army — Indian Campaigns

Rank and organization: Sergeant, Company C, 9th US Cavalry. Place and date: At Mimbres Mountains, N. Mex., 29 May 1879; at Cuchillo Negro River near Ojo Caliente, N. Mex., 27 September 1879. Entered service at: - --. Birth: Prince Georges County, Md. Date of issue: 6 January 1882.

Citation: Bravery in action.

Epilogue: Very little information was available about Boyne's life in the archives of the CMOHS. What is known is that he died in 1896 at the Old Soldiers Home in Washington, DC, and is buried in its cemetery.[36]

BROWN, BENJAMIN
US Army — Indian Campaigns

Rank and organization: Sergeant, Company C, 24th US Infantry. Place and date: Arizona, 11 May 1889. Entered service at: ------. Birth: Spotsylvania County, Va. Date of issue: 19 February 1890.

Citation: Although shot in the abdomen, in a fight between a paymaster's escort and robbers, did not leave the field until again wounded through both arms.

Epilogue: Brown died at the Old Soldiers Home in Washington, DC, in 1890 and is buried in its cemetery.[37]

DENNY, JOHN
US Army — Indian Campaigns

Rank and organization: Sergeant, Company C, 9th US Cavalry. Place and date: At Las Animas Canyon, N. Mex., 18 September 1879. Entered service at: 1867 Elmira, N.Y. Birth: Big Flats, N.Y. Date of issue: 27 November 1891.

Citation: Removed a wounded comrade, under a heavy fire, to a place of safety.

Epilogue: Denny was born a slave, but documents show that he was freed by his owner. He would remain in the Army for a number of years after receiving the Medal. He died at the Old Soldier's Home in Washington, DC, in 1901 and is buried in its cemetery.[38]

FACTOR, POMPEY
US Army — Indian Campaigns

Rank and organization: Private, Indian Scouts. Place and date: At Pecos River, Tex., 25 April 1875. Entered service at: ------. Birth: Arkansas. Date of issue: 28 May 1875.

Citation: With 3 other men, he participated in a charge against 25 hostiles while on a scouting patrol.

Epilogue: Factor was a Black Seminole Indian Scout for the Army. The action for which received the Medal was performed with a fellow Scout, John Ward, who also received the Medal. Factor would remain in the Army for several years after receiving the Medal, but violence and racism in the Army and the community near which his cavalry unit was based finally drove him back to Mexico. He died in 1928 and is buried in the Seminole Indian Scout Cemetery in Brackettville, Texas.[39]

GREAVES, CLINTON
US Army — Indian Campaigns

Rank and organization: Corporal, Company C, 9th US Cavalry. Place and date: At Florida Mountains, N. Mex., 24 January 1877. Entered service at: Prince George's County, Md. Birth: Madison County, Va. Date of issue: 26 June 1879.

Citation: While part of a small detachment to persuade a band of renegade Apache Indians to surrender, his group was surrounded. Cpl. Greaves in the center of the savage hand-to-hand fighting, managed to shoot and bash a gap through the swarming Apaches, permitting his companions to break free.

Epilogue: Greaves was born into slavery in 1855 in Madison, Virginia. His father was John Greaves, blacksmith, but the identity of his mother is unknown. Clinton was a laborer and a resident of Prince George's County when he enlisted in the Army in 1872. His enlistment papers describe him as five-feet-six-and-a-half inches tall, with black eyes, black hair, and black complexion. He could not write. He spent over twenty years in the Army, most of it with the 9th Cavalry as a Buffalo Soldier. After receiving the Medal, Greaves was reassigned to Columbus, Ohio, where he was a blacksmith. He married Bertha Williams in 1890 and had two children, both of whom died shortly after birth. Greaves was a well-known and respected member of the Columbus community and the Masonic Order. Due to poor health, he was discharged from the Army with a pension, receiving an extra $2 per month for receiving the Medal. After his discharge, he worked as a porter in downtown Columbus. He died in 1906 and is buried in Greenlawn Cemetery, Columbus.[40]

JOHNSON, HENRY
US Army — Indian Campaigns

Rank and organization: Sergeant, Company D, 9th US Cavalry. Place and date: At Milk River, Colo., 2-5 October 1879. Entered service at: ------. Birth: Boynton, Va. Date of issue: 22 September 1890.

Citation: Voluntarily left fortified shelter and under heavy fire at close range made the rounds of the pits to instruct the guards, fought his way to the creek and back to bring water to the wounded.

Epilogue: A Buffalo soldier, Johnson remained in the Army until he retired in 1898. He died in Washington, DC, in 1904 and is buried in Arlington National Cemetery.[41]

JORDAN, GEORGE
US Army — Indian Campaigns

Rank and organization: Sergeant, Company K, 9th US Cavalry. Place and date: At Fort Tularosa, N. Mex., 14 May 1880; at Carrizo Canyon, N. Mex., 12 August 1881. Entered service at: Nashville, Tenn. Birth: Williamson County, Tenn. Date of issue: 7 May 1890.

Citation: While commanding a detachment of 25 men at Fort Tularosa, N. Mex., repulsed a force of more than 100 Indians. At Carrizo Canyon, N. Mex., while commanding the right of a detachment of 19 men, on 12 August 1881, he stubbornly held his ground in an extremely exposed position and gallantly forced back a much superior number of the enemy, preventing them from surrounding the command.

Epilogue: Jordan died in 1890 and is buried in the Fort McPherson National Cemetery in Maxwell, Nebraska.[42]

MAYS, ISAIAH
US Army — Indian Campaigns

Rank and organization: Corporal, Company B, 24th US Infantry. Place and date: Arizona, 11 May 1889. Entered service at: Columbus Barracks, Ohio. Born: 16 February 1858, Carters Bridge, Va. Date of issue: 19 February 1890.

Citation: Gallantry in the fight between Paymaster Wham's escort and robbers. Mays walked and crawled 2 miles to a ranch for help.

Epilogue: Mays would remain in the Army after receiving the Medal. He died in 1925 in Phoenix, Arizona, and is buried in the Arizona State Hospital Cemetery.[43]

McBRYAR, WILLIAM
US Army — Indian Campaigns

Rank and organization: Sergeant, Company K, 10th US Cavalry. Place and date: Arizona, 7 March 1890. Entered service at: New York, N.Y. Birth: 14 February 1861, Elizabethtown, N.C. Date of issue: 15 May 1890.

Citation: Distinguished himself for coolness, bravery and marksmanship while his troop was in pursuit of hostile Apache Indians.

Epilogue: McBryar would remain in the Army for many years after receiving the Medal. He eventually received an officer's commission and served in the 49th US Volunteers Infantry as a second lieutenant. He died in 1941 in Philadelphia and is buried in Arlington National Cemetery.[44]

PAINE, ADAM
US Army — Indian Campaigns

Rank and organization: Private, Indian Scouts. Place and date: Canyon Blanco tributary of the Red River, Tex., 26-27 September 1874. Entered service at: Fort Duncan, Texas. Birth: Florida. Date of issue: 13 October 1875.

Citation: Rendered invaluable service to Col. R. S. Mackenzie, 4th US Cavalry, during this engagement.

Epilogue: From the records, all that is known about Paine is that he was a Seminole Indian Scout and died in 1877. He is buried in the Seminole Indian Scout Cemetery, Brackettville, Texas.

PAYNE, ISAAC
US Army — Indian Campaigns

Rank and organization: Trumpeter, Indian Scouts. Place and date: At Pecos River, Tex., 25 April 1875. Entered service at: ------. Birth: Mexico. Date of issue: 28 May 1875.

Citation: With 3 other men, he participated in a charge against 25 hostiles while on a scouting patrol.

Epilogue: Payne was a Black Seminole Indian, born and raised in Mexico. After his Army service, he returned to Mexico, where he died in 1904. He is buried in the Seminole Indian Scout Cemetery in Brackettville, Texas.[45]

SHAW, THOMAS
US Army — Indian Campaigns

Rank and organization: Sergeant, Company K, 9th US Cavalry. Place and date: At Carrizo Canyon, N. Mex., 12 August 1881. Entered service at: Pike County, Mo. Birth: Covington, Ky. Date of issue: 7 December 1890.

Citation: Forced the enemy back after stubbornly holding his ground in an extremely exposed position and prevented the enemy's superior numbers from surrounding his command.

Epilogue: Shaw was born in Kentucky, but the exact city or county is unknown, as different sources record different birthplaces. He was a slave, owned by Mary Shaw, who later filed a pension claim with a government program to reimburse owners whose slaves fought on the side of the Union. His enlistment papers indicate he was 5-feet-11-inches tall, with black eyes and hair, and of mixed parentage. Shaw's military records show he had numerous physical ailments, which may have caused him to leave the Army at age 38 for five years, during which he married Lara Luce and had one child, Lenoa. Shaw was later discharged from the Army with a medical pension but died before he could collect it. After his wife died in 1898, their daughter was adopted by Richard Tighman, who applied for, and received, Shaw's pension.[46] Shaw is buried in Arlington National Cemetery.

STANCE, EMANUEL
US Army — Indian Campaigns

Rank and organization: Sergeant, Company F, 9th US Cavalry. Place and date: At Kickapoo Springs, Tex., 20 May 1870. Entered service at: ------. Birth: Carroll Parish, La. Date of issue: 28 June 1870.

Citation: Gallantry on scout after Indians.

Epilogue: A native of Providence, Louisiana, Stance was the first Black to receive the Medal during the Indian Wars. He stood 5-feet-5-inches when he enlisted and entered farming as his primary occupation. Documents describe him as "learned and intelligent as evidenced by the composition of his scouting reports."[47] Stance was murdered in 1887 "along a public road" between Ft. Robinson and Crawford, Nebraska. He is buried in Fort McPherson National Cemetery, Nebraska.[48]

WALLEY, AUGUSTUS
US Army — Indian Campaigns

Rank and organization: Private, Company I, 9th US Cavalry. Place and date: At Cuchillo Negro Mountains, N. Mex., 16 August 1881. Entered service at: ------. Birth: Reistertown, Md. Date of issue: 1 October 1890.

Citation: Bravery in action with hostile Apaches.

Epilogue: Walley spent 30 years in the Army and retired with the rank of 1st Sergeant. It is customary for Medal of Honor recipients to have their rank designated on their gravestones, and in the 1990s, discovering that Walley's gravestone did not, researcher Houston Wedlock led a successful effort to correct this serious omission. In 1995, an elaborate ceremony was held, attended by Walley's 90-year-old niece and grandniece. Walley died in 1890 and, is buried in the cemetery of St. Luke's United Methodist Church in Reisterstown, Maryland.[49]

WARD, JOHN
US Army — Indian Campaigns

Rank and organization: Sergeant, 24th US Infantry Indian Scouts. Place and date: At Pecos River, Tex., 25 April 1875. Entered service at: Fort Duncan, Tex. Birth: Arkansas. Date of issue: 28 May 1875.

Citation: With 3 other men, he participated in a charge against 25 hostiles while on a scouting patrol.

Epilogue: Ward received his Medal along with fellow Black Seminole Indian Scout Pompey Factor for action against the Indians at the Pecos River.[50] Ward and Factor were probably born and raised in Mexico after their ancestors migrated there from the United States to escape slavery. Described as 5-feet-7-inches tall, with dark hair and dark skin, Ward remained in the Army for 24 years, despite the intense racism he experienced in the west. He was a private for 12 years, a corporal for six years, and a sergeant for six years. One night in January 1887, he lay on the ground to sleep, and the next morning, he was stiff and sore and unable to saddle his horse. Thereafter, he suffered from rheumatism and finally retired from the Army in 1895.[51] Ward died in 1911, probably in Texas, and is buried in the Seminole Indian Scout Cemetery, Brackettville, Texas.[52] Mrs. Ward received a widow's pension until her death in 1926.

WILLIAMS, MOSES
US Army — Indian Campaigns

Rank and organization: First Sergeant, Company I, 9th US Cavalry. Place and date: At foothills of the Cuchillo Negro Mountains, N. Mex., 16 August 1881. Entered service at: ------. Birth: Carrollton, La. Date of issue: 12 November 1896.

Citation: Rallied a detachment, skillfully conducted a running fight of 3 or 4 hours, and by his coolness, bravery, and unflinching devotion to duty in standing by his commanding officer in an exposed position under a heavy fire from a large party of Indians saved the lives of at least 3 of his comrades.

Epilogue: Probably born a slave, at the time of his enlistment in the Army, Williams listed his occupation as a farmer and signed with an X as his mark. In subsequent enlistment, he was able to sign his name. During the action for which he would receive the Medal, he was with two other men, one of whom, also named Williams, received the Medal soon after the battle.[53] When Moses Williams learned of his fellow soldier receiving the Medal, he petitioned the President of the United States and the Army to receive one as well. The Army rejected his petition, citing a lack of documents supporting his claim. However, an account of the battle, written by George Burnett, an officer attached to Williams' unit, supported Williams' claims. Williams finally received the Medal some fifteen years later. He retired from the Army in 1899 with a pension of $42.50 per month and settled in Vancouver, Washington, living in Kanaka Village, where Hawaiians, Chinese, and Blacks were segregated from Whites. When he died in August 1899, the commander of the Vancouver Barracks wrote that he "died alone and without friends." Among Williams' personal belongings was the Medal, which was buried with him in Vancouver's Post Cemetery.[54]

WILSON, WILLIAM
US Army — Indian Campaigns

Rank and organization: Sergeant, Company I, 4th US Cavalry. Place and date: At Colorado Valley, Tex., 28 March 1872. Entered service at: Philadelphia, Pa. Birth: Philadelphia, Pa. Date of issue: 27 April 1872. Second award.

Citation: In pursuit of a band of cattle thieves from New Mexico.

Epilogue: Information found in CMOHS records and data provided by the Department of Defense appear to conflict. As indicated above, Wilson is listed as having been born in Philadelphia, serving in the 4th Cavalry, and receiving the Medal for actions in Texas,[55] while CMOHS data indicate that he was born in Hagerstown, Maryland, served in the 9th Cavalry, and received the Medal for actions in South Dakota.[56] Judging from other, similar incidents, it is more likely that the Defense Department's information is inaccurate. CMOHS files contain numerous news clippings, letters, and research notes on Wilson that support its version. After his military service, this Wilson returned to Hagerstown, where he lived until his death and is buried. He had a controversial military career, accused of forgery and theft of a rifle. Both charges briefly held up his receipt of the Medal.[57] Wilson was the last American soldier to receive the nation's highest military award for battle on American soil. He fought at Wounded Knee.[58]

WOODS, BRENT
US Army — Indian Campaigns

Rank and organization: Sergeant, Company B, 9th US Cavalry. Place and date: New Mexico, 19 August 1881. Entered service at: Louisville, Ky. Birth: Pulaski County, Ky. Date of issue: 12 July 1894.

Citation: Saved the lives of his comrades and citizens of the detachment.

Epilogue: Woods was a slave (see APPENDIX C) prior to entering the Army, where he would remain for 25 years. His brief citation belies the heroic act for which he received the nation's highest military award for valor. With his commanders killed and only ten men, abandoned by the White settlers he was assigned to protect, he held off repeated charges by a large, hostile force of Apaches. After the Indians retreated, he collected the dead and wounded, regrouped the settlers, and restored security. Woods died in 1906 and is buried in White Springs National Cemetery, Nancy, Kentucky.[59]

ATKINS, DANIELS
US Navy — Interim Period

Rank and organization: Ship's Cook, First Class, US Navy. Born: 1867, Brunswick, Va. Accredited to: Virginia. G.O. No.: 489, 20 May 1898.

Citation: On board the U.S.S. Cushing, 11 February 1898. Showing gallant conduct, Atkins attempted to save the life of the late Ens. Joseph C. Breckenridge, U.S. Navy, who fell overboard at sea from that vessel on this date.

Epilogue: Atkins died in 1923 and is buried in the US Naval Cemetery, Portsmouth, Virginia, near his place of birth.[60]

GIRANDY, ALPHONSE
US Navy — Interim Period

Rank and Organization: Seaman, US Navy. Born: 21 January 1868, Guadeloupe, West Indies. Accredited to: Pennsylvania. G.O. No.: 85, 22 March 1902.

Citation: Serving on board the U.S.S. Petrel, for heroism and gallantry, fearlessly exposing his own life to danger for the saving of others, on the occasion of the fire on board that vessel, 31 March 1901.

Epilogue: Girandy died in 1941 in Philadelphia, Pennsylvania, and is buried in the Philadelphia National Cemetery.[61]

JOHNSON, JOHN
US Navy — Nicaraguan Campaign

Rank and organization: Seaman, US Navy. Born: 1839, Philadelphia, Pa. Accredited to: Pennsylvania. G.O. No.: 176, 9 July 1872.

Citation: Serving on board the U.S.S. Kansas near Greytown, Nicaragua 12 April 1872, Johnson displayed great coolness and self-possession at the time Comdr. A. F. Crosman and others were drowned and, by extraordinary heroism and personal exertion, prevented greater loss of life.

Epilogue: Very little information was available about Johnson's life in the archives of the CMOHS. He is lost to history.[62]

JOHNSON, WILLIAM
US Navy — Interim Period

Rank and organization: Cooper, US Navy. Born: 1855, St. Vincent West Indies. Accredited to: New York. G.O. No.: 326, 18 October 1884.

Citation: Serving on board the U.S.S. Adams at the Navy Yard, Mare Island, Calif., 14 November 1879, Johnson rescued Daniel W. Kloppen, a workman, from drowning.

Epilogue: Little is known about Johnson before or after he received the Medal. He died in 1905 and is buried in Arlington National Cemetery.[63]

NOIL, JOSEPH B.
US Navy — Interim Period

Rank and organization: Seaman, US Navy. Born: 1841, Nova Scotia. Accredited to: New York.

Citation: Serving on board the U.S.S. Powhatan at Norfolk, 26 December 1872, Noil saved Boatswain J. C. Walton from drowning.

Epilogue: No personal information was available in the CMOHS' archives for Noil. He is *lost to history.*[64]

SMITH, JOHN
US Navy — Interim Period

Rank and organization: Seaman, US Navy. Born: 1854, Bermuda. Accredited to: New York. G.O. No.: 326, 18 October 1884.

Citation: For jumping overboard from the U.S.S. Shenandoah, at Rio de Janeiro, Brazil,

19 September 1880, and rescuing from drowning James Grady, first class fireman.

Epilogue: Very little information was found in the archives for Smith except his citation. His life before and after receiving the Medal is *lost to history.*

SWEENEY, ROBERT
US Navy — Interim Period

Rank and organization: Ordinary Seaman, US Navy. Born: 1853 Montreal, Canada. Accredited to: New Jersey. G.O. No.: 326, 18 October 1884. Second award.

Citation: Serving on board the U.S.S. Kearsarge, at Hampton Roads, Va., 26 October 1881, Sweeney jumped overboard and assisted in saving from drowning a shipmate who had fallen overboard into a strongly running tide.

SECOND AWARD
Citation: Serving on board the U.S.S. Jamestown, at the Navy Yard New York, 20 December 1883, Sweeney rescued from drowning A. A. George, who had fallen overboard from that vessel.

Epilogue: Seaman Sweeney is only one of 19 to receive the Medal of Honor twice.[65] Although earlier Navy records show Seaman Sweeney was born in Canada, later records indicate he was born in Montserrat, West Indies. Before his death in 1890, he lived in New York City at 21 Minetta Lane. He is buried in Woodside Cemetery, New York.[66]

BAKER, EDWARD L., JR.
US Army — Spanish American War

Rank and organization: Sergeant Major, 10th US Cavalry. Place and date: At Santiago, Cuba, 1 July 1898. Entered service at: _____. Birth: Laramie County, Wyo. Date of issue: 3 July 1902.

Citation: Left cover and, under fire, rescued a wounded comrade from drowning.

Epilogue: A Buffalo Soldier serving with the 10th Cavalry in Cuba, Baker was born in Laramie County, Wyoming. He remained in the Army, rising to the rank of Captain, and died in 1913 at the Army's Presidio military base. He is buried in Rosedale Cemetery, Los Angeles, California.[67]

BELL, DENNIS
US Army — Spanish American War

Rank and organization: Private, Troop H, 10th US Cavalry. Place and date: At Tayabacoa, Cuba, 30 June 1898. Entered service at: Washington, D.C. Birth: Washington, DC. Date of issue: 23 June 1899.

Citation: Voluntarily went ashore in the face of the enemy and aided in the rescue of his wounded comrades; this after several previous attempts at rescue had been frustrated.

Epilogue: Bell died in 1953 and is buried in Arlington National Cemetery.[68]

LEE, FITZ
US Army — Spanish American War

Rank and organization: Private, Troop M, 10th US Cavalry. Place and date: At Tayabacoa, Cuba, 30 June 1898. Entered service at: Dinwiddie County, Va. Birth: Dinwiddie County, Va. Date of issue: 23 June 1899.

Citation: Voluntarily went ashore in the face of the enemy and aided in the rescue of his wounded comrades; this after several previous attempts had been frustrated.

Epilogue: Fitz died in Leavenworth, Kansas, and is buried in Leavenworth National Cemetery.[69]

PENN, ROBERT
US Navy — Spanish American War

Rank and organization: Fireman First Class, US Navy. Born: 10 October 1872, City Point, Va. Accredited to: Virginia. G.O. No.: 501, 14 December 1898.

Citation: On board the U.S.S. Iowa off Santiago de Cuba, 20 July 1898. Performing his duty at the risk of serious scalding at the time of the blowing out of the manhole gasket on board the vessel, Penn hauled the fire while standing on a board thrown across a coal bucket 1 foot above the boiling water which was still blowing from the boiler.

Epilogue: Penn died in Philadelphia in 1912. His burial site is unknown.[70]

THOMPKINS, WILLIAMS H.
US Army — Spanish American War

Rank and organization: Private, Troop G, 10th US Cavalry. Place and date: At Tayabacoa, Cuba, 30 June 1898. Entered service at: Paterson, N.J. Birth: Paterson, N.J. Date of issue: 23 June 1899.

Citation: Voluntarily went ashore in the face of the enemy and aided in the rescue of his wounded comrades; this after several previous attempts at rescue had been frustrated.

Epilogue: CMOHS records show that Thompkins retired from the Army and later died at the Presidio Army base hospital on September 24, 1918. He was buried in San Francisco National Cemetery at gravesite WS 1036A, row 11.[71]

WANTON, GEORGE H.
US Army — Spanish American War

Rank and organization: Private, Troop M, 10th US Cavalry. Place and date: At Tayabacoa, Cuba, 30 June 1898. Entered service at: Paterson, N.J. Birth: Paterson, N.J. Date of issue: 23 June 1899.

Citation: Voluntarily went ashore in the face of the enemy and aided in the rescue of his wounded comrades; this after several previous attempts at rescue had been frustrated.

Epilogue: Wanton had a most controversial and problematic life in the military. He was repeatedly court-martialed for sleeping on guard duty, fighting, insubordination, absent without leave, and a bout of the "loathsome disease," or gonorrhea, for which he spent 21 days in the hospital at Ft. Leavenworth. However, by 1889, he was maturing and had earned his first stripes as a Corporal.[72] Wanton retired from the Army as a Master Sergeant. He died in 1940 and is buried at Arlington National Cemetery.[73]

STOWERS, FREDDIE
US Army — World War I
Posthumous Award

Citation: Corporal Stowers, a native of Anderson County, South Carolina, distinguished himself by exceptional heroism on 28 September 1918, while serving as a squad leader in Company C, 371st Infantry Regiment, 93rd Infantry Division. His company was the lead company during the attack on Hill 188, Champagne Marne Sector, France, during World War I. A few minutes after the attack began, the enemy ceased firing and began climbing up onto the parapets of the trenches, holding up their arms as if wishing to surrender. The enemy's actions caused the American forces to cease fire and to come out into the open. As the company started forward and when within about 100 meters of the trench line, the enemy jumped back into their trenches and greeted Corporal Stowers' company with interlocking bands of machine gun fire and mortar fire causing well over fifty percent casualties. Faced with incredible enemy resistance, Corporal Stowers took charge, setting such a courageous example of personal bravery and leadership that he inspired his men to follow him in the attack. With extraordinary heroism and complete disregard of personal danger under devastating fire, he crawled forward leading his squad toward an enemy machine gun nest, which was causing heavy casualties to his company. After fierce fighting, the machine gun position was destroyed and the enemy soldiers were killed. Displaying great courage and intrepidity, Corporal Stowers continued to press the attack against a determined enemy. While crawling forward and urging his men to continue the attack on a second trench line, he was gravely wounded by machine gun fire. Although Corporal Stowers was mortally wounded, he pressed forward, urging on the members of his squad, until he died. Inspired by the heroism and display of bravery of Corporal Stowers, his company continued the attack against incredible odds, contributing to the capture of Hill 188 and causing heavy enemy casualties. Corporal Stowers' conspicuous gallantry, extraordinary heroism and supreme devotion to his men were well above and beyond the call of duty, follow the finest traditions of military service and reflect the utmost credit on him and the United States Army.

Epilogue: A native of Anderson County, South Carolina, Stowers was the first Black soldier to be awarded the Medal for service during World War I, and it took 72 years. Although he was nominated for the Medal, the recommendation was downgraded to the Distinguished Service Cross, the second highest medal for military valor (see APPENDIX D).[74] After an Army investigation, the Medal was finally presented to his two sisters, Georgina Palmer and Mary Bowens, by President Bush at a White House ceremony in 1991. At the time of his death, Stowers was survived by his wife Pearl and daughter Minnie Lee. He is buried in the Muse-Argonne Military Cemetery, France.[75]

BAKER, VERNON
US Army — World War II
European Theater

Citation: For extraordinary heroism in action on 5 and 6 April 1945, near Viareggio, Italy. Then Second Lieutenant Baker demonstrated outstanding courage and leadership in destroying enemy installations, personnel and equipment during his company's attack against a strongly entrenched enemy in mountainous terrain. When his company was stopped by the concentration of fire from several machine gun emplacements, he crawled to one position and destroyed it, killing three Germans. Continuing forward, he attacked an enemy observation post and killed two occupants. With the aid of one of his men, Lieutenant Baker attacked two more machine gun nests, killing or wounding the four enemy soldiers occupying these positions. He then covered the evacuation of the wounded personnel of his company by occupying an exposed position and drawing the enemy's fire. On the following night Lieutenant Baker voluntarily led a battalion advance through enemy mine fields and heavy fire toward the division objective. Second Lieutenant Baker's fighting spirit and daring leadership were an inspiration to his men and exemplify the highest traditions of the Armed Forces.

Epilogue: Orphaned when he was 4 years old, Baker enlisted in the Army six months before the start of World War II. He was commissioned in 1943 through Officer Candidate School. Baker is one of six Black Americans to receive the Medal through special legislation to redress a longstanding wrong and blatant racism by the War Department. Of the more than 432 Medals awarded for bravery during World War II, none was awarded to Blacks. A review of military records more than 50 years later finally corrected this injustice.[76] Baker is the only one of the six nominated and awarded the Medal who was still alive to receive it in person at a special White House ceremony. He made the Army his career, retiring in 1968 with the rank of Colonel. He and his wife moved to northern Idaho, where he still lives quietly with his second wife, Heidy.[77]

CARTER, EDWARD A., JR.
US Army — World War II
European Theater — Posthumous Award

Citation: For extraordinary heroism in action on 23 March 1945, near Speyer, Germany. When the tank on which he was riding received heavy bazooka and small arms fire, Sergeant Carter voluntarily attempted to lead a three-man group across an open field. Within a short time, two of his men were killed and the third seriously wounded. Continuing on alone, he was wounded five times and finally forced to take cover. As eight enemy riflemen attempted to capture him, Sergeant Carter killed six of them and captured the remaining two. He then crossed the field using as a shield his two prisoners from which he obtained valuable information concerning the disposition of enemy troops. Staff Sergeant Carter's extraordinary heroism was an inspiration to the officers and men of the Seventh Army Infantry Company Number 1 (Provisional) and exemplify the highest traditions of the Armed Forces.

Epilogue: The father of two sons, Carter entered the Army in 1941, survived the war, and died in 1963 from cancer. He was born and raised in Los Angeles, California, and as a child moved to China with his parents, who were missionaries. He ran away from home and made his way to Europe, where he joined the Abraham Lincoln Brigade to fight against the Fascists in Spain shortly before World War II. When he returned to the US and joined the Army, the military put him under surveillance because the Lincoln Brigade was thought to have communist ties, but no evidence was found against him. After the war in 1945, he became a Teamster truck driver in Gardena, California. He is buried in Arlington National Cemetery.

FOX, JOHN R.
US Army — World War II
European Theater — Posthumous Award

Citation: For extraordinary heroism against an armed enemy in the vicinity of Sommocolonia, Italy on 26 December 1944, while serving as a member of Cannon Company, 366th Infantry Regiment, 92d Infantry Division. During the preceding few weeks, Lieutenant Fox served with the 598th Field Artillery Battalion as a forward observer. On Christmas night, enemy soldiers gradually infiltrated the town of Sommocolonia in civilian clothes, and by early morning the town was largely in hostile hands. Commencing with a heavy barrage of enemy artillery at 0400 hours on 26 December 1944, an organized attack by uniformed German units began. Being greatly outnumbered, most of the United States Infantry forces were forced to withdraw from the town, but Lieutenant Fox and some other members of his observer party voluntarily remained on the second floor of a house to direct defensive artillery fire. At 0800 hours, Lieutenant Fox reported that the Germans were in the streets and attacking in strength. He then called for defensive artillery fire to slow the enemy advance. As the Germans continued to press the attack towards the area that Lieutenant Fox occupied, he adjusted the artillery fire closer to his position. Finally he was warned that the next adjustment would bring the deadly artillery right on top of his position. After acknowledging the danger, Lieutenant Fox insisted that the last adjustment be fired as this was the only way to defeat the attacking soldiers. Later, when a counterattack retook the position from the Germans, Lieutenant Fox's body was found with the bodies of approximately 100 German soldiers. Lieutenant Fox's gallant and courageous actions, at the supreme sacrifice of his own life, contributed greatly to delaying the enemy advance until other infantry and artillery units could reorganize to repel the attack. His extraordinary valorous actions were in keeping with the most cherished traditions of military service, and reflect the utmost credit on him, his unit, and the United States Army.

Epilogue: Fox was born and raised in Ohio and attended Wilberforce College, where he met Arlene, his future wife. Upon graduation, he immediately entered the Army and was felled in action in 1944. At the time of his death, he had one daughter, Sandra, who later grew up to be an anesthetist. His widow, Arlene, worked for many years at the local VA hospital.

Fox's family fought for years to have his achievements properly recognized. Finally, his Bronze Star was upgraded to a Distinguished Service Cross (DSC), the second highest award for valor. The DSC was presented to his family at Ft. Devens, Massachusetts, the post where Sandra was born when Fox was shipped out to Europe. Fox's Medal of Honor was a result of an Army study and recommendation to the President. No African-American soldier had been awarded the Medal of Honor in World War II. A study by Shaw University reviewed and recommended upgrades of 7 Distinguished Service Crosses to the Medal of Honor. Congress passed legislation accepting the recommendation, and President Clinton presented the Medal of Honor to the one recipient still living and to the next-of-kin of six others. Fox's widow Arlene accepted the Medal from President Clinton in 1997, 52 years after his death.[78] Carter is buried in Colebrook Cemetery, Whitman, Massachusetts.

JAMES, WILLY F., JR.
US Army — World War II
European Theater — Posthumous Award

Citation: For extraordinary heroism in action on 7 April 1945 near Lippoldsberg, Germany. As lead scout during a maneuver to secure and expand a vital bridgehead, Private First Class James was the first to draw enemy fire. He was pinned down for over an hour, during which time he observed enemy positions in detail. Returning to his platoon, he assisted in working out a new plan of maneuver. He then led a squad in the assault, accurately designating targets as he advanced, until he was killed by enemy machine gun fire while going to the aid of his fatally wounded platoon leader. Private First Class James' fearless, self-assigned actions, coupled with his diligent devotion to duty exemplified the finest traditions of the Armed Forces.

Epilogue: James was born and raised in Kansas City, Missouri, and entered the Army in 1942. At the time of his death, he was survived by his widow Valencia James. James's body was never returned to the US and is buried at the American Military Cemetery, Margraten, The Netherlands.[79] In 2001, the US Army Reserve Center in Bamberg, Germany, was named in his honor.[80]

RIVERS, RUBEN
US Army — World War II
European Theater — Posthumous Award

Citation: For extraordinary heroism in action during the 15-19 November 1944, toward Guebling, France. Though severely wounded in the leg, Sergeant Rivers refused medical treatment and evacuation, took command of another tank, and advanced with his company in Guebling the next day. Repeatedly refusing evacuation, Sergeant Rivers continued to direct his tank's fire at enemy positions through the morning of 19 November 1944. At dawn, Company A's tanks began to advance towards Bougaktroff, but were stopped by enemy fire. Sergeant Rivers, joined by another tank, opened fire on the enemy tanks, covering company A as they withdrew. While doing so, Sergeant River's tank was hit, killing him and wounding the crew. Staff Sergeant Rivers' fighting spirit and daring leadership were an inspiration to his unit and exemplify the highest traditions of military service.

Epilogue: Of mixed ethnicity (Black and American Indian), Rivers was born and raised in Oklahoma and taught by his father to be proud of his mixed heritage. Like other heroes from World War II, Rivers had to wait over fifty years to receive his long overdue recognition through a special act of Congress. Because Rivers had no next of kin, the Medal was instead presented to the Sergeant Major of the Army for safe-keeping by President Clinton in 1997. Rivers is buried in the American Battle Monument Cemetery, France.[81]

THOMAS, CHARLES L.
US Army — World War II
European Theater — Posthumous Award

Citation: For extraordinary heroism in action on 14 December 1944, near Climbach, France. While riding in the lead vehicle of a task force organized to storm and capture the village of Climbach, France, then First Lieutenant Thomas's armored scout car was subjected to intense enemy artillery, self-propelled gun, and small arms fire. Although wounded by the initial burst of hostile fire, Lieutenant Thomas signaled the remainder of the column to halt and, despite the severity of his wounds, assisted the crew of the wrecked car in dismounting. Upon leaving the scant protection which the vehicle afforded, Lieutenant Thomas was again subjected to a hail of enemy fire which inflicted multiple gunshot wounds in his chest, legs, and left arm. Despite the intense pain caused by these wounds, Lieutenant Thomas ordered and directed the dispersion and emplacement of two antitank guns which in a few moments were promptly and effectively returning the enemy fire. Realizing that he could no longer remain in command of the platoon, he signaled to the platoon commander to join him. Lieutenant Thomas then thoroughly oriented him on enemy gun dispositions and the general situation. Only after he was certain that his junior officer was in full control of the situation did he permit himself to be evacuated. First Lieutenant Thomas' outstanding heroism were an inspiration to his men and exemplify the highest traditions of the Armed Forces.

Epilogue: A native of Detroit, Thomas survived the war, remained in the army until 1947, when he was discharged with the rank of Major. Thomas died in 1980 and was survived by his wife Bertha.

WATSON, GEORGE
US Army — World War II
Pacific Theater — Posthumous Award

Citation: For extraordinary heroism in action on 8 March 1943. Private Watson was on board a ship which was attacked and hit by enemy bombers. When the ship was abandoned, Private Watson, instead of seeking to save himself, remained in the water assisting several soldiers who could not swim to reach the safety of the raft. This heroic action, which subsequently cost him his life, resulted in the saving of several of his comrades. Weakened by his exertions, he was dragged down by the suction of the sinking ship and was drowned. Private Watson's extraordinarily valorous actions, daring leadership, and self-sacrificing devotion to his fellow-man exemplify the finest traditions of military service.

Epilogue: Born and raised in Birmingham, Alabama, Watson was 29 when he died, pulled down by a sinking ship. When the Medal was finally awarded to recognize his actions some fifty years later, there was no next of kin to receive it. The Medal was instead given to the Army's Sergeant Major for safe-keeping. Watson's body was never recovered.[82]

CHARLTON, CORNELIUS H.
US Army — Korean War
Posthumous Award

Rank and organization: Sergeant, US Army, Company C, 24th Infantry Regiment, 25th Infantry Division. Place and date: Near Chipori, Korea, 2 June 1951. Entered service at: Bronx, N.Y. Born: 24 July 1929, East Gulf, W. Va. G.O. No.: 30, 19 March 1952.

Citation: Sgt. Charlton, a member of Company C, distinguished himself by conspicuous gallantry and intrepidity above and beyond the call of duty in action against the enemy. His platoon was attacking heavily defended hostile positions on commanding ground when the leader was wounded and evacuated. Sgt. Charlton assumed command, rallied the men, and spearheaded the assault against the hill. Personally eliminating 2 hostile positions and killing 6 of the enemy with his rifle fire and grenades, he continued up the slope until the unit suffered heavy casualties and became pinned down. Regrouping the men he led them forward only to be again hurled back by a shower of grenades. Despite a severe chest wound, Sgt. Charlton refused medical attention and led a third daring charge which carried to the crest of the ridge. Observing that the remaining emplacement which had retarded the advance was situated on the reverse slope, he charged it alone, was again hit by a grenade but raked the position with a devastating fire which eliminated it and routed the defenders. The wounds received during his daring exploits resulted in his death but his indomitable courage, superb leadership, and gallant self-sacrifice reflect the highest credit upon himself the infantry, and the military service.

Epilogue: Born and raised in East Gulf, West Virginia, Charlton was one of seventeen children.[83] He weighed fifteen pounds at birth. His father was a coal miner and his family lived in primitive, company-owned housing in Raleigh County. Charlton and some family members eventually moved to

New York, where he finished high school and joined the Army in 1947.[84] He saw duty in Okinawa before landing in Korea with the all-Black 24th Infantry Regiment in October 1950. Charlton was killed in the action for which he would receive the Medal. When his body was brought back to the United States, the Army failed to offer the family the option of burying him in Arlington National Cemetery and later called it an administrative error. Instead, Charlton was buried in a segregated cemetery, which is also shared with Jews. Through the efforts of a local citizen, today he is buried in the American Legion Cemetery, Beckley, West Virginia.[85]

THOMPSON, WILLIAM
US Army — Korean War
Posthumous Award

Rank and organization: Private First Class, US Army, 24th Company M, 24th Infantry Regiment, 25th Infantry Division. Place and date: Near Haman, Korea, 6 August 1950. Entered service at: Bronx, N.Y. Birth: New York, N.Y. G.O. No.: 63, 2 August 1951.

Citation: Pfc. Thompson, distinguished himself by conspicuous gallantry and intrepidity above and beyond the call of duty in action against the enemy. While his platoon was reorganizing under cover of darkness, fanatical enemy forces in overwhelming strength launched a surprise attack on the unit. Pfc. Thompson set up his machine gun in the path of the onslaught and swept the enemy with withering fire, pinning them down momentarily thus permitting the remainder of his platoon to withdraw to a more tenable position. Although hit repeatedly by grenade fragments and small-arms fire, he resisted all efforts of his comrades to induce him to withdraw, steadfastly remained at his machine gun and continued to deliver deadly, accurate fire until mortally wounded by an enemy grenade. Pfc. Thompson's dauntless courage and gallant self-sacrifice reflect the highest credit on himself and uphold the esteemed traditions of military service.

Epilogue: The first Black to receive the Medal since the Spanish American War was found on a "cold bench" in Brooklyn when he was 15 years old by the Rev. Harvey Eva, who was director of a Bronx orphanage. Rev. Eva said, "The boy followed my wife and I home at day and remained several years before entering the army." His home of record was listed as the orphanage. Eva described Thompson as "helpful, cheerful and willing and very close to us." While at the orphanage, Thompson became a member of the choir and was one of its best singers.[86] Had it not been for the persistence of Thompson's commanders, he might not have ever been recognized for his heroic acts. When the recommendation for the Medal was submitted to general headquarters, it was initially rejected. The reviewers saw no significance in a Black soldier dying for his country.[87] Thompson's Medal was presented to his mother, Mrs. Mary Henderson, by General Omar Bradley at a Pentagon ceremony. Thompson was buried in Brooklyn, New York. Both his mother and father attended the services.

ANDERSON, JAMES, JR.
US Marine Corps — Vietnam War
Posthumous Award

Rank and organization: Private First Class, US Marine Corps, 2nd Platoon, Company F, 2nd Battalion, 3rd Marines, 3rd Marine Division. Place and date: Republic of Vietnam, 28 February 1967. Entered service at: Los Angeles, Calif. Born: 22 January 1947, Los Angeles, Calif.

Citation: For conspicuous gallantry and intrepidity at the risk of his life above and beyond the call of duty. Company F was advancing in dense jungle northwest of Cam Lo in an effort to extract a heavily besieged reconnaissance patrol. Pfc. Anderson's platoon was the lead element and had advanced only about 200 meters when they were brought under extremely intense enemy small-arms and automatic weapons fire. The platoon reacted swiftly, getting on line as best they could in the thick terrain, and began returning fire. Pfc. Anderson found himself tightly bunched together with the other members of the platoon only 20 meters from the enemy positions. As the fire fight continued several of the men were wounded by the deadly enemy assault. Suddenly, an enemy grenade landed in the midst of the marines and rolled alongside Pfc. Anderson's head. Unhesitatingly and with complete disregard for his personal safety, he reached out, grasped the grenade, pulled it to his chest and curled around it as it went off. Although several marines received shrapnel from the grenade, his body absorbed the major force of the explosion. In this singularly heroic act, Pfc. Anderson saved his comrades from serious injury and possible death. His personal heroism, extraordinary valor, and inspirational supreme self-sacrifice reflected great credit upon himself and the Marine Corps and upheld the highest traditions of the U.S. Naval Service. He gallantly gave his life for his country.

Epilogue: Anderson was born and raised in Los Angeles, California, where he attended Carver Elementary School, Willowbrook Junior High School, Centennial High School, and Los Harbor Junior College prior to entering the Marines in 1966.[88] He became the first Black to receive the Medal in the history of the Marine Corps. He died when he used his body to smother an enemy hand grenade, saving the life of his fellow Marines. At the time of death, he was survived by his parents, five sisters, and one brother. He is buried in Lincoln Memorial Park Cemetery, Los Angeles.[89]

ANDERSON, WEBSTER
US Army — Vietnam War

Rank and organization: Sergeant First Class, US Army, Battery A, 2nd Battalion, 320th Field Artillery, 101st Airborne Infantry Division (Airmobile). Place and date: Tam Ky, Republic of Vietnam, 15 October 1967. Entered service at: Winnsboro, S.C. Born: 15 July 1933, Winnsboro, S.C.

Citation: Sfc. Anderson (then S/Sgt.), distinguished himself by conspicuous gallantry and intrepidity in action while serving as chief of section in Battery A, against a hostile force. During the early morning hours Battery A's defensive position was attacked by a determined North Vietnamese Army infantry unit supported by heavy mortar, recoilless rifle, rocket propelled grenade and automatic weapon fire. The initial enemy onslaught breached the battery defensive perimeter. Sfc. Anderson, with complete disregard for his personal safety, mounted the exposed parapet of his howitzer position and became the mainstay of the defense of the battery position. Sfc. Anderson directed devastating direct howitzer fire on the assaulting enemy while providing rifle and grenade defensive fire against enemy soldiers attempting to overrun his gun section position. While protecting his crew and directing their fire against the enemy from his exposed position, 2 enemy grenades exploded at his feet knocking him down and severely wounding him in the legs. Despite the excruciating pain and though not able to stand, Sfc. Anderson valorously propped himself on the parapet and continued to direct howitzer fire upon the closing enemy and to encourage his men to fight on. Seeing an enemy grenade land within the gun pit near a wounded member of his gun crew, Sfc. Anderson heedless of his own safety, seized the grenade and attempted to throw it over the parapet to save his men. As the grenade was thrown from the position it exploded and Sfc. Anderson was again grievously wounded. Although only partially conscious and severely wounded, Sfc. Anderson refused medical evacuation and continued to encourage his men in the defense of the position. Sfc. Anderson by his inspirational leadership, professionalism, devotion to duty and complete disregard for his welfare was able to maintain the defense of his section position and to defeat a determined attack. Sfc. Anderson's gallantry and extraordinary heroism at the risk of his life above and beyond the call of duty are in the highest traditions of the military service and reflect great credit upon himself, his unit, and the U.S. Army.

Epilogue: Anderson was born and raised in South Carolina, although he lived briefly in Philadelphia before entering the Army in 1953. He was a career soldier and served in Germany and the Dominican Republic before reassignment to Vietnam with the 101st Airborne Division. He lost both legs and an arm during the battle for which he received the Medal but is one of the few Black Medal recipients to survive. After discharge from the Army, he returned to Winnsboro, South Carolina, where he worked part-time in a television and radio repair business.[90] He also actively volunteered his time to participate in various community service causes and projects. The last few years of his life were very challenging. He became a caretaker for his wife, who is gravely ill; his oldest son lost a leg to cancer; and his business failed. Anderson died in 2005 and is buried in Blackjack Baptist Cemetery, Winnsboro, South Carolina.[91]

ASHLEY, EUGENE, JR.
US Army — Vietnam War
Posthumous Award

Rank and organization: Sergeant First Class, US Army, Company C, 5th Special Forces Group (Airborne), 1st Special Forces. Place and date: Near Lang Vei, Republic of Vietnam, 6 and 7 February 1968. Entered service at: New York, N.Y. Born: 12 October 1931, Wilmington, N.C.

Citation: Sfc. Ashley, distinguished himself by conspicuous gallantry and intrepidity while serving with Detachment A-101, Company C. Sfc. Ashley was the senior special forces Advisor of a hastily organized assault force whose mission was to rescue entrapped U.S. special forces advisors at Camp Lang Vei. During the initial attack on the special forces camp by North Vietnamese army forces, Sfc. Ashley supported the camp with high explosive and illumination mortar rounds. When communications were lost with the main camp, he assumed the additional responsibility of directing air strikes and artillery support. Sfc. Ashley organized and equipped a small assault force composed of local friendly personnel. During the ensuing battle, Sfc. Ashley led a total of 5 vigorous assaults against the enemy, continuously exposing himself to a voluminous hail of enemy grenades, machine gun and automatic weapons fire. Throughout these assaults, he was plagued by numerous booby-trapped satchel charges in all bunkers on his avenue of approach. During his fifth and final assault, he adjusted air strikes nearly on top of his assault element, forcing the enemy to withdraw and resulting in friendly control of the summit of the hill. While exposing himself to intense enemy fire, he was seriously wounded by machine gun fire but continued his mission without regard for his personal safety. After the fifth assault he lost consciousness and was carried from the summit by his comrades only to suffer a fatal wound when an enemy artillery round landed in the area. Sfc. Ashley displayed extraordinary heroism in risking his life in an attempt to save the lives of his entrapped comrades and commanding officer. His total disregard for his personal safety while exposed to enemy observation and automatic weapons fire was an inspiration to all men committed to the assault. The resolute valor with which he led 5 gallant charges placed critical diversionary pressure on the attacking enemy and his valiant efforts carved a channel in the overpowering enemy forces and weapons positions through which the survivors of Camp Lang Vei eventually escaped to freedom. Sfc. Ashley's bravery at the cost of his life was in the highest traditions of the military service, and reflects great credit upon himself, his unit, and the U.S. Army.

Epilogue: Ashley was born in Wilmington, North Carolina. He moved to Brooklyn, New York, as a child and graduated from Alexander Hamilton High School prior to entering the Army in 1951. Before his assignment to Vietnam, he was stationed in Korea, Germany, Okinawa, and the Dominican Republic.[92] At the time of his death, he was survived by his wife, Barbara; five children, Larry, Charles, Michael, Darrin, and Tracy; and mother, Cornelia. Ashley is buried in Rockfish Memorial Cemetery, Fayetteville, North Carolina.[93]

AUSTIN, OSCAR .P.
US Marine Corps — Vietnam War
Posthumous Award

Rank and organization: Private First Class, US Marine Corps, Company E, 2nd Battalion, 7th Marines, 1st Marine Division, (Rein), FMF. Place and date: West of Da Nang, Republic of Vietnam, 23 February 1969. Entered service at: Phoenix, Ariz. Born: 15 January 1948, Nacogdoches, Tex.

Citation: For conspicuous gallantry and intrepidity at the risk of his life above and beyond the call of duty while serving as an assistant machine gunner with Company E, in connection with operations against enemy forces. During the early morning hours Pfc. Austin's observation post was subjected to a fierce ground attack by a large North Vietnamese Army force supported by a heavy volume of hand grenades, satchel charges, and small arms fire. Observing that 1 of his wounded companions had fallen unconscious in a position dangerously exposed to the hostile fire, Pfc. Austin unhesitatingly left the relative security of his fighting hole and, with complete disregard for his safety, raced across the fire-swept terrain to assist the marine to a covered location. As he neared the casualty, he observed an enemy grenade land nearby and, reacting instantly, leaped between the injured marine and the lethal object, absorbing the effects of its detonation. As he ignored his painful injuries and turned to examine the wounded man, he saw a North Vietnamese Army soldier aiming a weapon at his unconscious companion. With full knowledge of the probable consequences and thinking only to protect the marine, Pfc. Austin resolutely threw himself between the casualty and the hostile soldier, and, in doing, was mortally wounded. Pfc. Austin's indomitable courage, inspiring initiative and selfless devotion to duty upheld the highest traditions of the Marine Corps and the U.S. Naval Service. He gallantly gave his life for his country.

Epilogue: Austin was born and raised in Nacogdoches, Texas, where he attended Booker T. Washington Elementary School and Phoenix Union High School. He joined the Marines in 1968 and received his initial training at the Recruit Depot, San Diego, and at Camp Pendleton. At the time of the action for which he received the Medal, he was assigned to the 7th Marines in Vietnam. At the time of his death, he was survived by his mother, Mildred, father, Frank, four sisters, and one brother. Austin is buried in Greenwood Cemetery, Phoenix, Arizona.[94]

BRYANT, WILLIAM MAUD
US Army — Vietnam War
Posthumous Award

Rank and organization: Sergeant First Class, US Army, Company A, 5th Special Forces Group, 1st Special Forces. Place and date: Long Khanh Province, Republic of Vietnam, 24 March 1969. Entered service at: Detroit, Mich. Born: 16 February 1933, Cochran, Ga.

Citation: For conspicuous gallantry and intrepidity in action at the risk of his life above and beyond the call of duty. Sfc. Bryant, assigned to Company A, distinguished himself while serving as commanding officer of Civilian Irregular Defense Group Company 321, 2d Battalion, 3d Mobile Strike Force Command, during combat operations. The battalion came under heavy fire and became surrounded by the elements of 3 enemy regiments. Sfc. Bryant displayed extraordinary heroism throughout the succeeding 34 hours of incessant attack as he moved throughout the company position heedless of the intense hostile fire while establishing and improving the defensive perimeter, directing fire during critical phases of the battle, distributing ammunition, assisting the wounded, and providing the leadership and inspirational example of courage to his men. When a helicopter drop of ammunition was made to re-supply the beleaguered force, Sfc. Bryant with complete disregard for his safety ran through the heavy enemy fire to retrieve the scattered ammunition boxes and distributed needed ammunition to his men. During a lull in the intense fighting, Sfc. Bryant led a patrol outside the perimeter to obtain information of the enemy. The patrol came under intense automatic weapons fire and was pinned down. Sfc. Bryant single-handedly repulsed 1 enemy attack on his small force and by his heroic action inspired his men to fight off other assaults. Seeing a wounded enemy soldier some distance from the patrol location, Sfc. Bryant crawled forward alone under heavy fire to retrieve the soldier for intelligence purposes. Finding that the enemy soldier had expired, Sfc. Bryant crawled back to his patrol and led his men back to the company position where he again took command of the defense. As the siege continued, Sfc. Bryant organized and led a patrol in a daring attempt to break through the enemy encirclement. The patrol had advanced some 200 meters by heavy fighting when it was pinned down by the intense automatic weapons fire from heavily fortified bunkers and Sfc. Bryant was severely wounded. Despite his wounds he rallied his men, called for helicopter gunship support, and directed heavy suppressive fire upon the enemy positions. Following the last gunship attack, Sfc. Bryant fearlessly charged an enemy automatic weapons position, overrunning it, and single-handedly destroying its 3 defenders. Inspired by his heroic example, his men renewed their attack on the entrenched enemy. While regrouping his small force for the final assault against the enemy, Sfc. Bryant fell mortally wounded by an enemy rocket. Sfc. Bryant's selfless concern for his comrades, at the cost of his life above and beyond the call of duty are in keeping with the highest traditions of the military service and reflect great credit upon himself, his unit, and the U.S. Army.

Epilogue: Bryant was born in Cochran, Georgia, and enlisted in the Army in 1953 in Detroit. By most measures, he was a trained elite warrior; he had completed the Airborne, Ranger, Special Forces, heavy weapons, and intelligence courses. In addition to assignments throughout the United States, he served in Germany just prior to reassignment to Vietnam in 1968. At the time of his death, he was survived by his wife, Lizzie, and four children, Nancyrette, Angela, Gregory, and Kelvin. The Medal was presented to his family by President Nixon at a White House ceremony. Bryant is buried in Raleigh National Cemetery, North Carolina. [95]

DAVIS, RODNEY MAXWELL
US Marine Corps — Vietnam War
Posthumous Award

Rank and organization: Sergeant, US Marine Corps, Company B, 1st Battalion, 5th Marines, 1st Marine Division. Place and date: Quang Nam Province, Republic of Vietnam, 6 September 1967. Entered service at: Macon, Ga. Born: 7 April 1942, Macon, Ga.

Citation: For conspicuous gallantry and intrepidity at the risk of his life above and beyond the call of duty while serving as the right guide of the 2d Platoon, Company B, in action against enemy forces. Elements of the 2d Platoon were pinned down by a numerically superior force of attacking North Vietnamese Army Regulars. Remnants of the platoon were located in a trench line where Sgt. Davis was directing the fire of his men in an attempt to repel the enemy attack. Disregarding the enemy hand grenades and high volume of small arms and mortar fire, Sgt. Davis moved from man to man shouting words of encouragement to each of them while firing and throwing grenades at the onrushing enemy. When an enemy grenade landed in the trench in the midst of his men, Sgt. Davis, realizing the gravity of the situation, and in a final valiant act of complete self-sacrifice, instantly threw himself upon the grenade, absorbing with his body the full and terrific force of the explosion. Through his extraordinary initiative and inspiring valor in the face of almost certain death, Sgt. Davis saved his comrades from injury and possible loss of life, enabled his platoon to hold its vital position, and upheld the highest traditions of the Marine Corps and the U.S. Naval Service. He gallantly gave his life for his country.

Epilogue: Davis was born and raised in Macon, Georgia. He entered the Marine Corps after graduating from Pete G Appling High School in 1961. He completed boot camp at Parris Island and received infantry training at Camp Lejeune. Prior to assignment to Vietnam, he was a Marine guard in London. At the time of his death, Davis was survived by his wife, Judy, two children, Jane and Samantha, his parents, Mr. & Mrs. George Davis, three brothers, and one sister.[96] A Navy ship was named in his honor in 1972. Davis is buried in Linwood Cemetery, Macon, Georgia.

JENKINS, ROBERT H., JR.

US Marine Corps — Vietnam War
Posthumous Award

Rank and organization: Private First Class, US Marine Corps, 3rd Reconnaissance Battalion, 3rd Marine Division (Rein), FMF. Place and date: Fire Support Base Argonne, Republic of Vietnam, 5 March 1969. Entered service at: Jacksonville, Fla. Born: 1 June 1948, Interlachen, Fla.

Citation: For conspicuous gallantry and intrepidity at the risk of his life above and beyond the call of duty while serving as a machine gunner with Company C, 3d Reconnaissance Battalion, in connection with operations against enemy forces. Early in the morning Pfc. Jenkins' 12-man reconnaissance team was occupying a defensive position at Fire Support Base Argonne south of the Demilitarized Zone. Suddenly, the marines were assaulted by a North Vietnamese Army platoon employing mortars, automatic weapons, and hand grenades. Reacting instantly, Pfc. Jenkins and another marine quickly moved into a 2-man fighting emplacement, and as they boldly delivered accurate machine gun fire against the enemy, a North Vietnamese soldier threw a hand grenade into the friendly emplacement. Fully realizing the inevitable results of his actions, Pfc. Jenkins quickly seized his comrade, and pushing the man to the ground, he leaped on top of the marine to shield him from the explosion. Absorbing the full impact of the detonation, Pfc. Jenkins was seriously injured and subsequently succumbed to his wounds. His courage, inspiring valor and selfless devotion to duty saved a fellow marine from serious injury or possible death and upheld the highest traditions of the Marine Corps and the U.S. Naval Service. He gallantly gave his life for his country.

Epilogue: Jenkins was born and raised in Interlachen, Florida, where he attended Oak Grove Elementary and Central Academy High Schools prior to entering the Marine Corps in 1968. He completed his basics at Parris Island and advance training in Camp Lejeune before being assigned to the 3rd Marine Division in the Republic of Vietnam, where he was killed in the action for which he would receive the Medal. Jenkins was survived by his father, Robert, mother, Willie Mae, three sisters, and one brother.[97] The man whose life Jenkins saved when he fell on the hand grenade returned the favor in a small but very meaningful way. Fred Ostrom was with Jenkins the night the soldiers of North Vietnam attempted to overrun their position. Because of what Jenkins did, Ostrom lived, and from that day on, Ostrom carried a photo of Jenkins wherever he went. In 1995, when Ostrom learned that Jenkins's grave had been badly neglected, he started a campaign to restore it. The effort quickly gained support from various veteran's groups and public officials. At the official ceremony, all of Jenkins's local family and friends were present, including Ostrom and a special representative from the White House. Jenkins is buried at Sister Spring Baptist Cemetery, Interlachen, Florida.[98]

JOEL, LAWRENCE
US Army — Vietnam War

Rank and organization: Specialist Sixth Class (then Sp5c), US Army, Headquarters and Headquarters Company, 1st Battalion (Airborne), 503rd Infantry, 173rd Airborne Brigade. Place and date: Republic of Vietnam, 8 November 1965, Entered service at: New York City, N.Y. G.O. No.: 15, 5 April 1967. Born: 22 February 1928, Winston-Salem, N.C.

Citation: For conspicuous gallantry and intrepidity at the risk of life above and beyond the call of duty. Sp6c. Joel demonstrated indomitable courage, determination, and professional skill when a numerically superior and well-concealed Viet Cong element launched a vicious attack which wounded or killed nearly every man in the lead squad of the company. After treating the men wounded by the initial burst of gunfire, he bravely moved forward to assist others who were wounded while proceeding to their objective. While moving from man to man, he was struck in the right leg by machine gun fire. Although painfully wounded his desire to aid his fellow soldiers transcended all personal feeling. He bandaged his own wound and self-administered morphine to deaden the pain enabling him to continue his dangerous undertaking. Through this period of time, he constantly shouted words of encouragement to all around him. Then, completely ignoring the warnings of others, and his pain, he continued his search for wounded, exposing himself to hostile fire; and, as bullets dug up the dirt around him, he held plasma bottles high while kneeling completely engrossed in his life saving mission. Then, after being struck a second time and with a bullet lodged in his thigh, he dragged himself over the battlefield and succeeded in treating 13 more men before his medical supplies ran out. Displaying resourcefulness, he saved the life of 1 man by placing a plastic bag over a severe chest wound to congeal the blood. As 1 of the platoons pursued the Viet Cong, an insurgent force in concealed positions opened fire on the platoon and wounded many more soldiers. With a new stock of medical supplies, Sp6c. Joel again shouted words of encouragement as he crawled through an intense hail of gunfire to the wounded men. After the 24 hour battle subsided and the Viet Cong dead numbered 410, snipers continued to harass the company. Throughout the long battle, Sp6c. Joel never lost sight of his mission as a medical aidman and continued to comfort and treat the wounded until his own evacuation was ordered. His meticulous attention to duty saved a large number of lives and his unselfish, daring example under most adverse conditions was an inspiration to all. Sp6c. Joel's profound concern for his fellow soldiers, at the risk of his life above and beyond the call of duty are in the highest traditions of the U.S. Army and reflect great credit upon himself and the Armed Forces of his country.

Epilogue: Joel was born in poverty in Winston-Salem, North Carolina. The segregated south offered few opportunities for Blacks,[99] and to lessen the economic burden of raising the Joel family, his father placed him in a foster home. He was raised by Mr. & Mrs. Samuels, who had five daughters and no sons. He attended the Woodland Avenue and the 14th Street Elementary Schools and graduated from Atkins High School. Finding few opportunities, he first enlisted in the Army in 1947 and again in 1949. Joel would remain in the Army until his retirement in 1969. He returned to Winston-Salem, where he worked for the Veterans Administration for a number of years until his death in 1984. He was survived by his wife and two children and is buried in Arlington National Cemetery.[100]

JOHNSON, DWIGHT H.
US Army — Vietnam War

Rank and organization: Specialist Fifth Class, US Army, Company B, 1st Battalion, 69th Armor, 4th Infantry Division. Place and date: Near Dak To, Kontum Province, Republic of Vietnam, 15 January 1968. Entered service at: Detriot, Mich. Born: 7 May 1947, Detroit, Mich.

Citation: For conspicuous gallantry and intrepidity at the risk of his life above and beyond the call of duty. Sp5c. Johnson, a tank driver with Company B, was a member of a reaction force moving to aid other elements of his platoon, which was in heavy contact with a battalion size North Vietnamese force. Sp5c. Johnson's tank, upon reaching the point of contact, threw a track and became immobilized. Realizing that he could do no more as a driver, he climbed out of the vehicle, armed only with a .45 caliber pistol. Despite intense hostile fire, Sp5c. Johnson killed several enemy soldiers before he had expended his ammunition. Returning to his tank through a heavy volume of antitank rocket, small arms and automatic weapons fire, he obtained a sub-machine gun with which to continue his fight against the advancing enemy. Armed with this weapon, Sp5c. Johnson again braved deadly enemy fire to return to the center of the ambush site where he courageously eliminated more of the determined foe. Engaged in extremely close combat when the last of his ammunition was expended, he killed an enemy soldier with the stock end of his submachine gun. Now weaponless, Sp5c. Johnson ignored the enemy fire around him, climbed into his platoon sergeant's tank, extricated a wounded crewmember and carried him to an armored personnel carrier. He then returned to the same tank and assisted in firing the main gun until it jammed. In a magnificent display of courage, Sp5c. Johnson exited the tank and again armed only with a .45 caliber pistol, engaged several North Vietnamese troops in close proximity to the vehicle. Fighting his way through devastating fire and remounting his own immobilized tank, he remained fully exposed to the enemy as he bravely and skillfully engaged them with the tank's externally-mounted .50 caliber machine gun; where he remained until the situation was brought under control. Sp5c. Johnson's profound concern for his fellow soldiers, at the risk of his life above and beyond the call of duty are in keeping with the highest traditions of the military service and reflect great credit upon himself and the U.S. Army.

Epilogue: Johnson was born and raised in a dreary Detroit housing project. Growing up, he was remembered by neighbors as someone who was gentle and hated to fight.[101] When he was shot and killed while trying to rob a Detroit grocery store shortly after he returned from Vietnam and before his 24th birthday, his death might have gone unnoticed, as he was one of many who died that year in similar circumstances. However, it was later learned that he had received the Medal of Honor for heroic actions in Vietnam. Many articles would be written about him to try to explain and to understand his death. Sociologists, psychologists, politicians would debate and ponder the tragedy. Was it racism? Was he a victim of the aftermath of a senseless war? Some would say his death was a precursor of what would follow: tens of thousands of Vietnam veterans who had difficulty adjusting to civilian life after fighting in a savage war. The Veterans Administration ruled that he was incompetent at the time of his death, which meant that his widow could receive a $300 monthly pension.[102] Johnson is buried in Arlington National Cemetery.[103]

JOHNSON, RALPH H.
US Marine Corps — Vietnam War
Posthumous Award

Rank and organization: Private First Class, US Marine Corps, Company A, 1st Reconnaissance Battalion, 1st Marine Division (Rein), FMF. Place and date: Near the Quan Duc Valley, Republic of Vietnam, 5 March 1968. Entered service at: Oakland, Calif. Born: 11 January 1949, Charleston, S.C.

Citation: For conspicuous gallantry and intrepidity at the risk of his life above and beyond the call of duty while serving as a reconnaissance scout with Company A, in action against the North Vietnamese Army and Viet Cong forces. In the early morning hours during Operation ROCK, Pfc. Johnson was a member of a 15-man reconnaissance patrol manning an observation post on Hill 146 overlooking the Quan Duc Valley deep in enemy controlled territory. They were attacked by a platoon-size hostile force employing automatic weapons, satchel charges and hand grenades. Suddenly, a hand grenade landed in the 3-man fighting hole occupied by Pfc. Johnson and 2 fellow marines. Realizing the inherent danger to his 2 comrades, he shouted a warning and unhesitatingly hurled himself upon the explosive device. When the grenade exploded, Pfc. Johnson absorbed the tremendous impact of the blast and was killed instantly. His prompt and heroic act saved the life of 1 marine at the cost of his life and undoubtedly prevented the enemy from penetrating his sector of the patrol's perimeter. Pfc. Johnson's courage, inspiring valor and selfless devotion to duty were in keeping with the highest traditions of the Marine Corps and the U.S. Naval Service. He gallantly gave his life for his country.

Epilogue: Johnson was born and raised in Charleston, South Carolina, where he attended public school prior to entering the Marine Corps in 1967. He completed his basic training at Parris Island and advanced training in infantry at Camp Pendleton. At the time of his death, Johnson was survived by his mother, Rebecca, father, Luther, five brothers, and five sisters.[104] When he fell on the hand grenade that took his life and for which he received the Medal, he saved many others, including Clebe McClary, a fellow Marine who was with Johnson when the enemy grenade was thrown into their foxhole. McClary said Johnson was the bravest man he ever knew and talks about him three or four times a day. "He saved my life," said McClary.[105] One of many honors for Johnson was the 1990 renaming of Charleston's Veterans Administration Medical Center in his name.[106]

LANGHORN, GARFIELD M.
US Army — Vietnam War
Posthumous Award

Rank and organization: Private First class, US Army, Troop C, 7th Squadron (Airmobile), 17th Cavalry, 1st Aviation Brigade. Place and date: Pleiku province, Republic of Vietnam, 15 January 1969. Entered service at: Brooklyn, N.Y. Born: 10 September 1948, Cumberland, Va.

Citation: For conspicuous gallantry and intrepidity in action at the risk of his life above and beyond the call of duty. Pfc. Langhorn distinguished himself while serving as a radio operator with Troop C, near Plei Djereng in Pleiku province. Pfc. Langhorn's platoon was inserted into a landing zone to rescue 2 pilots of a Cobra helicopter shot down by enemy fire on a heavily timbered slope. He provided radio coordination with the command-and-control aircraft overhead while the troops hacked their way through dense undergrowth to the wreckage, where both aviators were found dead. As the men were taking the bodies to a pickup site, they suddenly came under intense fire from North Vietnamese soldiers in camouflaged bunkers to the front and right flank, and within minutes they were surrounded. Pfc. Langhorn immediately radioed for help from the orbiting gunships, which began to place minigun and rocket fire on the aggressors. He then lay between the platoon leader and another man, operating the radio and providing covering fire for the wounded who had been moved to the center of the small perimeter. Darkness soon fell, making it impossible for the gunships to give accurate support, and the aggressors began to probe the perimeter. An enemy hand grenade landed in front of Pfc. Langhorn and a few feet from personnel who had become casualties. Choosing to protect these wounded, he unhesitatingly threw himself on the grenade, scooped it beneath his body and absorbed the blast. By sacrificing himself, he saved the lives of his comrades. Pfc. Langhorn's extraordinary heroism at the cost of his life was in keeping with the highest traditions of the military service and reflect great credit on himself, his unit, and the U.S. Army.

Epilogue: Langhorn was a star athlete in high school, especially in track. His father, Garfield Langhorn, a retired janitor, said his son wanted to "go into data processing" before he was drafted into the Army. His mother, Mary, a retired garment worker, said her son often wrote to her from Vietnam that "killing people was nonsense." Langhorn died when he threw himself on a hand grenade to save the lives of his fellow soldiers. In addition to his parents, he was survived by two sisters.[107] He is buried at Riverhead Cemetery, Riverhead, New York.[108]

LEONARD, MATTHEW
US Army — Vietnam War
Posthumous Award

Rank and organization: Platoon Sergeant, US Army, Company B, 1st Battalion, 16th Infantry, 1st Infantry Division. Place and date: Near Suoi Da, Republic of Vietnam, 28 February 1967. Entered service at: Birmingham, Ala. Born: 26 November 1929, Eutaw, Ala.

Citation: For conspicuous gallantry and intrepidity in action at the risk of his life above and beyond the call of duty. His platoon was suddenly attacked by a large enemy force employing small arms, automatic weapons, and hand grenades. Although the platoon leader and several other key leaders were among the first wounded, P/Sgt. Leonard quickly rallied his men to throw back the initial enemy assaults. During the short pause that followed, he organized a defensive perimeter, redistributed ammunition, and inspired his comrades through his forceful leadership and words of encouragement. Noticing a wounded companion outside the perimeter, he dragged the man to safety but was struck by a sniper's bullet which shattered his left hand. Refusing medical attention and continuously exposing himself to the increasing fire as the enemy again assaulted the perimeter, P/Sgt. Leonard moved from position to position to direct the fire of his men against the well camouflaged foe. Under the cover of the main attack, the enemy moved a machine gun into a location where it could sweep the entire perimeter. This threat was magnified when the platoon machine gun in this area malfunctioned. P/Sgt. Leonard quickly crawled to the gun position and was helping to clear the malfunction when the gunner and other men in the vicinity were wounded by fire from the enemy machine gun. P/Sgt. Leonard rose to his feet, charged the enemy gun and destroyed the hostile crew despite being hit several times by enemy fire. He moved to a tree, propped himself against it, and continued to engage the enemy until he succumbed to his many wounds. His fighting spirit, heroic leadership, and valiant acts inspired the remaining members of his platoon to hold back the enemy until assistance arrived. P/Sgt. Leonard's profound courage and devotion to his men are in keeping with the highest traditions of the military service, and his gallant actions reflect great credit upon himself and the U.S. Army.

Epilogue: Leonard was born and raised in Alabama and graduated from A P. Parker High School before entering the Army in 1947. Before Vietnam, he served in combat during the Korean War from 1951-1953. At the time of his death, he was survived by his wife, Lois, and five children: Carl (21), Lavon (17), Brenda (16), Wanda (13), and Paula (8). The Medal was presented to his wife by Army Secretary Resor at a Pentagon ceremony. Leonard is buried at Fort Mitchell National Cemetery, Fort Mitchell, Alabama.[109]

LONG, DONALD RUSSELL
US Army — Vietnam War
Posthumous Award

Rank and organization: Sergeant, US Army, Troop C, 1st Squadron, 4th Cavalry, 1st Infantry Division. Place and date: Republic of Vietnam, 30 June 1966. Entered service at: Ashland, Ky. Born: 27 August 1939, Blackfork, Ohio. G.O. No.: 13, 4 April 1968.

Citation: For conspicuous gallantry and intrepidity in action at the risk of his life above and beyond the call of duty. Troops B and C, while conducting a reconnaissance mission along a road were suddenly attacked by a Viet Cong regiment, supported by mortars, recoilless rifles and machine guns, from concealed positions astride the road. Sgt. Long abandoned the relative safety of his armored personnel carrier and braved a withering hail of enemy fire to carry wounded men to evacuation helicopters. As the platoon fought its way forward to resupply advanced elements, Sgt. Long repeatedly exposed himself to enemy fire at point blank range to provide the needed supplies. While assaulting the Viet Cong position, Sgt. Long inspired his comrades by fearlessly standing unprotected to repel the enemy with rifle fire and grenades as they attempted to mount his carrier. When the enemy threatened to overrun a disabled carrier nearby, Sgt. Long again disregarded his own safety to help the severely wounded crew to safety. As he was handing arms to the less seriously wounded and reorganizing them to press the attack, an enemy grenade was hurled onto the carrier deck. Immediately recognizing the imminent danger, he instinctively shouted a warning to the crew and pushed to safety one man who had not heard his warning over the roar of battle. Realizing that these actions would not fully protect the exposed crewmen from the deadly explosion, he threw himself over the grenade to absorb the blast and thereby saved the lives of 8 of his comrades at the expense of his life. Throughout the battle, Sgt. Long's extraordinary heroism, courage and supreme devotion to his men were in the finest tradition of the military service, and reflect great credit upon himself and the U.S. Army.

Epilogue: Long was born and raised in Blackfork, Ohio, where he attended public school prior to entering the Army in 1963. He completed basic training at Fort Knox, Kentucky, and advanced training at Fort Jackson and served in Hawaii before he was assigned to the 1st Infantry Division in Vietnam. At the time of his death, both his parents were deceased. His sister, Marva Gordon, and 40 members of his extended family received the Medal from the Secretary of the Army at a Pentagon ceremony. He is buried in Union Baptist Church Cemetery, Blackfork, Ohio.[110]

OLIVE, MILTON L III
US Army — Vietnam War
Posthumous Award

Rank and organization: Private First Class, US Army, Company B, 2nd Battalion (Airborne), 503rd Infantry, 173rd Airborne Brigade. Place and date: Phu Cuong, Republic of Vietnam, 22 October 1965. Entered service at: Chicago, Ill. Born: 7 November 1946, Chicago, Ill. C.O. No.: 18, 26 April 1966.

Citation: For conspicuous gallantry and intrepidity at the risk of his life above and beyond the call of duty. Pfc. Olive was a member of the 3d Platoon of Company B, as it moved through the jungle to find the Viet Cong operating in the area. Although the platoon was subjected to a heavy volume of enemy gunfire and pinned down temporarily, it retaliated by assaulting the Viet Cong positions, causing the enemy to flee. As the platoon pursued the insurgents, Pfc. Olive and 4 other soldiers were moving through the jungle together with a grenade was thrown into their midst. Pfc. Olive saw the grenade, and then saved the lives of his fellow soldiers at the sacrifice of his by grabbing the grenade in his hand and falling on it to absorb the blast with his body. Through his bravery, unhesitating actions, and complete disregard for his safety, he prevented additional loss of life or injury to the members of his platoon. Pfc. Olive's extraordinary heroism, at the risk of his life above and beyond the call of duty are in the highest traditions of the U.S. Army and reflect great credit upon himself and the Armed Forces of his country.

Epilogue: Olive was born and raised in Chicago, where he attended Fuller, Copernicus, Beals, and St. Raphael grammar schools and Saints Junior College High School prior to entering the Army in 1964. His father thought it was a good decision because it was difficult for young Black men to make a respectable living without a high school education. Olive was called "Preacher" because, while in Vietnam, he frequently quoted the Bible.[111] When Olive earned his first Purple Heart for wounds received in combat, he kept it a secret from his parents because he didn't want them to worry. As the citation indicates, he died falling on a hand grenade to save his fellow soldiers. He was just 18 years old. The Medal was presented to Olive's father by President Johnson at a White House ceremony in 1966. Olive was survived by both parents and is buried at West Grove Cemetery,

Lexington, Mississippi.[112] One of many honors paid him was the renaming of a local park after him. A stone monument was also erected at Ohio Street and Lake Shore Drive in Chicago, with an image of Johnson's now-famous photo as a paratrooper. In 1970, someone vandalized it, knocking down the stones with a sledge hammer. The monument was quickly restored.

Olive's deeds received a lot of press coverage, partly because he was the first Black to receive the Medal for heroism during the Vietnam War, and partly because of the tense racial climate in the country at the time. All of the major media outlets did stories on his life and the action for which he received the Medal. His story struck a chord. I was in the 8th grade when I learned about Olive and his deeds and remember vividly the black community's reaction and admiration for this hero. Somehow, Olive's sacrifice of his life to save others, including Whites, bridged the racial divide. Two recent newspaper articles, both appearing in Philadelphia,[113] illustrate this point. Robert Toporek was one of the men Olive saved. He was an 18-year-old White from South Carolina, who never got along with Olive, a Black Chicagoan. In fact, one day they fought to a draw behind their tent. After the fight, Toporek said, they became the best of friends. Their friendship changed the racial dynamics in their unit for the better, soon ending self-segregation by race. Olive changed Toporek's life; now, more than 40 years later, he spends his spare time working with inner-city Black children and offering free message services in the ghettos of Philadelphia.[112]

PITTS, RILEY L.
US Army — Vietnam War
Posthumous Award

Rank and organization: Captain, US Army, Company C, 2nd Battalion, 27th Infantry, 25th Infantry Division. Place and date: Ap Dong, Republic of Vietnam, 31 October 1967. Entered service at: Wichita, Kans. Born: 15 October 1937, Fallis, Okla.

Citation: Distinguishing himself by exceptional heroism while serving as company commander during an airmobile assault. Immediately after his company landed in the area, several Viet Cong opened fire with automatic weapons. Despite the enemy fire, Capt. Pitts forcefully led an assault which overran the enemy positions. Shortly thereafter, Capt. Pitts was ordered to move his unit to the north to reinforce another company heavily engaged against a strong enemy force. As Capt. Pitts' company moved forward to engage the enemy, intense fire was received from 3 directions, including fire from 4 enemy bunkers, 2 of which were within 15 meters of Capt. Pitts' position. The severity of the incoming fire prevented Capt. Pitts from maneuvering his company. His rifle fire proving ineffective against the enemy due to the dense jungle foliage, he picked up an M-79 grenade launcher and began pinpointing the targets. Seizing a Chinese Communist grenade which had been taken from a captured Viet Cong's web gear, Capt. Pitts lobbed the grenade at a bunker to his front, but it hit the dense jungle foliage and rebounded. Without hesitation, Capt. Pitts threw himself on top of the grenade which, fortunately, failed to explode. Capt. Pitts then directed the repositioning of the company to permit friendly artillery to be fired. Upon completion of the artillery fire mission, Capt. Pitts again led his men toward the enemy positions, personally killing at least 1 more Viet Cong. The jungle growth still prevented effective fire to be placed on the enemy bunkers. Capt. Pitts, displaying complete disregard for his life and personal safety, quickly moved to a position which permitted him to place effective fire on the enemy. He maintained a continuous fire, pinpointing the enemy's fortified positions, while at the same time directing and urging his men forward, until he was mortally wounded. Capt. Pitts' conspicuous gallantry, extraordinary heroism, and intrepidity at the cost of his life, above and beyond the call of duty, are in the highest traditions of the U.S. Army and reflect great credit upon himself, his unit, and the Armed Forces of his country.

Epilogue: Riley was born and raised in Oklahoma City, graduating from Douglas Junior-Senior High School before entering the University of Wichita in 1960. A career Army officer, he was stationed for three years in France and reassigned to Vietnam in 1967. During the action for which he received the Medal, he threw himself on an enemy hand grenade that turned out to be a dud. At the time of his death, he was survived by his wife, Eula, and two small children, a boy, Mark, and a girl, Stacie. He was the first officer to receive the Medal, which was presented to his wife by President Johnson at the White House. [114]

ROGER, CHARLES CALVIN
US Army — Vietnam War

Rank and organization: Lieutenant Colonel, US Army, 1st Battalion, 5th Artillery, 1st Infantry Division. Place and date: Fishhook, near the Cambodian border, Republic of Vietnam, 1 November 1968. Entered service at: Institute, W. Va. Born: 6 September 1929, Claremont, W. Va.

Citation: For conspicuous gallantry and intrepidity in action at the risk of his life above and beyond the call of duty. Lt. Col. Rogers, Field Artillery, distinguished himself in action while serving as commanding officer, 1st Battalion, during the defense of a forward fire support base. In the early morning hours, the fire support base was subjected to a concentrated bombardment of heavy mortar, rocket and rocket propelled grenade fire. Simultaneously the position was struck by a human wave ground assault, led by sappers who breached the defensive barriers with bangalore torpedoes and penetrated the defensive perimeter. Lt. Col. Rogers with complete disregard for his safety moved through the hail of fragments from bursting enemy rounds to the embattled area. He aggressively rallied the dazed artillery crewmen to man their howitzers and he directed their fire on the assaulting enemy. Although knocked to the ground and wounded by an exploding round, Lt. Col. Rogers sprang to his feet and led a small counterattack force against an enemy element that had penetrated the howitzer positions. Although painfully wounded a second time during the assault, Lt. Col. Rogers pressed the attack killing several of the enemy and driving the remainder from the positions. Refusing medical treatment, Lt. Col. Rogers reestablished and reinforced the defensive positions. As a second human wave attack was launched against another sector of the perimeter, Lt. Col. Rogers directed artillery fire on the assaulting enemy and led a second counterattack against the charging forces. His valorous example rallied the beleaguered defenders to repulse and defeat the enemy onslaught. Lt. Col. Rogers moved from position to position through the heavy enemy fire, giving encouragement and direction to his men. At dawn the determined enemy launched a third assault against the fire base in an attempt to overrun the position. Lt. Col. Rogers moved to the threatened area and directed lethal fire on the enemy forces. Seeing a howitzer inoperative due to casualties, Lt. Col. Rogers joined the surviving members of the crew to return the howitzer to action. While directing the position defense, Lt. Col. Rogers was seriously wounded by fragments from a heavy mortar round which exploded on the parapet of the gun position. Although too severely wounded to physically lead the defenders, Lt. Col. Rogers continued to give encouragement and direction to his men in the defeating and repelling of the enemy attack. Lt. Col. Rogers' dauntless courage and heroism inspired the defenders of the fire support base to the heights of valor to defeat a determined and numerically superior enemy force. His relentless spirit of aggressiveness in action are in the highest traditions of the military service and reflects great credit upon himself, his unit, and the U.S. Army.

Epilogue: Rogers was born and raised in West Virginia and has the distinction of being the highest ranking Black American ever to receive the Medal. He was a Lieutenant Colonel then and eventually became a Two-Star General. Rogers was educated at West Virginia State College prior to entering the Army in 1951.[115] After receiving the Medal in 1968, he continued to excel in the Army. He died in 1990 at the age of 61 from cancer. At the time of his death, he was survived by his wife, Margarete, and three children: Jackie, Linda, and Barbara. Rogers is buried in Arlington National Cemetery.[116]

SARGENT, RUPERT L.
US Army — Vietnam War
Posthumous Award

Rank and organization: First Lieutenant, US Army, Company B, 4th Battalion, 9th Infantry, 25th Infantry Division. Place and date: Hau Nghia Province, Republic of Vietnam, 15 March 1967. Entered service at: Richmond, Va. Born: 6 January 1938, Hampton, Va.

Citation: For conspicuous gallantry and intrepidity in action at the risk of his life above and beyond the call of duty. While leading a platoon of Company B, 1st Lt. Sargent was investigating a reported Viet Cong meeting house and weapons cache. A tunnel entrance which 1st Lt. Sargent observed was booby trapped. He tried to destroy the booby trap and blow the cover from the tunnel using hand grenades, but this attempt was not successful. He and his demolition man moved in to destroy the booby trap and cover which flushed a Viet Cong soldier from the tunnel, who was immediately killed by the nearby platoon sergeant. 1st Lt. Sargent, the platoon sergeant, and a forward observer moved toward the tunnel entrance. As they approached, another Viet Cong emerged and threw 2 hand grenades that landed in the midst of the group. 1st Lt. Sargent fired 3 shots at the enemy then turned and unhesitatingly threw himself over the 2 grenades. He was mortally wounded, and his 2 companions were lightly wounded when the grenades exploded. By his courageous and selfless act of exceptional heroism, he saved the lives of the platoon sergeant and forward observer and prevented the injury or death of several other nearby comrades. 1st Lt. Sargent's actions were in keeping with the highest traditions of the military services and reflect great credit upon himself and the U.S. Army.

Epilogue: Sargent's Medal was presented to his widow in a first-of-its-kind private ceremony held at her house in Hampton, Virginia. The presentation was delayed for several months when Mrs. Sargent refused to accept the award on religious grounds. She is a Jehovah's Witness. Sargent was born and raised in Hampton and attended George P. Phoenix High School, Hampton Institute, and Virginia State College before entering the Army in 1961.[118] At the time of his death, he was survived by his wife, Mary Jo; two children, Stephen and Cheryl; and his parents, Woodrow and Janet.[119]

SASSER, CLARENCE EUGENE
US Army — Vietnam War

Rank and organization: Specialist Fifth Class (then Pfc.), US Army, Headquarters Company, 3rd Battalion, 60th Infantry, 9th Infantry Division. Place and date: Ding Tuong Province, Republic of Vietnam, 10 January 1968. Entered service at: Houston, Tex. Born: 12 September 1947, Chenango, Tex.

Citation: For conspicuous gallantry and intrepidity in action at the risk of his life above and beyond the call of duty. Sp5c. Sasser distinguished himself while assigned to Headquarters and Headquarters Company, 3d Battalion. He was serving as a medical aidman with Company A, 3d Battalion, on a reconnaissance in force operation. His company was making an air assault when suddenly it was taken under heavy small arms, recoilless rifle, machinegun and rocket fire from well fortified enemy positions on 3 sides of the landing zone. During the first few minutes, over 30 casualties were sustained. Without hesitation, Sp5c Sasser ran across an open rice paddy through a hail of fire to assist the wounded. After helping 1 man to safety, was painfully wounded in the left shoulder by fragments of an exploding rocket. Refusing medical attention, he ran through a barrage of rocket and automatic weapons fire to aid casualties of the initial attack and, after giving them urgently needed treatment, continued to search for other wounded. Despite 2 additional wounds immobilizing his legs, he dragged himself through the mud toward another soldier 100 meters away. Although in agonizing pain and faint from loss of blood, Sp5c. Sasser reached the man, treated him, and proceeded on to encourage another group of soldiers to crawl 200 meters to relative safety. There he attended their wounds for 5 hours until they were evacuated. Sp5c. Sasser's extraordinary heroism is in keeping with the highest traditions of the military service and reflects great credit upon himself, his unit, and the U.S. Army.

Epilogue: Sasser came home from Vietnam with much fanfare and optimism. He was showered with gifts, money, jobs, and a scholarship to Texas A & M but still found it difficult to adjust to the constant "fear of death." He soon moved to Los Angeles and held several odd jobs before returning to Houston and a job at Dow Chemical, working as a "sledger"—someone who removes carbon deposits from furnaces. He resides today in Houston, Texas with his wife, Ethyl, and children.

SIMS, CLIFFORD CHESTER
US Army — Vietnam War
Posthumous Award

Rank and organization: Staff Sergeant, US Army, Company D, 2nd Battalion (Airborne), 501st Infantry, 101st Airborne Division. Place and date: Near Hue, Republic of Vietnam, 21 February 1968. Entered service at: Jacksonville, Fla. Born: 18 June 1942, Port St. Joe, Fla.

Citation: For conspicuous gallantry and intrepidity in action at the risk of his life above and beyond the call of duty. S/Sgt. Sims distinguished himself while serving as a squad leader with Company D. Company D was assaulting a heavily fortified enemy position concealed within a dense wooded area when it encountered strong enemy defensive fire. Once within the woodline, S/Sgt. Sims led his squad in a furious attack against an enemy force which had pinned down the 1st Platoon and threatened to overrun it. His skillful leadership provided the platoon with freedom of movement and enabled it to regain the initiative. S/Sgt. Sims was then ordered to move his squad to a position where he could provide covering fire for the company command group and to link up with the 3d Platoon, which was under heavy enemy pressure. After moving no more than 30 meters S/Sgt. Sims noticed that a brick structure in which ammunition was stocked was on fire. Realizing the danger, S/Sgt. Sims took immediate action to move his squad from this position. Though in the process of leaving the area 2 members of his squad were injured by the subsequent explosion of the ammunition, S/Sgt. Sims' prompt actions undoubtedly prevented more serious casualties from occurring. While continuing through the dense woods amidst heavy enemy fire, S/Sgt. Sims and his squad were approaching a bunker when they heard the unmistakable noise of a concealed booby trap being triggered immediately to their front. S/Sgt. Sims warned his comrades of the danger and unhesitatingly hurled himself upon the device as it exploded, taking the full impact of the blast. In so protecting his fellow soldiers, he willingly sacrificed his life. S/Sgt. Sims' extraordinary heroism at the cost of his life is in keeping with the highest traditions of the military service and reflects great credit upon himself and the U.S. Army.

Epilogue: Sims was born and raised in Port Saint Joe, Florida, and graduated from Washington High School before entering the Army in 1961. Prior to his Vietnam assignment, Simms served with the 82nd Airborne Division in the Dominican Republic in 1966 during a brief police action. In addition to the Medal, he was also awarded the Silver Star, Bronze Star, and the Purple Heart. At the time of Sims's death, he was survived by his wife, Mary, and daughter, Gina. Sims was buried in Barrancas National Cemetery, Pensacola, Florida.[120]

WARREN, JOHN E., JR.

US Army — Vietnam War

Posthumous Award

Rank and organization: First Lieutenant, US Army, Company C, 2nd Battalion, (Mechanized), 22nd Infantry, 25th Infantry Division. Place and date: Tay Ninh Province, Republic of Vietnam, 14 January 1969. Entered service at: New York, N.Y. Born: 16 November 1946, Brooklyn, N.Y.

Citation: For conspicuous gallantry and intrepidity in action at the risk of his life above and beyond the call of duty. 1st Lt. Warren, distinguished himself at the cost of his life while serving as a platoon leader with Company C. While moving through a rubber plantation to reinforce another friendly unit, Company C came under intense fire from a well-fortified enemy force. Disregarding his safety, 1st Lt. Warren with several of his men began maneuvering through the hail of enemy fire toward the hostile positions. When he had come to within 6 feet of one of the enemy bunkers and was preparing to toss a hand grenade into it, an enemy grenade was suddenly thrown into the middle of his small group. Thinking only of his men, 1st Lt. Warren fell in the direction of the grenade, thus shielding those around him from the blast. His action, performed at the cost of his life, saved 3 men from serious or mortal injury. First Lt. Warren's ultimate action of sacrifice to save the lives of his men was in keeping with the highest traditions of the military service and reflects great credit on him, his unit, and the U.S. Army.

Epilogue: Warren was born and raised in Brooklyn, New York, where he attended Boys High School and Brooklyn College prior to entering the Army. He completed his basic and advanced individual training (Infantry) at Forts Jackson and McClellan before entering OCS at Fort Benning, Georgia, where he was commissioned a second lieutenant of Infantry. He served with the 25th Infantry Division at the time of the action for which he would posthumously receive the Medal. He was survived by his mother, Lilliam Warren, and father John Warren, Sr. He is buried at Long island National Cemetery, New York.[121]

ASIAN AND PACIFIC ISLANDER RECIPIENTS OF THE MEDAL OF HONOR

CALUGAS, JOSE
US Army — World War II
Pacific Theater

Rank and organization: Sergeant, US Army, Battery B, 88th Field Artillery, Philippine Scouts. Place and date: At Culis, Bataan Province, Philippine Islands, 16 January 1942. Entered service at: Fort Stotsenburg, Philippine Islands. Born: 29 December 1907, Barrio Tagsing, Leon, Iloilo, Philippine Islands. G.O. No.: 10, 24 February 1942.

Citation: The action for which the award was made took place near Culis, Bataan Province, Philippine Islands, on 16 January 1942. A battery gun position was bombed and shelled by the enemy until 1 gun was put out of commission and all the cannoneers were killed or wounded. Sgt. Calugas, a mess sergeant of another battery, voluntarily and without orders ran 1,000 yards across the shell-swept area to the gun position. There he organized a volunteer squad which placed the gun back in commission and fired effectively against the enemy, although the position remained under constant and heavy Japanese artillery fire.

Epilogue: Born and raised in the Philippines, Calugas was captured during World War II by the Japanese and survived the infamous Death March. When released, he joined the guerillas. He relocated to Puget Sound after the war, graduated from college, and worked for Boeing until his retirement. Calugas and his wife, Nora, have three children.

MENDONCA, LEROY A.
US Army — Korean War
Posthumous Award

Rank and organization: Sergeant, US Army, Company B, 7th Infantry Regiment, 3rd Infantry Division. Place and date: Near Chich-on, Korea, 4 July 1951. Entered service at: Honolulu, T.H. Birth: Honolulu, T.H. G.O. No.: 83, 3 September 1952.

Citation: Sgt. LeRoy A. Mendonca, distinguished himself by conspicuous gallantry above and beyond the call of duty in action against the enemy. After his platoon, in an exhaustive fight, had captured Hill 586, the newly won positions were assaulted during the night by a numerically superior enemy force. When the 1st Platoon positions were outflanked and under great pressure and the platoon was ordered to withdraw to a secondary line of defense, Sgt. Mendonca voluntarily remained in an exposed position and covered the platoon's withdrawal. Although under murderous enemy fire, he fired his weapon and hurled grenades at the onrushing enemy until his supply of ammunition was exhausted. He fought on, clubbing with his rifle and using his bayonet until he was mortally wounded. After the action it was estimated that Sgt. Mendonca had accounted for 37 enemy casualties. His daring actions stalled the crushing assault, protecting the platoon's withdrawal to secondary positions, and enabling the entire unit to repel the enemy attack and retain possession of the vital hilltop position. Sgt. Mendonca's extraordinary gallantry and exemplary valor are in keeping with the highest traditions of the U.S. Army.

Epilogue: Mendonca was born and raised in Hawaii. He died in Korea while serving with the 3rd Infantry Division. He was survived by his mother, Genevieve, and is buried in the National Memorial Cemetery of the Pacific, Honolulu, Hawaii.

MIYAMURA, HIROSHI H.
US Army — Korean War

Rank and organization: Corporal, US Army, Company H, 7th Infantry Regiment, 3rd Infantry Division. Place and date: Near Taejonni, Korea, 24 and 25 April 1951. Entered service at: Gallup, N. Mex. Birth: Gallup, N. Mex. G.O. No.: 85, 4 November 1953.

Citation: Cpl. Miyamura, a member of Company H, distinguished himself by conspicuous gallantry and intrepidity above and beyond the call of duty in action against the enemy. On the night of 24 April, Company H was occupying a defensive position when the enemy fanatically attacked threatening to overrun the position. Cpl. Miyamura, a machine gun squad leader, aware of the imminent danger to his men unhesitatingly jumped from his shelter wielding his bayonet in close hand-to-hand combat killing approximately 10 of the enemy. Returning to his position, he administered first aid to the wounded and directed their evacuation. As another savage assault hit the line, he manned his machine gun and delivered withering fire until his ammunition was expended. He ordered the squad to withdraw while he stayed behind to render the gun inoperative. He then bayoneted his way through infiltrated enemy soldiers to a second gun emplacement and assisted in its operation. When the intensity of the attack necessitated the withdrawal of the company Cpl. Miyamura ordered his men to fall back while he remained to cover their movement. He killed more than 50 of the enemy before his ammunition was depleted and he was severely wounded. He maintained his magnificent stand despite his painful wounds, continuing to repel the attack until his position was overrun. When last seen he was fighting ferociously against an overwhelming number of enemy soldiers. Cpl. Miyamura's indomitable heroism and consummate devotion to duty reflect the utmost glory on himself and uphold the illustrious traditions on the military service.

Epilogue: Just 15 when Pearl Harbor was bombed, Miyamura's parents made it clear that, when called upon, they would always fight in defense of the United States. Raised in Gallup, New Mexico, where his parents owned and operated a restaurant, Miyamura joined the Army after high school and married a Japanese-American woman who was in an internment camp for three years. He was shipped to the Korean peninsula at the beginning of the Korean War with the 24th Infantry Division. After the action for which he received the Medal, he was taken prisoner by the North Koreans. Fearing reprisals by his capturers, the Army kept secret that Miyamura was awarded the Medal for over 18 months until he was released in 1953. The Medal was presented to him by President Dwight D. Eisenhower in 1953.[122]

PILILAAU, HERBERT K.
US Army — Korean War
Posthumous Award

Rank and organization: Private First Class, US Army, Company C, 23d Infantry Regiment, 2nd Infantry Division. Place and date: Near Pia-ri, Korea, 17 September 1951. Entered service at: Oahu, T.H. Born: 10 October 1928, Waianae, Oahu, T.H. G.O. No.: 58, 18 June 1952.

Citation: Pfc. Pililaau, a member of Company C, distinguished himself by conspicuous gallantry and outstanding courage above and beyond the call of duty in action against the enemy. The enemy sent wave after wave of fanatical troops against his platoon which held a key terrain feature on "Heartbreak Ridge." Valiantly defending its position, the unit repulsed each attack until ammunition became practically exhausted and it was ordered to withdraw to a new position. Voluntarily remaining behind to cover the withdrawal, Pfc. Pililaau fired his automatic weapon into the ranks of the assailants, threw all his grenades and, with ammunition exhausted, closed with the foe in hand-to-hand combat, courageously fighting with his trench knife and bare fists until finally overcome and mortally wounded. When the position was subsequently retaken, more than 40 enemy dead were counted in the area he had so valiantly defended. His heroic devotion to duty, indomitable fighting spirit, and gallant self-sacrifice reflect the highest credit upon himself, the infantry, and the U.S. Army.

Epilogue: Born and raised in Hawaii and described as a pure Hawaiian, Pililaau very likely witnessed the Japanese attack on Pearl Harbor in 1941. He earned the Medal at Heartbreak Ridge, which was the name of a film later made by Clint Eastwood. He was tall, soft-spoken, and mostly kept to himself. At the time of his death, he was survived by his parents and is buried in National Memorial Cemetery of the Pacific, Honolulu.

SMITH, ELMELINDO R.
US Army — Vietnam War
Posthumous Award

Rank and organization: Platoon Sergeant (then S/Sgt.), US Army, 1st Platoon, Company C, 2nd Battalion, 8th Infantry, 4th Infantry Division. Place and date: Republic of Vietnam, 16 February 1967. Entered service at: Honolulu, Hawaii. Born: 27 July 1935, Honolulu, Hawaii.

Citation: For conspicuous gallantry and intrepidity at the risk of his life above and beyond the call of duty. During a reconnaissance patrol. his platoon was suddenly engaged by intense machinegun fire hemming in the platoon on 3 sides. A defensive perimeter was hastily established, but the enemy added mortar and rocket fire to the deadly fusillade and assaulted the position from several directions. With complete disregard for his safety, P/Sgt. Smith moved through the deadly fire along the defensive line, positioning soldiers, distributing ammunition and encouraging his men to repeal the enemy attack. Struck to the ground by enemy fire which caused a severe shoulder wound, he regained his feet, killed the enemy soldier and continued to move about the perimeter. He was again wounded in the shoulder and stomach but continued moving on his knees to assist in the defense. Noting the enemy massing at a weakened point on the perimeter, he crawled into the open and poured deadly fire into the enemy ranks. As he crawled on, he was struck by a rocket. Moments later, he regained consciousness, and drawing on his fast dwindling strength, continued to crawl from man to man. When he could move no farther, he chose to remain in the open where he could alert the perimeter to the approaching enemy. P/Sgt. Smith perished, never relenting in his determined effort against the enemy. The valorous acts and heroic leadership of this outstanding soldier inspired those remaining members of his platoon to beat back the enemy assaults. P/Sgt. Smith's gallant actions were in keeping with the highest traditions of the U.S. Army and they reflect great credit upon him and the Armed Forces of his country .

Epilogue: Smith was born and raised in Hawaii. He attended Leilehua High School and upon graduation, entered the Army with the intention of making it a career. At the time of his death, he was survived by his wife, Jane, and two children, Kathleen and Pamela. He is buried in the National Memorial Cemetery of the Pacific, Honolulu.

KARAMURA, TERRY T.
US Army — Vietnam War
Posthumous Award

Rank and organization: Corporal, US Army, 173d Engineer Company, 173d Airborne Brigade, Republic of Vietnam. Place and date: Camp Radcliff, Republic of Vietnam, 20 March 1969. Entered service at: Oahu, Hawaii. Born. 10 December 1949, Wahiawa, Oahu, Hawaii.

Citation: For conspicuous gallantry and intrepidity in action at the risk of his life above and beyond the call of duty. Cpl. Kawamura distinguished himself by heroic action while serving as a member of the 173d Engineer Company. An enemy demolition team infiltrated the unit quarters area and opened fire with automatic weapons. Disregarding the intense fire, Cpl. Kawamura ran for his weapon. At that moment, a violent explosion tore a hole in the roof and stunned the occupants of the room. Cpl. Kawamura jumped to his feet, secured his weapon and, as he ran toward the door to return the enemy fire, he observed that another explosive charge had been thrown through the hole in the roof to the floor. He immediately realized that 2 stunned fellow soldiers were in great peril and shouted a warning. Although in a position to escape, Cpl. Kawamura unhesitatingly wheeled around and threw himself on the charge. In completely disregarding his safety, Cpl. Kawamura prevented serious injury or death to several members of his unit. The extraordinary courage and selflessness displayed by Cpl. Kawamura are in the highest traditions of the military service and reflect great credit upon himself, his unit, and the U.S. Army.

Epilogue: Kawamura was born and raised in Hawaii. He was an Army brat, as his father, Harry, was a career enlisted man. Kawamura entered the Army after graduating from Leilehua High School in 1967. He completed basic training at Ft. Ord, advanced training (AIT) at Ft. Leonard Wood, and Airborne School at Ft. Benning. At the time of the action for which he received the Medal, he was assigned to the 173rd Airborne Brigade. At the time of his death, he was survived by both parents, who received the Medal from President Richard Nixon. Kawamura is buried at Mililani Memorial Cemetery, Pearl City, Hawaii.

YANO, RODNEY
US Army — Vietnam War
Posthumous Award

Rank and organization: Sergeant First Class, US Army, Air Cavalry Troop, 11th Armored Cavalry Regiment. Place and date: Near Bien Hao, Republic of Vietnam, 1 January 1969. Entered service at: Honolulu, Hawaii. Born: 13 December 1943, Kealakekua Kona, Hawaii.

Citation: Sfc. Yano distinguished himself while serving with the Air Cavalry Troop. Sfc. Yano was performing the duties of crew chief aboard the troop's command-and-control helicopter during action against enemy forces entrenched in dense jungle. From an exposed position in the face of intense small arms and antiaircraft fire he delivered suppressive fire upon the enemy forces and marked their positions with smoke and white phosphorous grenades, thus enabling his troop commander to direct accurate and effective artillery fire against the hostile emplacements. A grenade, exploding prematurely, covered him with burning phosphorous, and left him severely wounded. Flaming fragments within the helicopter caused supplies and ammunition to detonate. Dense white smoke filled the aircraft, obscuring the pilot's vision and causing him to lose control. Although having the use of only 1 arm and being partially blinded by the initial explosion, Sfc. Yano completely disregarded his welfare and began hurling blazing ammunition from the helicopter. In so doing he inflicted additional wounds upon himself, yet he persisted until the danger was past. Sfc. Yano's indomitable courage and profound concern for his comrades averted loss of life and additional injury to the rest of the crew. By his conspicuous gallantry at the cost of his life, in the highest traditions of the military service, Sfc. Yano has reflected great credit on himself, his unit, and the U.S. Army.

Epilogue: Yano was born and raised in Kona, Hawaii, where his family made a living from sea fishing. He attended public school, graduating from Kona High School in 1961. He immediately entered the Army with the intention of making it a career. Prior to assignment to Vietnam, he served in Germany with various transportation units. At the time of his death, he was survived by his parents and two brothers. He is buried in the National Memorial Cemetery of the Pacific, Honolulu, Hawaii.[123] Yano's Medal was presented to his parents by President Richard Nixon at a White House ceremony.

TRINIDAD, TELESFORO
US Navy — Interim Period

Rank and organization: Fireman Second Class, US Navy. Born: 25 November 1890, New Washington Capig, Philippine Islands. Accredited to: Philippine Islands. G.O. No.: 142, 1 April 1915.

Citation: For extraordinary heroism in the line of his profession at the time of the boiler explosion on board the U.S.S. San Diego, 21 January 1915. Trinidad was driven out of fireroom No. 2 by the explosion, but at once returned and picked up R.E. Daly, fireman, second class, whom he saw to be injured, and proceeded to bring him out. While coming into No. 4 fireroom, Trinidad was just in time to catch the explosion in No. 3 fireroom, but without consideration for his own safety, passed Daly on and then assisted in rescuing another injured man from No. 3 fireroom. Trinidad was himself burned about the face by the blast from the explosion in No. 3 fireroom.

Epilogue: Little information about Trinidad was found in the archives. He was born in New Washington in the Philippine Islands and died in 1968. He is buried in Imus Cemetery, Cavite.

DAVILA, RUDOLPH B.
US Army — World War II
European Theater

Citation: Staff Sergeant Rudolph B. Davila distinguished himself by extraordinary heroism in action, on 28 May 1944, near Artena, Italy. During the offensive which broke through the German mountain strongholds surrounding the Anzio beachhead, Staff Sergeant Davila risked death to provide heavy weapons support for a beleaguered rifle company. Caught on an exposed hillside by heavy, grazing fire from a well-entrenched German force, his machine gunners were reluctant to risk putting their guns into action. Crawling fifty yards to the nearest machine gun, Staff Sergeant Davila set it up alone and opened fire on the enemy. In order to observe the effect of his fire, Sergeant Davila fired from the kneeling position, ignoring the enemy fire that struck the tripod and passed between his legs. Ordering a gunner to take over, he crawled forward to a vantage point and directed the fire-fight with hand and arm signals until both hostile machine guns were silenced. Bringing his three remaining machine guns into action, he drove the enemy to a reserve position two hundred yards to the rear. When he received a painful wound in the leg, he dashed to a burned tank and, despite the crash of bullets on the hull, engaged a second enemy force from the tank's turret. Dismounting, he advanced 130 yards in short rushes, crawled 20 yards and charged into an enemy-held house to eliminate the defending force of five with a hand grenade and rifle fire. Climbing to the attic, he straddled a large shell hole in the wall and opened fire on the enemy. Although the walls of the house were crumbling, he continued to fire until he had destroyed two more machine guns. His intrepid actions brought desperately needed heavy weapons support to a hard-pressed rifle company and silenced four machine gunners, which forced the enemy to abandon their prepared positions. Staff Sergeant Davila's extraordinary heroism and devotion to duty are in keeping with the highest traditions of military service and reflect great credit on him, his unit, and the United States Army.

Epilogue: Davila was born in El Paso, Texas, and raised in Los Angeles, California, by his Hispanic father and Filipino mother. He entered the Army in 1941 and saw combat in Italy, for which he would receive the Medal over forty years later. Davila was medically retired from the Army in 1951. He graduated from the University of Southern California with two degrees and worked for many years as a high school history teacher. Davila died in 2000 from cancer; his wife died in 1999. At the time of his death, he was survived by three sons and two daughters.

NISPEROS, JOSE B.
US Army — Philippine Insurrection

Rank and organization: Private, 34th Company, Philippine Scouts. Place and date: At Lapurap, Basilan, Philippine Islands, 24 September 1911. Entered service at: San Fernandos Union, P.I. Birth: San Fernandos Union, P.I. Date of issue: Unknown.

Citation: Having been badly wounded (his left arm was broken and lacerated and he had received several spear wounds in the body so that he could not stand) continued to fire his rifle with one hand until the enemy was repulsed, thereby aiding materially in preventing the annihilation of his party and the mutilation of their bodies.

Epilogue: Little information is available on Nisperos. He was born and raised in the Philippine Islands, entered the Army, and was assigned to the Philippine Scouts. Nisperos's Medal was presented to him by Mrs. J. Franklin Bell, wife of Major General Bell, in 1913. Nisperos died in 1922 and is buried in San Fernandos Union's New Municipal Cemetery, Philippines.

HAJIRO, BARNEY
US Army — World War II
European Theater

Citation: Private Barney F. Hajiro distinguished himself by extraordinary heroism in action on 19, 22, and 29 October 1944, in the vicinity of Bruyeres and Biffontaine, eastern France. Private Hajiro, while acting as a sentry on top of an embankment on 19 October 1944, in the vicinity of Bruyeres, France, rendered assistance to allied troops attacking a house 200 yards away by exposing himself to enemy fire and directing fire at an enemy strong point. He assisted the unit on his right by firing his automatic rifle and killing or wounding two enemy snipers. On 22 October 1944, he and one comrade took up an outpost security position about 50 yards to the right front of their platoon, concealed themselves, and ambushed an 18-man, heavily armed, enemy patrol, killing two, wounding one, and taking the remainder as prisoners. On 29 October 1944, in a wooded area in the vicinity of Biffontaine, France, Private Hajiro initiated an attack up the slope of a hill referred to as "Suicide Hill" by running forward approximately 100 yards under fire. He then advanced ahead of his comrades about 10 yards, drawing fire and spotting camouflaged machine gun nests. He fearlessly met fire with fire and single-handedly destroyed two machine gun nests and killed two enemy snipers. As a result of Private Hajiro's heroic actions, the attack was successful. Private Hajiro's extraordinary heroism and devotion to duty are in keeping with the highest traditions of military service and reflect great credit upon him, his unit, and the United States Army.

Epilogue: A biographical summary compiled by the CMOHS indicates that little is known about Hajiro before or after his military service. He was born in 1916 in Punene, Hawaii, the eldest of nine children. He left the 8th grade to work in the sugar-cane fields for 10 cents an hour, 10 hours a day to help support his family, and was never able to pursue his dream to compete in high school and college track. He entered the service in Honolulu and currently resides in Maui, Hawaii.

HASEMOTO, MIKIO
US Army — World War II
European Theater — Posthumous Award

Citation: Private Mikio Hasemoto distinguished himself by extraordinary heroism in action on 29 November 1943, in the vicinity of Cerasuolo, Italy. A force of approximately 40 enemy soldiers, armed with machine guns, machine pistols, rifles, and grenades, attacked the left flank of his platoon. Two enemy soldiers with machine guns advanced forward, firing their weapons. Private Hasemoto, an automatic rifleman, challenged these two machine gunners. After firing four magazines at the approaching enemy, his weapon was shot and damaged. Unhesitatingly, he ran 10 yards to the rear, secured another automatic rifle and continued to fire until his weapon jammed. At this point, Private Hasemoto and his squad leader had killed approximately 20 enemy soldiers. Again, Private Hasemoto ran through a barrage of enemy machine gun fire to pick up an M-1 rifle. Continuing their fire, Private Hasemoto and his squad leader killed 10 more enemy soldiers. With only three enemy soldiers left, he and his squad leader charged courageously forward, killing one, wounding one, and capturing another. The following day, Private Hasemoto continued to repel enemy attacks until he was killed by enemy fire. Private Hasemoto's extraordinary heroism and devotion to duty are in keeping with the highest traditions of military service and reflect great credit on him, his unit, and the United States Army.

Epilogue: Hasemoto was killed by the actions for which he received the

Medal. He is buried in the National Memorial Cemetery of the Pacific, Section D, Grave 338.

HAYASHI, JOE
US Army — World War II
European Theater — Posthumous Award

Citation: Private Joe Hayashi distinguished himself by extraordinary heroism in action on 20 and 22 April 1945, near Tendola, Italy. On 20 April 1945, ordered to attack a strongly defended hill that commanded all approaches to the village of Tendola, Private Hayashi skillfully led his men to a point within 75 yards of enemy positions before they were detected and fired upon. After dragging his wounded comrades to safety, he returned alone and exposed himself to small arms fire in order to direct and adjust mortar fire against hostile emplacements. Boldly attacking the hill with the remaining men of his squad, he attained his objective and discovered that the mortars had neutralized three machine guns, killed 27 men, and wounded many others. On 22 April 1945, attacking the village of Tendola, Private Hayashi maneuvered his squad up a steep, terraced hill to within 100 yards of the enemy. Crawling under intense fire to a hostile machine gun position, he threw a grenade, killing one enemy soldier and forcing the other members of the gun crew to surrender. Seeing four enemy machine guns delivering deadly fire upon other elements of his platoon, he threw another grenade, destroying a machine gun nest. He then crawled to the right flank of another machine gun position where he killed four enemy soldiers and forced the others to flee. Attempting to pursue the enemy, he was mortally wounded by a burst of machine pistol fire. The dauntless courage and exemplary leadership of Private Hayashi enabled his company to attain its objective. Private Hayashi's extraordinary heroism and devotion to duty are in keeping with the highest traditions of military service and reflect great credit on him, his unit, and the United States Army.

Epilogue: Hayashi was killed in the action for which he received the Medal and is buried in Evergreen Memorial Cemetery, Los Angeles, California.

HAYASHI, SHIZUYA
US Army — World War II
European Theater

Citation: Private Shizuya Hayashi distinguished himself by extraordinary heroism in action on 29 November 1943, near Cerasuolo, Italy. During a flank assault on high ground held by the enemy, Private Hayashi rose alone in the face of grenade, rifle, and machine gun fire. Firing his automatic rifle from the hip, he charged and overtook an enemy machine gun position, killing seven men in the nest and two more as they fled. After his platoon advanced 200 yards from this point, an enemy antiaircraft gun opened fire on the men. Private Hayashi returned fire at the hostile position, killing nine of the enemy, taking four prisoners, and forcing the remainder of the force to withdraw from the hill. Private Hayashi's extraordinary heroism and devotion to duty are in keeping with the highest traditions of military service and reflect great credit on him, his unit, and the United States Army.

Epilogue: Hayashi, who was born and raised in Hawaii, was already in the Army at the time of Pearl Harbor. He may have witnessed the attack. His unit was transferred to Wisconsin, formed into the 100th Infantry Battalion, and reassigned to Italy, where it served with great distinction. After the war, Hayashi returned to Hawaii, where he resides today.

IINOUYE, DANIEL K.
US Army — World War II
European Theater

Citation: Second Lieutenant Daniel K. Inouye distinguished himself by extraordinary heroism in action on 21 April 1945, in the vicinity of San Terenzo, Italy. While attacking a defended ridge guarding an important road junction, Second Lieutenant Inouye skillfully directed his platoon through a hail of automatic weapon and small arms fire, in a swift enveloping movement that resulted in the capture of an artillery and mortar post and brought his men to within 40 yards of the hostile force. Emplaced in bunkers and rock formations, the enemy halted the advance with crossfire from three machine guns. With complete disregard for his personal safety, Second Lieutenant Inouye crawled up the treacherous slope to within five yards of the nearest machine gun and hurled two grenades, destroying the emplacement. Before the enemy could retaliate, he stood up and neutralized a second machine gun nest. Although wounded by a sniper's bullet, he continued to engage other hostile positions at close range until an exploding grenade shattered his right arm. Despite the intense pain, he refused evacuation and continued to direct his platoon until enemy resistance was broken and his men were again deployed in defensive positions. In the attack, 25 enemy soldiers were killed and eight others captured. By his gallant, aggressive tactics and by his indomitable leadership, Second Lieutenant Inouye enabled his platoon to advance through formidable resistance, and was instrumental in the capture of the ridge. Second Lieutenant Inouye's extraordinary heroism and devotion to duty are in keeping with the highest traditions of military service and reflect great credit on him, his unit, and the United States Army.

Epilogue: Probably the best known of the Japanese World War II recipients, Inouye went on to have a distinguished career as a Member of Congress. He is currently Senator for the state of Hawaii.

KOBASHIGAWA, YEIKI
US Army — World War II
European Theater

Citation: Technical Sergeant Yeiki Kobashigawa distinguished himself by extraordinary heroism in action on 2 June 1944, in the vicinity of Lanuvio, Italy. During an attack, Technical Sergeant Kobashigawa's platoon encountered strong enemy resistance from a series of machine guns providing supporting fire. Observing a machine gun nest 50 yards from his position, Technical Sergeant Kobashigawa crawled forward with one of his men, threw a grenade and then charged the enemy with his submachine gun while a fellow soldier provided covering fire. He killed one enemy soldier and captured two prisoners. Meanwhile, Technical Sergeant Kobashigawa and his comrade were fired upon by another machine gun 50 yards ahead. Directing a squad to advance to his first position, Technical Sergeant Kobashigawa again moved forward with a fellow soldier to subdue the second machine gun nest. After throwing grenades into the position, Technical Sergeant Kobashigawa provided close supporting fire while a fellow soldier charged, capturing four prisoners. On the alert for other machine gun nests, Technical Sergeant Kobashigawa discovered four more, and skillfully led a squad in neutralizing two of them. Technical Sergeant Kobashigawa's extraordinary heroism and devotion to duty are in keeping with the highest traditions of military service and reflect great credit on him, his unit, and the United States Army.

Epilogue: Kobashigawa was born in Waiakea on the Big Island and never got beyond the seventh grade at Waianae Intermediate and High School after his family moved to Oahu. Kobashigawa, nicknamed Lefty, played baseball with the Waianae Plantation Company and the Rural Japanese Leagues. Throughout his youth, he worked days for the plantation then went home to help on the family truck farm. After registering for the draft, he was inducted on November 16, 1941. He was 18. On December 7, 1941, Kobashigawa, then assigned to the Hawaii Army National Guard's 298th Regiment, still didn't know how to load his rifle. He was on leave at home in Waianae, preparing for a Sunday baseball game, when the Japanese attacked Pearl Harbor. "I caught an Army truck which took us through Kolekole Pass back to Schofield ... but shortly after that, they took away our rifles. I don't know what they thought we would do."[125] Kobashigawa died March 31, 2005, and is buried in the National Memorial Cemetery of the Pacific.

KURODA, ROBERT T.
US Army — World War II
European Theater — Posthumous Award

Citation: Staff Sergeant Robert T. Kuroda distinguished himself by extraordinary heroism in action, on 20 October 1944, near Bruyeres, France. Leading his men in an advance to destroy snipers and machine gun nests, Staff Sergeant Kuroda encountered heavy fire from enemy soldiers occupying a heavily wooded slope. Unable to pinpoint the hostile machine gun, he boldly made his way through heavy fire to the crest of the ridge. Once he located the machine gun, Staff Sergeant Kuroda advanced to a point within ten yards of the nest and killed three enemy gunners with grenades. He then fired clip after clip of rifle ammunition, killing or wounding at least three of the enemy. As he expended the last of his ammunition, he observed that an American officer had been struck by a burst of fire from a hostile machine gun located on an adjacent hill. Rushing to the officer's assistance, he found that the officer had been killed. Picking up the officer's submachine gun, Staff Sergeant Kuroda advanced through continuous fire toward a second machine gun emplacement and destroyed the position. As he turned to fire upon additional enemy soldiers, he was killed by a sniper. Staff Sergeant Kuroda's courageous actions and indomitable fighting spirit ensured the destruction of enemy resistance in the sector. Staff Sergeant Kuroda's extraordinary heroism and devotion to duty are in keeping with the highest traditions of military service and reflect great credit on him, his unit, and the United States Army.

Epilogue: Born and raised in Hawaii, Kuroda was killed by the actions that earned him the Medal. He is buried in the National Memorial Cemetery of the Pacific, Section D, Grave 93.

MOTO, KAORU
US Army — World War II,
European Theate — Posthumous Award

Citation: Private First Class Kaoru Moto distinguished himself by extraordinary heroism in action on 7 July 1944, near Castellina, Italy. While serving as first scout, Private First Class Moto observed a machine gun nest that was hindering his platoon's progress. On his own initiative, he made his way to a point ten paces from the hostile position, and killed the enemy machine gunner. Immediately, the enemy assistant gunner opened fire in the direction of Private First Class Moto. Crawling to the rear of the position, Private First Class Moto surprised the enemy soldier, who quickly surrendered. Taking his prisoner with him, Private First Class Moto took a position a few yards from a house to prevent the enemy from using the building as an observation post. While guarding the house and his prisoner, he observed an enemy machine gun team moving into position. He engaged them, and with deadly fire forced the enemy to withdraw. An enemy sniper located in another house fired at Private First Class Moto, severely wounding him. Applying first aid to his wound, he changed position to elude the sniper fire and to advance. Finally relieved of his position, he made his way to the rear for treatment. Crossing a road, he spotted an enemy machine gun nest. Opening fire, he wounded two of the three soldiers occupying the position. Not satisfied with this accomplishment, he then crawled forward to a better position and ordered the enemy soldier to surrender. Receiving no answer, Private First Class Moto fired at the position, and the soldiers surrendered. Private First Class Moto's extraordinary heroism and devotion to duty are in keeping with the highest traditions of military service and reflect great credit on him, his unit, and the United States Army. Epilogue: Born and raised in Hawaii and a career Army man after the war, Moto died in 1992 and is buried in the National Memorial Cemetery of the Pacific, Section CT2-F, Row 400, Grave 422.

MURANAGA, KIYOSHI K.
US Army — World War II,
]European Theater — Posthumous Award

Citation: Private First Class Kiyoshi K. Muranaga distinguished himself by extraordinary heroism in action on 26 June 1944, near Suvereto, Italy. Private First Class Muranaga's company encountered a strong enemy force in commanding positions and with superior firepower. An enemy 88mm self-propelled gun opened direct fire on the company, causing the men to disperse and seek cover. Private First Class Muranaga's mortar squad was ordered to action, but the terrain made it impossible to set up their weapons. The squad leader, realizing the vulnerability of the mortar position, moved his men away from the gun to positions of relative safety. Because of the heavy casualties being inflicted on his company, Private First Class Muranaga, who served as a gunner, attempted to neutralize the 88mm weapon alone. Voluntarily remaining at his gun position, Private First Class Muranaga manned the mortar himself and opened fire on the enemy gun at a range of approximately 400 yards. With his third round, he was able to correct his fire so that the shell landed directly in front of the enemy gun. Meanwhile, the enemy crew, immediately aware of the source of mortar fire, turned their 88mm weapon directly on Private First Class

Muranaga's position. Before Private First Class Muranaga could fire a fourth round, an 88mm shell scored a direct hit on his position, killing him instantly. Because of the accuracy of Private First Class Muranaga's previous fire, the enemy soldiers decided not to risk further exposure and immediately abandoned their position. Private First Class Muranaga's extraordinary heroism and devotion to duty are in keeping with the highest traditions of military service and reflect great credit on him, his unit, and the United States Army.

Epilogue: Muranaga was killed in the action for which he received the Medal some 54 years later. He is buried in Evergreen Memorial Cemetery, Los Angeles, California.

NAKAE, MASATO
US Army — World War II,
European Theater — Posthumous Award

Citation: Private Masato Nakae distinguished himself by extraordinary heroism in action on 19 August 1944, near Pisa, Italy. When his submachine gun was damaged by a shell fragment during a fierce attack by a superior enemy force, Private Nakae quickly picked up his wounded comrade's M-1 rifle and fired rifle grenades at the steadily advancing enemy. As the hostile force continued to close in on his position, Private Nakae threw six grenades and forced them to withdraw. During a concentrated enemy mortar barrage that preceded the next assault by the enemy force, a mortar shell fragment seriously wounded Private Nakae. Despite his injury, he refused to surrender his position and continued firing at the advancing enemy. By inflicting heavy casualties on the enemy force, he finally succeeded in breaking up the attack and caused the enemy to withdraw. Private Nakae's extraordinary heroism and devotion to duty are in keeping with the highest traditions of military service and reflect great credit on him, his unit, and the United States Army.

Epilogue: Nakae was born and raised in Hawaii. He died in 1998 and is buried in the National Memorial Cemetery of the Pacific, Section O, Row O, Grave 1446.

NAKAMINE, SHINYEI
US Army— World War II
European Theater — Posthumous Award

Citation: Private Shinyei Nakamine distinguished himself by extraordinary heroism in action on 2 June 1944, near La Torreto, Italy. During an attack, Private Nakamine's platoon became pinned down by intense machine gun crossfire from a small knoll 200 yards to the front. On his own initiative, Private Nakamine crawled toward one of the hostile weapons. Reaching a point 25 yards from the enemy, he charged the machine gun nest, firing his submachine gun, and killed three enemy soldiers and captured two. Later that afternoon, Private Nakamine discovered an enemy soldier on the right flank of his platoon's position. Crawling 25 yards from his position, Private Nakamine opened fire and killed the soldier. Then, seeing a machine gun nest to his front approximately 75 yards away, he returned to his platoon and led an automatic rifle team toward the enemy. Under covering fire from his team, Private Nakamine crawled to a point 25 yards from the nest and threw hand grenades at the enemy soldiers, wounding one and capturing four. Spotting another machine gun nest 100 yards to his right flank, he led the automatic rifle team toward the hostile position but was killed by a burst of machine gun fire. Private Nakamine's extraordinary heroism and devotion to duty are in keeping with the highest traditions of military service and reflect great credit on him, his unit, and the United States Army.

Epilogue: Born and raised in Hawaii, Nakamine was killed in the action for which he received the Medal. He is buried in the National Memorial Cemetery of the Pacific in Honolulu, Section D, Grave 402.

NAKAMURA, WILLIAM K.
US Army — World War II
European Theater

Private First Class William K. Nakamura distinguished himself by extraordinary heroism in action on 4 July 1944, near Castellina, Italy. During a fierce firefight, Private First Class Nakamura's platoon became pinned down by enemy machine gun fire from a concealed position. On his own initiative, Private First Class Nakamura crawled 20 yards toward the hostile nest with fire from the enemy machine gun barely missing him. Reaching a point 15 yards from the position, he quickly raised himself to a kneeling position and threw four hand grenades, killing or wounding at least three of the enemy soldiers. The enemy weapon silenced, Private First Class Nakamura crawled back to his platoon, which was able to continue its advance as a result of his courageous action. Later, his company was ordered to withdraw from the crest of a hill so that a mortar barrage could be placed on the ridge. On his own initiative, Private First Class Nakamura remained in position to cover his comrades' withdrawal. While moving toward the safety of a wooded draw, his platoon became pinned down by deadly machine gun fire. Crawling to a point from which he could fire on the enemy position, Private First Class Nakamura quickly and accurately fired his weapon to pin down the enemy machine gunners. His platoon was then able to withdraw to safety without further casualties. Private First Class Nakamura was killed during this heroic stand. Private First Class Nakamura's extraordinary heroism and devotion to duty are in keeping with the highest traditions of military service and reflect great credit on him, his unit, and the United States Army.

Epilogue: Nakamura received the Medal some 55 years after earning it. Along with 21 other Japanese-Americans, he was denied the Medal for generations solely because of race. Nakamura was as American as anyone could be. He played baseball and football at Garfield High School in Seattle and was a popular and carefree boy. His high school nickname was Rhino.[126] Like most Japanese of that era and region, Nakamura went north in the summers to work in the salmon canneries and studied at the University of Washington until Pearl Harbor. After the attack, his entire family was relocated to Minidoka, a "hellish dusty internment camp in Idaho".[127] He was nominated for the Medal by his commander in 1944 but instead received the Distinguished Service Cross, the second highest award for valor. He was killed in action. His family and community did not learn of his death until it appeared in a local newspaper. The Medal was presented to his sister, June Oshima, by President Clinton at a White House ceremony.

NISHIMOTO, JOE E.
US Army — World War II
European Theater — Posthumous Award

Citation: Private First Class Joe M. Nishimoto distinguished himself by extraordinary heroism in action on 7 November 1944, near La Houssiere, France. After three days of unsuccessful attempts by his company to dislodge the enemy from a strongly defended ridge, Private First Class Nishimoto, as acting squad leader, boldly crawled forward through a heavily mined and booby-trapped area. Spotting a machine gun nest, he hurled a grenade and destroyed the emplacement. Then, circling to the rear of another machine gun position, he fired his submachine gun at point-blank range, killing one gunner and wounding another. Pursuing two enemy riflemen, Private First Class Nishimoto killed one, while the other hastily retreated. Continuing his determined assault, he drove another machine gun crew from its position. The enemy, with their key strong points taken, were forced to withdraw from this sector. Private First Class Nishimoto's extraordinary heroism and devotion to duty are in keeping with the highest traditions of military service and reflect great credit on him, his unit, and the United States Army.

Epilogue: Born and raised in Fresno, California, he was killed in action and buried in Washington Colony Cemetery, Fresno, California.

OHATA, ALLAN M.
US Army — World War II
European Theater — Posthumous Award

Citation: Sergeant Allan M. Ohata distinguished himself by extraordinary heroism in action on 29 and 30 November 1943, near Cerasuolo, Italy. Sergeant Ohata, his squad leader, and three men were ordered to protect his platoon's left flank against an attacking enemy force of 40 men, armed with machine guns, machine pistols, and rifles. He posted one of his men, an automatic rifleman, on the extreme left, 15 yards from his own position. Taking his position, Sergeant Ohata delivered effective fire against the advancing enemy. The man to his left called for assistance when his automatic rifle was shot and damaged. With utter disregard for his personal safety, Sergeant Ohata left his position and advanced 15 yards through heavy machine gun fire. Reaching his comrade's position, he immediately fired upon the enemy, killing 10 enemy soldiers and successfully covering his comrade's withdrawal to replace his damaged weapon. Sergeant Ohata and the automatic rifleman held their position and killed 37 enemy soldiers. Both men then charged the three remaining soldiers and captured them. Later, Sergeant Ohata and the automatic rifleman stopped another attacking force of 14, killing four and wounding three while the others fled. The following day he and the automatic rifleman held their flank with grim determination and staved off all attacks. Staff Sergeant Ohata's extraordinary heroism and devotion to duty are in keeping with the highest traditions of military service and reflect great credit on him, his unit, and the United States Army.

Epilogue: Ohata was born and raised in Honolulu, Hawaii. He died in Hawaii in 1977 and is buried at the National Memorial Cemetery of the Pacific in Honolulu, Section III, Row 0, Grave 474.

OKUBO, JAMES K.
US Army — World War II
European Theater — Posthumous Award

Citation: Technician Fifth Grade James K. Okubo distinguished himself by extraordinary heroism in action on 28 and 29 October and 4 November 1944, in the Foret Domaniale de Champ, near Biffontaine, eastern France. On 28 October, under strong enemy fire coming from behind mine fields and roadblocks, Technician Fifth Grade Okubo, a medic, crawled 150 yards to within 40 yards of the enemy lines. Two grenades were thrown at him while he left his last covered position to carry back wounded comrades. Under constant barrages of enemy small arms and machine gun fire, he treated 17 men on 28 October and 8 more men on 29 October. On 4 November, Technician Fifth Grade Okubo ran 75 yards under grazing machine gun fire and, while exposed to hostile fire directed at him, evacuated and treated a seriously wounded crewman from a burning tank, who otherwise would have died. Technician Fifth Grade James K. Okubo's extraordinary heroism and devotion to duty are in keeping with the highest traditions of military service and reflect great credit on him, his unit, and the United States Army.

Epilogue: Okubo survived the war, returned home, and became a dentist. He taught for many years at the University of Detroit Dental School, where he was known as a tough instructor. He died in 1967 in a car accident and was survived by his wife, Nobuyo, who lives in Walled Lake, Michigan. More than 300 of his family and friends attended the dedication of a new veteran's medical facility,. Like a great number of other Japanese Americans during the early days of the war, Okubo and his family were interned at a "relocation" camp. He joined the Army when he was 23 years old, in part, to prove his loyalty to his country.

OKUTSU, YUKIO
US Army — World War II,
European Theater

Citation: Technical Sergeant Yukio Okutsu distinguished himself by extraordinary heroism in action on 7 April 1945, on Mount Belvedere, Italy. While his platoon was halted by the crossfire of three machine guns, Technical Sergeant Okutsu boldly crawled to within 30 yards of the nearest enemy emplacement through heavy fire. He destroyed the position with two accurately placed hand grenades, killing three machine gunners. Crawling and dashing from cover to cover, he threw another grenade, silencing a second machine gun, wounding two enemy soldiers, and forcing two others to surrender. Seeing a third machine gun, which obstructed his platoon's advance, he moved forward through heavy small arms fire and was stunned momentarily by rifle fire, which glanced off his helmet. Recovering, he bravely charged several enemy riflemen with his submachine gun, forcing them to withdraw from their positions. Then, rushing the machine gun nest, he captured the weapon and its entire crew of four. By these single-handed actions he enabled his platoon to resume its assault on a vital objective. The courageous performance of Technical Sergeant Okutsu against formidable odds was an inspiration to all. Technical Sergeant Okutsu's extraordinary heroism and devotion to duty are in keeping with the highest traditions of military service and reflect great credit on him, his unit, and the United States Army.

Epilogue: Okutsu was born and raised in Hawaii, the fourth of 11 children of Chozuchi and Otoshi Okutsu. He attended public school prior to entering the Army, volunteering for the 442nd RCT in 1943 because he didn't want to stay in Koloa and work in his father's manju store. After the war, Okutsu attended a watch making school in Kansas City, worked on the federal clean up of Bikini and Eniwetok islands, and then worked for Hawaii County as a mechanic until he retired in 1985. He and his wife, Elaine, tended an acre-and-a-half anthurium farm until his death in 2003 at the age of 81 from cancer. He is survived by his wife of 53 years and two sons and buried in Hawaii Veterans Cemetery No. 2, Hilo, Hawaii.

ONO, FRANK H.
US Army — World War II
European Theater — Posthumous Award

Citation: Private First Class Frank H. Ono distinguished himself by extraordinary heroism in action on 4 July 1944, near Castellina, Italy. In attacking a heavily defended hill, Private First Class Ono's squad was caught in a hail of formidable fire from the well-entrenched enemy. Private First Class Ono opened fire with his automatic rifle and silenced one machine gun 300 hundred yards to the right front. Advancing through incessant fire, he killed a sniper with another burst of fire, and while his squad leader reorganized the rest of the platoon in the rear, he alone defended the critical position. His weapon was then wrenched from his grasp by a burst of enemy machine pistol fire as enemy troops attempted to close in on him. Hurling hand grenades, Private First Class Ono forced the enemy to abandon the attempt, resolutely defending the newly won ground until the rest of the platoon moved forward. Taking a wounded comrade's rifle, Private First Class Ono again joined in the assault. After killing two more enemy soldiers, he boldly ran through withering automatic, small arms, and mortar fire to render first aid to his platoon leader and a seriously wounded rifleman. In danger of being encircled, the platoon was ordered to withdraw. Volunteering to cover the platoon, Private First Class Ono occupied virtually unprotected positions near the crest of the hill, engaging an enemy machine gun emplaced on an adjoining ridge and exchanging fire with snipers armed with machine pistols. Completely disregarding his own safety, he made himself the constant target of concentrated enemy fire until the platoon reached the comparative safety of a draw. He then descended the hill in stages, firing his rifle, until he rejoined the platoon. Private First Class Ono's extraordinary heroism and devotion to duty are in keeping with the highest traditions of military service and reflect great credit on him, his unit, and the United States Army.

Epilogue: Very little information was available in the CMOHS's archives for Ono. What is known is the he died in 1980 and is buried in Highland Cemetery, North Ludson, Indiana, Section VII, Lot 47, Grave C.

OTANI, KAZUO
US Army — World War II
European Theater — Posthumous Award

Citation: Staff Sergeant Kazuo Otani distinguished himself by extraordinary heroism in action on 15 July 1944, near Pieve Di S. Luce, Italy. Advancing to attack a hill objective, Staff Sergeant Otani's platoon became pinned down in a wheat field by concentrated fire from enemy machine gun and sniper positions. Realizing the danger confronting his platoon, Staff Sergeant Otani left his cover and shot and killed a sniper who was firing with deadly effect upon the platoon. Followed by a steady stream of machine gun bullets, Staff Sergeant Otani then dashed across the open wheat field toward the foot of a cliff, and directed his men to crawl to the cover of the cliff. When the movement of the platoon drew heavy enemy fire, he dashed along the cliff toward the left flank, exposing himself to enemy fire. By attracting the attention of the enemy, he enabled the men closest to the cliff to reach cover. Organizing these men to guard against possible enemy counterattack, Staff Sergeant Otani again made his way across the open field, shouting instructions to the stranded men while continuing to draw enemy fire. Reaching the rear of the platoon position, he took partial cover in a shallow ditch and directed covering fire for the men who had begun to move forward. At this point, one of his men became seriously wounded. Ordering his men to remain under cover, Staff Sergeant Otani crawled to the wounded soldier who was lying on open ground in full view of the enemy. Dragging the wounded soldier to a shallow ditch, Staff Sergeant Otani proceeded to render first aid treatment, but was mortally wounded by machine gun fire. Staff Sergeant Otani's extraordinary heroism and devotion to duty are in keeping with the highest traditions of military service and reflect great credit on him, his unit, and the United States Army.

Epilogue: Otani was born and raised in Sanger, California, the son of Yoichi and Shizuo Ishizaki Otani. He graduated from Visalia Union High School and worked for several years on the Martin Ranch in Woodlake, packing grapes, making boxes, and putting labels on navel oranges. At the time of his death, he was survived by his parents. The location of his burial site is unknown.

SAKATO, GEORGE T.
US Army — World War II
European Theater

Citation: Private George T. Sakato distinguished himself by extraordinary heroism in action on 29 October 1944, on hill 617 in the vicinity of Biffontaine, France. After his platoon had virtually destroyed two enemy defense lines, during which he personally killed five enemy soldiers and captured four, his unit was pinned down by heavy enemy fire. Disregarding the enemy fire, Private Sakato made a one-man rush that encouraged his platoon to charge and destroy the enemy strongpoint. While his platoon was reorganizing, he proved to be the inspiration of his squad in halting a counter-attack on the left flank during which his squad leader was killed. Taking charge of the squad, he continued his relentless tactics, using an enemy rifle and P-38 pistol to stop an organized enemy attack. During this entire action, he killed 12 and wounded two, personally captured four and assisted his platoon in taking 34 prisoners. By continuously ignoring enemy fire, and by his gallant courage and fighting spirit, he turned impending defeat into victory and helped his platoon complete its mission. Private Sakato's extraordinary heroism and devotion to duty are in keeping with the highest traditions of military service and reflect great credit on him, his unit, and the United States Army.

Epilogue: Sakato received his Medal over forty years after the action for which it was earned. The retired postal worker from Denver received the Medal from President Clinton at a White House ceremony. He is one of seven still alive to receive the Medal after it was issued by special legislation. Sakato was born and raised in Colton, California, and interned in Utah during the early years of World War II with his entire family. He entered the Army, in part, to prove his loyalty to his country.

TANOUYE, TED T.
US Army — World War II
European Theater — Posthumous Award

Citation: Technical Sergeant Ted T. Tanouye distinguished himself by extraordinary heroism in action on 7 July 1944, near Molino A Ventoabbto, Italy. Technical Sergeant Tanouye led his platoon in an attack to capture the crest of a strategically important hill that afforded little cover. Observing an enemy machine gun crew placing its gun in position to his left front, Technical Sergeant Tanouye crept forward a few yards and opened fire on the position, killing or wounding three and causing two others to disperse. Immediately, an enemy machine pistol opened fire on him. He returned the fire and killed or wounded three more enemy soldiers. While advancing forward, Technical Sergeant Tanouye was subjected to grenade bursts, which severely wounded his left arm. Sighting an enemy-held trench, he raked the position with fire from his submachine gun and wounded several of the enemy. Running out of ammunition, he crawled 20 yards to obtain several clips from a comrade on his left flank. Next, sighting an enemy machine pistol that had pinned down his men, Technical Sergeant Tanouye crawled forward a few yards and threw a hand grenade into the position, silencing the pistol. He then located another enemy machine gun firing down the slope of the hill, opened fire on it, and silenced that position. Drawing fire from a machine pistol nest located above him, he opened fire on it and wounded three of its occupants. Finally taking his objective, Technical Sergeant Tanouye organized a defensive position on the reverse slope of the hill before accepting first aid treatment and evacuation. Technical Sergeant Tanouye's extraordinary heroism and devotion to duty are in keeping with the highest traditions of military service and reflect great credit on him, his unit, and the United States Army.

Epilogue: Very little information was available in the CMOHS' archives for Tanouye. What is known is that he is buried in Evergreen Memorial Cemetery, Los Angeles, California, Section A, Lot 2734, Grave 1.

WAI, FRANCIS B.
US Army — World War II
Pacific Theater — Posthumous Award

Citation: Captain Francis B. Wai distinguished himself by extraordinary heroism in action, on 20 October 1944, in Leyte, Philippine Islands. Captain Wai landed at Red Beach, Leyte, in the face of accurate, concentrated enemy fire from gun positions advantageously located in a palm grove bounded by submerged rice paddies. Finding the first four waves of American soldiers leaderless, disorganized, and pinned down on the open beach, he immediately assumed command. Issuing clear and concise orders, and disregarding heavy enemy machine gun and rifle fire, he began to move inland through the rice paddies without cover. The men, inspired by his cool demeanor and heroic example, rose from their positions and followed him. During the advance, Captain Wai repeatedly determined the locations of enemy strong points by deliberately exposing himself to draw their fire. In leading an assault upon the last remaining Japanese pillbox in the area, he was killed by its occupants. Captain Wai's courageous, aggressive leadership inspired the men, even after his death, to advance and destroy the enemy. His intrepid and determined efforts were largely responsible for the rapidity with which the initial beachhead was secured. Captain Wai's extraordinary heroism and devotion to duty are in keeping with the highest traditions of military service and reflect great credit on him, his unit, and the United States Army.

Epilogue: Very little information was available in the CMOHS' archives for Wai. What is known is that he is buried in the National Memorial Cemetery of the Pacific, Section O, Row O, Grave 1194.

HISPANIC-AMERICAN RECIPIENT OF THE MEDAL OF HONOR

ADAMS, LUCIAN
US Army — World War II
European Theater

Rank and organization: Staff Sergeant, US Army, 30th Infantry, 3d Infantry Division. Place and date: Near St. Die, France, 28 October 1944. Entered service at: Port Arthur, Tex. Birth: Port Arthur, Tex. G.O. No.: 20, 29 March 1945.

Citation: For conspicuous gallantry and intrepidity at risk of life above and beyond the call of duty on 28 October 1944, near St. Die, France. When his company was stopped in its effort to drive through the Mortagne Forest to reopen the supply line to the isolated third battalion, S/Sgt. Adams braved the concentrated fire of machineguns in a lone assault on a force of German troops. Although his company had progressed less than 10 yards and had lost 3 killed and 6 wounded, S/Sgt. Adams charged forward dodging from tree to tree firing a borrowed BAR from the hip. Despite intense machinegun fire which the enemy directed at him and rifle grenades which struck the trees over his head showering him with broken twigs and branches, S/Sgt. Adams made his way to within 10 yards of the closest machinegun and killed the gunner with a hand grenade. An enemy soldier threw hand grenades at him from a position only 10 yards distant; however, S/Sgt. Adams dispatched him with a single burst of BAR fire. Charging into the vortex of the enemy fire, he killed another machinegunner at 15 yards range with a hand grenade and forced the surrender of 2 supporting infantrymen. Although the remainder of the German group concentrated the full force of its automatic weapons fire in a desperate effort to knock him out, he proceeded through the woods to find and exterminate 5 more of the enemy. Finally, when the third German machinegun opened up on him at a range of 20 yards, S/Sgt. Adams killed the gunner with BAR fire. In the course of the action, he personally killed 9 Germans, eliminated 3 enemy machineguns, vanquished a specialized force which was armed with automatic weapons and grenade launchers, cleared the woods of hostile elements, and reopened the severed supply lines to the assault companies of his battalion.

Epilogue: Very little information was available in the CMOHS's archives for Adams. He survived the war and returned home to Texas. He died in San Antonio in 2003.

BACA, JOHN P
US Army — Vietnam War

Rank and organization: Specialist Fourth Class, US Army, Company D, 1st Battalion, 12th Cavalry, 1st Cavalry Division. Place and date: Phuoc Long Province, Republic of Vietnam, 10 February 1970. Entered service at: Fort Ord, Calif. Born: 10 January 1949, Providence, R.I.

Citation: For conspicuous gallantry and intrepidity in action at the risk of his life above and beyond the call of duty. Sp4c. Baca, Company D, distinguished himself while serving on a recoilless rifle team during a night ambush mission A platoon from his company was sent to investigate the detonation of an automatic ambush device forward of his unit's main position and soon came under intense enemy fire from concealed positions along the trail. Hearing the heavy firing from the platoon position and realizing that his recoilless rifle team could assist the members of the besieged patrol, Sp4c. Baca led his team through the hail of enemy fire to a firing position within the patrol's defensive perimeter. As they prepared to engage the enemy, a fragmentation grenade was thrown into the midst of the patrol. Fully aware of the danger to his comrades, Sp4c. Baca unhesitatingly, and with complete disregard for his own safety, covered the grenade with his steel helmet and fell on it as the grenade exploded, thereby absorbing the lethal fragments and concussion with his body. His gallant action and total disregard for his personal well-being directly saved 8 men from certain serious injury or death. The extraordinary courage and selflessness displayed by Sp4c. Baca, at the risk of his life, are in the highest traditions of the military service and reflect great credit on him, his unit, and the U.S. Army.

Epilogue: Baca was a Navy brat, as his father was a career naval officer, who moved the family to California, where Baca attended school in Los Angeles and San Diego. After joining the Army in 1969, he was assigned to the 1st Cavalry Division in Vietnam, and seven months later, he jumped on a live hand grenade to save the lives of his buddies, an act for which he received the Medal. He said, "I saw it. I don't know if anybody else saw it. All I could do was think about putting my helmet on it and covering it up. The explosion threw me on my back. I was awake. I could see my stomach just pouring out of me. It was a numbing feeling. It was a peaceful feeling. I thought I was going to die, and I knew I would meet it in a peaceful attitude." Baca received the Medal from President Nixon at a White House ceremony. After his discharge, he worked for the Post Office, attended Bible college, and worked for the Veterans Administration in Los Angeles. In 1993, he lived on a farm owned by one of his Army buddies in California and got by on a monthly disability check from the VA. In 1990, Baca went to Vietnam with a fellow veteran to help build medical clinics. He said in a 1993 interview, "Sometimes I curse the Medal, how it raises you above who you are."

BARKELEY, DAVID B.
US Army — World War I
Posthumous Award

Rank and organization: Private, US Army, Company A, 356th Infantry, 89th Division. Place and date: Near Pouilly, France, 9 November 1918. Entered service at: San Antonio, Tex. Birth: Laredo, Tex. G.O. No.: 20, W.D., 1919.

Citation: When information was desired as to the enemy's position on the opposite side of the Meuse River, Pvt. Barkeley, with another soldier, volunteered without hesitation and swam the river to reconnoiter the exact location. He succeeded in reaching the opposite bank, despite the evident determination of the enemy to prevent a crossing. Having obtained his information, he again entered the water for his return, but before his goal was reached, he was seized with cramps and drowned.

Epilogue: Barkeley's mother was Mexican, and his father Anglo and an American soldier. Despite the mixed heritage, Barkeley was not recognized as Hispanic until 1989, when he was proclaimed as the first Hispanic-American to receive the Medal of Honor. For reasons we may never know, he kept his background secret. He was born in Laredo, Texas. The family moved briefly to San Antonio and shortly thereafter relocated to Pennsylvania. He attended Brackenridge Elementary School and worked part-time after school as a newsboy. He was an avid swimmer, enjoyed singing, and once had a role in a play. He quit school at 13 to work full-time as a delivery boy for a local merchant. At the onset of WWI, he joined the Texas National Guard and was later transferred to the 356th Infantry regiment, which was sent to France in 1918. Barkeley did not survive the war. He was buried in France and later his remains were brought back to the United States at his mother's request. He is buried at Fort Sam Houston Post Cemetery (now Fort Sam Houston National Cemetery). Initially, his headstone misspelled his name, but it was later corrected. He had one living sister, Amelia, who was present when the City of San Antonio organized a tribute to her brother's achievement in 1989.

BAZAAR, PHILIP

US Navy — Spanish American War

Rank and organization: Ordinary Seaman, US Navy. Born: Chile, South America. Accredited to: Massachusetts. G.O. No.: 59, 22 June 1865.

Citation: On board the U.S.S. Santiago de Cuba during the assault on Fort Fisher on 15 January 1865. As one of a boat crew detailed to one of the generals on shore, O.S. Bazaar bravely entered the fort in the assault and accompanied his party in carrying dispatches at the height of the battle. He was 1 of 6 men who entered the fort in the assault from the fleet.

Epilogue: Very little information was available in the CMOHS's archives for Bazaar. What is known is that a year after receiving the Medal, Bazaar deserted the Navy, lived under the assumed name of Phillipe Bazin, and is *lost to history.*[128]

VERSACE, HUMBERT R

US Army — Vietnam War
Posthumous Award

Citation: Captain Humbert R. Versace distinguished himself by extraordinary heroism during the period of 29 October 1963 to 26 September 1965, while serving as S-2 Advisor, Military Assistance Advisory Group, Detachment 52, Ca Mau, Republic of Vietnam. While accompanying a Civilian Irregular Defense Group patrol engaged in combat operations in Thoi Binh District, An Xuyen Province, Captain Versace and the patrol came under sudden and intense mortar, automatic weapons, and small arms fire from elements of a heavily armed enemy battalion. As the battle raged, Captain Versace, although severely wounded in the knee and back by hostile fire, fought valiantly and continued to engage enemy targets. Weakened by his wounds and fatigued by the fierce firefight, Captain Versace stubbornly resisted capture by the over-powering Viet Cong force with the last full measure of his strength and ammunition. Taken prisoner by the Viet Cong, he exemplified the tenets of the Code of Conduct from the time he entered into Prisoner of War status. Captain Versace assumed command of his fellow American soldiers, scorned the enemy's exhaustive interrogation and indoctrination efforts, and made three unsuccessful attempts to escape, despite his weakened condition which was brought about by his wounds and the extreme privation and hardships he was forced to endure. During his captivity, Captain Versace was segregated in an isolated prisoner of war cage, manacled in irons for prolonged periods of time, and placed on extremely reduced ration. The enemy was unable to break his indomitable will, his faith in God, and his trust in the United States of America. Captain Versace, an American fighting man who epitomized the principles of his country and the Code of Conduct, was executed by the Viet Cong on 26 September 1965. Captain Versace's gallant actions in close contact with an enemy force and unyielding courage and bravery while a prisoner of war are in the highest traditions of the military service and reflect the utmost credit upon himself and the United States Army.

Epilogue: The Medal was awarded to Versace 38 years after the action in Vietnam, which also led to his death. After being held for two years, he was executed by his Viet Cong capturers. His original recommendation by Major Nick Rowe was downgraded to a Silver Star, the third highest award for valor. Born in Hawaii, son of a West Point graduate and a graduate himself as well as a special officer, Versace was a native of Alexandria, Virginia. His Medal was finally awarded to him by President Bush in 2002. He is buried in Arlington National Cemetery.

BENAVIDEZ, ROY
US Army — Vietnam War

Rank and Organization: Master Sergeant, Detachment B-56, 5th Special Forces Group, Republic of Vietnam. Place and Date: West of Loc Ninh on 2 May 1968. Entered Service at: Houston, Texas, June 1955. Date and Place of Birth: 5 August 1935, DeWitt County, Cuero, Texas.

Citation: Master Sergeant (then Staff Sergeant) Roy P. Benavidez United States Army, who distinguished himself by a series of daring and extremely valorous actions on 2 May 1968 while assigned to Detachment B56, 5th Special Forces Group (Airborne), 1st Special Forces, Republic of Vietnam. On the morning of 2 May 1968, a 12-man Special Forces Reconnaissance Team was inserted by helicopters in a dense jungle area west of Loc Ninh, Vietnam to gather intelligence information about confirmed large-scale enemy activity. This area was controlled and routinely patrolled by the North Vietnamese Army. After a short period of time on the ground, the team met heavy enemy resistance, and requested emergency extraction. Three helicopters attempted extraction, but were unable to land due to intense enemy small arms and anti-aircraft fire. Sergeant Benavidez was at the Forward Operating Base in Loc Ninh monitoring the operation by radio when these helicopters returned to off-load wounded crewmembers and to assess aircraft damage. Sergeant Benavidez voluntarily boarded a returning aircraft to assist in another extraction attempt. Realizing that all the team members were either dead or wounded and unable to move to the pickup zone, he directed the aircraft to a nearby clearing where he jumped from the hovering helicopter, and ran approximately 75 meters under withering small arms fire to the crippled team. Prior to reaching the team's position he was wounded in his right leg, face, and head. Despite these painful injuries, he took charge, repositioning the team members and directing their fire to facilitate the landing of an extraction aircraft, and the loading of wounded and dead team members. He then threw smoke canisters to direct the aircraft to the team's position. Despite his severe wounds and under intense enemy fire, he carried and dragged half of the wounded team members to the awaiting aircraft. He then provided protective fire by running alongside the aircraft as it moved to pick up the remaining team members. As the enemy's fire intensified, he hurried to recover the body and classified documents on the dead team leader. When he reached the leader's body, Sergeant Benavidez was severely wounded by small arms fire in the abdomen and grenade fragments in his back. At nearly the same moment, the aircraft pilot was mortally wounded, and his helicopter crashed. Although in extremely critical condition due to his multiple wounds, Sergeant Benavidez secured the classified documents and made his way back to the wreckage, where he aided the wounded out of the overturned aircraft, and gathered the stunned survivors into a defensive perimeter. Under increasing enemy automatic weapons and grenade fire, he moved around the perimeter distributing water and ammunition to his weary men, reinstilling in them a will to live and fight. Facing a buildup of enemy opposition with a beleaguered team, Sergeant Benavidez mustered his strength, began calling in tactical air strikes and directed the fire from supporting gunships to suppress the enemy's fire and so permit another extraction attempt. He was wounded again in his thigh by small arms fire while administering first aid to a wounded team member just before another extraction helicopter was able to land. His indomitable spirit kept him going as he began to ferry his comrades to the craft. On his second trip with the wounded, he was clubbed from additional wounds to his head and arms before killing his adversary. He then continued under devastating fire to carry the wounded to the helicopter. Upon reaching the aircraft, he spotted and killed two enemy soldiers who were rushing the craft from an angle that prevented the aircraft door gunner from firing upon them. With little strength remaining, he made one last trip to the perimeter to ensure that all classified material had been collected or destroyed, and to bring in the remaining wounded. Only then, in extremely serious condition from numerous wounds and loss of blood, did he allow himself to be pulled into the extraction aircraft. Sergeant Benavidez' gallant choice to join voluntarily his comrades who were in critical straits, to expose himself constantly to withering enemy fire, and his refusal to be stopped despite numerous severe wounds, saved the lives of at least eight men. His fearless personal leadership, tenacious devotion to duty, and extremely valorous actions in the face of overwhelming odds were in keeping with the highest traditions of the military service, and reflect the utmost credit on him and the United States Army. Benavidez

Epilogue: Benavidez, who died in 1998 in San Antonio, was by all accounts a soldier's soldier. Loyalty and a strong sense of duty drove him to save a Special Forces unit in a vicious firefight, even after he was shot, stabbed, and clubbed. He was fluent in many languages, could talk with eloquence and confidence on many subjects, and had amazing physical stamina. He is survived by his wife, Hilaria, a son Noel, and two daughters, Denice and Yvette. [129]

DE CASTRO, JOSEPH H.
US Army — American Civil War

Rank and organization: Corporal, Company I, 19th Massachusetts Infantry. Place and date: At Gettysburg, Pa., 3 July 1863. Entered service at: ------. Birth: Boston, Mass. Date of issue: 1 December 1864.

Citation: Capture of flag of 19th Virginia regiment (C.S.A.).

Epilogue: No personal information was available in the CMOHS' archives for De Castro. He is *lost to history.*

DE LA GARZA, EMILO A., JR.
US Marine Corps — Vietnam War
Posthumous Award

Rank and organization: Lance Corporal, US Marine Corps, Company E, 2nd Battalion, 1st Marines, 1st Marine Division. Place and date: Near Da Nang, Republic of Vietnam, 11 April 1970. Entered service at: Chicago, 111. Born: 23 June 1949, East Chicago, Ind.

Citation: For conspicuous gallantry and intrepidity at the risk of his life above and beyond the call of duty while serving as a machine gunner with Company E. Returning with his squad from a night ambush operation, L/Cpl. De La Garza joined his platoon commander and another marine in searching for 2 enemy soldiers who had been observed fleeing for cover toward a small pond. Moments later, he located 1 of the enemy soldiers hiding among the reeds and brush. As the 3 marines attempted to remove the resisting soldier from the pond, L/Cpl. De La Garza observed him pull the pin on a grenade. Shouting a warning, L/Cpl. De La Garza placed himself between the other 2 marines and the ensuing blast from the grenade, thereby saving the lives of his comrades at the sacrifice of his life. By his prompt and decisive action, and his great personal valor in the face of almost certain death, L/Cpl. De La Garza upheld and further enhanced the finest traditions of the Marine Corps and the U.S. Naval Service.

Epilogue: Born and raised in East Chicago, Indiana, after graduating from Washington High School and working briefly for a local merchant, De La Garza enlisted in the Marines in 1969. He was awarded the Medal for throwing his body on an enemy hand grenade to save the lives of his fellow Marines in Vietnam. Three years after his next of kin received the award, the East Chicago city council proposed to change the name of Main Street to De La Garza Street. Merchants complained and opposed the idea, saying they would have to buy new stationery and that outsiders would get lost. Following charges of racism and the intervention of the local chapter of the American Legion, the city council approved the change. In subsequent years, a recreation center and an American Legion post were also named in his honor. The Medal was presented to De La Garza's wife, Rosemary, and his daughter, Renee, by Vice-President Spiro Agnew at a White House ceremony. De La Garza is buried in St John's Cemetery, Hammond, Indiana.

DIAS, RALPH E.
US Marine Corps — Vietnam War
Posthumous Award

Rank and organization: Private First Class, US Marine Corps, 3rd Platoon, Company D, 1st Battalion, 7th Marines, 1st Marine Division (Rein) FMF. Place and date: Que Son Mountains, Republic of Vietnam, 12 November 1969. Entered service at: Pittsburgh, Pa. Born: 15 July 1950, Shelocta, Indiana County, Pa.

Citation: As a member of a reaction force which was pinned down by enemy fire while assisting a platoon in the same circumstance, Pfc. Dias, observing that both units were sustaining casualties, initiated an aggressive assault against an enemy machine gun bunker which was the principal source of hostile fire. Severely wounded by enemy snipers while charging across the open area, he pulled himself to the shelter of a nearby rock. Braving enemy fire for a second time, Pfc. Dias was again wounded. Unable to walk, he crawled 15 meters to the protection of a rock located near his objective and, repeatedly exposing himself to intense hostile fire, unsuccessfully threw several hand grenades at the machine gun emplacement. Still determined to destroy the emplacement, Pfc. Dias again moved into the open and was wounded a third time by sniper fire. As he threw a last grenade which destroyed the enemy position, he was mortally wounded by another enemy round. Pfc. Dias' indomitable courage, dynamic initiative, and selfless devotion to duty upheld the highest traditions of the Marine Corps and the U.S. Naval Service. He gallantly gave his life in the service to his country.

Epilogue: Dias was born and raised in Indiana, Pennsylvania, and graduated from Elderton High School before entering the Marine Corps in 1967. He completed basic training at Parris Island, special infantry training at Camp Lejeune, and was assigned to the 5th Marines at Camp Pendleton before being ordered to Vietnam in 1969. Dias was killed in action. He was survived by his parents, Melvin and Anna Dias, four sisters, and two brothers. The Medal was presented to his mother by Vice-President Gerald Ford at the Blair House.[130]

FERNANDEZ, DANIEL
US Army — Vietnam War
Posthumous Award

Rank and organization: Specialist Fourth Class, US Army, Company C, 1st Battalion, 5th Infantry (Mechanized), 25th Infantry Division. Place and date: Cu Chi, Hau Nghia Province, Republic of Vietnam, 18 February 1966. Entered service at: Albuquerque, N. Mex. Born: 30 June 1944, Albuquerque, N. Mex. c.o. No.: 21, 26 April 1967.

Citation: For conspicuous gallantry and intrepidity at the risk of his life above and beyond the call of duty. Sp4c. Fernandez demonstrated indomitable courage when the patrol was ambushed by a Viet Cong rifle company and driven back by the intense enemy automatic weapons fire before it could evacuate an American soldier who had been wounded in the Viet Cong attack. Sp4c. Fernandez, a sergeant and 2 other volunteers immediately fought their way through devastating fire and exploding grenades to reach the fallen soldier. Upon reaching their fallen comrade the sergeant was struck in the knee by machine gun fire and immobilized. Sp4c. Fernandez took charge, rallied the left flank of his patrol and began to assist in the recovery of the wounded sergeant. While first aid was being administered to the wounded man, a sudden increase in the accuracy and intensity of enemy fire forced the volunteer group to take cover. As they did, an enemy grenade landed in the midst of the group, although some men did not see it. Realizing there was no time for the wounded sergeant or the other men to protect themselves from the grenade blast, Sp4c. Fernandez vaulted over the wounded sergeant and threw himself on the grenade as it exploded, saving the lives of his 4 comrades at the sacrifice of his life. Sp4c. Fernandez' profound concern for his fellow soldiers, at the risk of his life above and beyond the call of duty are in the highest traditions of the U.S. Army and reflect great credit upon himself and the Armed Forces of his country.

Epilogue: Fernandez was from Los Lunas, a sleepy New Mexico town of 1200 along the Rio Grande. When asked why he would sacrifice his life to save others, he father, Jose, said, "Daniel was no different than any other American boy… we have many here… and there are many in the US. But, he was a very generous boy. He liked to help people." Jose told his son before he was shipped to Vietnam, "You don't always have to volunteer. You've earned your medals. Please don't do more than you are asked." Fernandez was active in the 4-H Club and played football before dropping out of high school to join the Army. He worked hard to be good soldier, some of his buddies said. "He was a fine soldier and a good friend." At the time of his death, he was survived by his parents, Mr. & Mrs. Jose Fernandez, his sister, Rita, and brothers Peter and James. The Medal was presented to his parents by President Johnson at a White House ceremony. He is buried in Santa Fe National Cemetery, New Mexico.

GARCIA, MARCARO
US Army — World War II
European Theater

Rank and organization: Staff Sergeant, US Army, Company B, 22nd Infantry, 4th Infantry Division. Place and date: Near Grosshau, Germany, 27 November 1944. Entered service at: Sugarland, Tex. Born: 20 January 1920, Villa de Castano, Mexico. G.O. No.: 74, 1 September 1945.

Citation: While an acting squad leader of Company B, 22d Infantry, on 27 November 1944, near Grosshau, Germany, he single-handedly assaulted 2 enemy machinegun emplacements. Attacking prepared positions on a wooded hill, which could be approached only through meager cover, his company was pinned down by intense machinegun fire and subjected to a concentrated artillery and mortar barrage. Although painfully wounded, he refused to be evacuated and on his own initiative crawled forward alone until he reached a position near an enemy emplacement. Hurling grenades, he boldly assaulted the position, destroyed the gun, and with his rifle killed 3 of the enemy who attempted to escape. When he rejoined his company, a second machinegun opened fire and again the intrepid soldier went forward, utterly disregarding his own safety. He stormed the position and destroyed the gun, killed 3 more Germans, and captured 4 prisoners. He fought on with his unit until the objective was taken and only then did he permit himself to be removed for medical care. S/Sgt. (then private) Garcia's conspicuous heroism, his inspiring, courageous conduct, and his complete disregard for his personal safety wiped out 2 enemy emplacements and enabled his company to advance and secure its objective.

Epilogue: When Garcia returned home to Texas after receiving the Medal, he got into a fight with a café owner who refused to serve him because he was a Mexican-American. He was charged with assault and held over for trial. His friends and family raised money for his trial, and he was acquitted of the charges. He worked for many years as a contract employee of the Veterans Administration until he was killed in an auto accident in 1972 near his home in Sugarland, Texas. He was 52. He is buried in Houston National Cemetery.[131]

GARCIA, FERNANDO L.
US Marine Corps — Korean War
Posthumous Award

Rank and organization: Private First Class, US Marine Corps, Company I, 3rd Battalion, 5th Marines, 1st Marine Division (Rein.). Place and date: Korea, 5 September 1952. Entered service at: San Juan, P.R. Born: 14 October 1929, Utuado, P.R.

Citation: For conspicuous gallantry and intrepidity at the risk of his life above and beyond the call of duty while serving as a member of Company I, in action against enemy aggressor forces. While participating in the defense of a combat outpost located more than 1 mile forward of the main line of resistance during a savage night attack by a fanatical enemy force employing grenades, mortars, and artillery, Pfc. Garcia, although suffering painful wounds, moved through the intense hail of hostile fire to a supply point to secure more hand grenades. Quick to act when a hostile grenade landed nearby, endangering the life of another marine, as well as his own, he unhesitatingly chose to sacrifice himself and immediately threw his body upon the deadly missile, receiving the full impact of the explosion. His great personal valor and cool decision in the face of almost certain death sustain and enhance the finest traditions of the U.S. Naval Service. He gallantly gave his life for his country.

Epilogue: Garcia was born and raised in Puerto Rico, where he attended elementary and high school. He was working as a file clerk when he was drafted into the Marine Corps in 1951. He completed boot camp at Parris Island, South Carolina, and was sent to Camp Pendleton, California, for further training. In 1952, he was assigned to the 5th Marines in Korea, where he was killed in action. At the time of his death, he was survived by his parents, Mr. & Mrs. German Garcia-Toledo, two sisters, Daisy and Carmen, and a brother, Hector. Garcia's body was never recovered. In 1953, a ceremony was held at Utuado, Puerto Rico, where Garcia's parents were presented with the Medal, and later, a US Navy ship was named in his honor..[132]

GOMEZ, EDWARD

US Marine Corps — Korean War
Posthumous Award

Rank and organization: Private First Class, US Marine Corps, Reserve, Company E, 2nd Battalion, 1st Marines, 1st Marine Division (Rein.). Place and date: Korea, Hill 749, 14 September 1951. Entered service at: Omaha, Nebr. Born: 10 August 1932, Omaha, Nebr.

Citation: For conspicuous gallantry and intrepidity at the risk of his life above and beyond the call of duty while serving as an ammunition bearer in Company E, in action against enemy aggressor forces. Bolding advancing with his squad in support of a group of riflemen assaulting a series of strongly fortified and bitterly defended hostile positions on Hill 749, Pfc. Gomez consistently exposed himself to the withering barrage to keep his machine gun supplied with ammunition during the drive forward to seize the objective. As his squad deployed to meet an imminent counterattack, he voluntarily moved down an abandoned trench to search for a new location for the gun and, when a hostile grenade landed between himself and his weapon, shouted a warning to those around him as he grasped the activated charge in his hand. Determined to save his comrades, he unhesitatingly chose to sacrifice himself and, diving into the ditch with the deadly missile, absorbed the shattering violence of the explosion in his body. By his stouthearted courage, incomparable valor, and decisive spirit of self-sacrifice, Pfc. Gomez inspired the others to heroic efforts in subsequently repelling the outnumbering foe, and his valiant conduct throughout sustained and enhanced the finest traditions of the U.S. Naval Service. He gallantly gave his life for his country.

Epilogue: Gomez was born and raised in Omaha and enlisted in the Marines at 17 after graduating from Omaha High School in 1949. He was 19 when he used his body to smother an enemy hand grenade to save his fellow Marines. At the time of his death, his parents, Mr. & Mrs. Modesta Gomez, lived in Omaha at 2505 Washington Street. Gomez is buried in St. Mary's Cemetery, Omaha..[133]

GONSALVES, HAROLD

US Marine Corps — World War II
Pacific Theater — Posthumous Award

Rank and organization: Private First Class, US Marine Corps Reserve. Born: 28 January 1926, Alameda, Calif. Accredited to: California.

Citation: For conspicuous gallantry and intrepidity at the risk of his life above and beyond the call of duty while serving as Acting Scout Sergeant with the 4th Battalion, 15th Marines, 6th Marine Division, during action against enemy Japanese forces on Okinawa Shima in the Ryukyu Chain, 15 April 1945. Undaunted by the powerfully organized opposition encountered on Motobu Peninsula during the fierce assault waged by his battalion against the Japanese stronghold at Mount Yaetake, Pfc. Gonsalves repeatedly braved the terrific enemy bombardment to aid his forward observation team in directing well-placed artillery fire. When his commanding officer determined to move into the front lines in order to register a more effective bombardment in the enemy's defensive position, he unhesitatingly advanced uphill with the officer and another Marine despite a slashing barrage of enemy mortar and rifle fire. As they reached the front and a Japanese grenade fell close within the group, instantly Pfc. Gonsalves dived on the deadly missile, absorbing the exploding charge in his own body and thereby protecting the others from serious and perhaps fatal wounds. Stouthearted and indomitable, Pfc. Gonsalves readily yielded his own chances of survival that his fellow marines might carry on the relentless battle against a fanatic enemy and his cool decision, prompt action and valiant spirit of self-sacrifice in the face of certain death reflect the highest credit upon himself and upon the U.S. Naval Service.

Epilogue: Gonsalves threw himself on a hand grenade to save the lives of his fellow Marines. He was born and raised in Alameda, California. He father was from Massachusetts, and his mother from Hawaii. He attended high school for only two years, dropping out to work as a stock clerk at Montgomery Ward department store. When he enlisted in the Marines, he was 5'9" and weighed 178 pounds. He completed boot camp in San Diego and trained to become a Raider, an elite combat unit, at Camp Pendleton. During the War in the Pacific, Gonsalves participated in the assault and occupation of Engebi, Parry Island, Eniwetok, Kwajalein, Guadalcanal, Guam, and Okinawa, where he died. He was buried with full military honors in Golden Gate National Cemetery in San Bruno, California. His parents, John and Marie, lived in their Alameda home at 1818 Oak Street for many years after his death.[134]

GONZALES, ALFREDO

US Marine Corps — Vietnam War
Posthumous Award

Rank and organization: Sergeant, US Marine Corps, Company A, 1st Battalion, 1st Marines, 1st Marine Division (Rein), FMF. Place and date: Near Thua Thien, Republic of Vietnam, 4 February 1968. Entered service at: San Antonio, Tex. Born: 23 May 1946, Edinburg Tex.

Citation: For conspicuous gallantry and intrepidity at the risk of his life above and beyond the call of duty while serving as platoon commander, 3d Platoon, Company A. On 31 January 1968, during the initial phase of Operation Hue City, Sgt. Gonzalez' unit was formed as a reaction force and deployed to Hue to relieve the pressure on the beleaguered city. While moving by truck convoy along Route No. 1, near the village of Lang Van Lrong, the marines received a heavy volume of enemy fire. Sgt. Gonzalez aggressively maneuvered the marines in his platoon, and directed their fire until the area was cleared of snipers. Immediately after crossing a river south of Hue, the column was again hit by intense enemy fire. One of the marines on top of a tank was wounded and fell to the ground in an exposed position. With complete disregard for his safety, Sgt. Gonzalez ran through the fire-swept area to the assistance of his injured comrade. He lifted him up and though receiving fragmentation wounds during the rescue, he carried the wounded marine to a covered position for treatment. Due to the increased volume and accuracy of enemy fire from a fortified machine gun bunker on the side of the road, the company was temporarily halted. Realizing the gravity of the situation, Sgt. Gonzalez exposed himself to the enemy fire and moved his platoon along the east side of a bordering rice paddy to a dike directly across from the bunker. Though fully aware of the danger involved, he moved to the fire-swept road and destroyed the hostile position with hand grenades. Although seriously wounded again on 3 February, he steadfastly refused medical treatment and continued to supervise his men and lead the attack. On 4 February, the enemy had again pinned the company down, inflicting heavy casualties with automatic weapons and rocket fire. Sgt. Gonzalez, utilizing a number of light antitank assault weapons, fearlessly moved from position to position firing numerous rounds at the heavily fortified enemy emplacements. He successfully knocked out a rocket position and suppressed much of the enemy fire before falling mortally wounded. The heroism, courage, and dynamic leadership displayed by Sgt. Gonzalez reflected great credit upon himself and the Marine Corps, and were in keeping with the highest traditions of the U.S. Naval Service. He gallantly gave his life for his country.

Epilogue: Gonzales was born and raised in Edinburg, Texas, by his mother, Dolia, while she worked as a waitress, a job she held until she retired, He attended Lamar Grammar School and, upon graduation from Edinburg High School in 1965, immediately entered the Marine Corps, despite his mother's wishes. She said she wanted him to go to college, but ever since he was eight, he had wanted to join the Marines.[135] Gonzales received numerous honors, including the naming of a new US Navy Aegis destroyer. Gonzales is buried in Hillcrest Cemetery, Edinburg, Texas.[136]

GONZALES, DAVID M.
US Army — World War II
Pacific Theater — Posthumous Award

Rank and organization: Private First Class, US Army, Company A, 127th Infantry, 32nd Infantry Division. Place and date: Villa Verde Trail, Luzon, Philippine Islands, 25 April 1945. Entered service at: Pacoima, Calif. Birth: Pacoima, Calif. G.O. No.: 115, 8 December 1945.

Citation: He was pinned down with his company. As enemy fire swept the area, making any movement extremely hazardous, a 500-pound bomb smashed into the company's perimeter, burying 5 men with its explosion. Pfc. Gonzales, without hesitation, seized an entrenching tool and under a hail of fire crawled 15 yards to his entombed comrades, where his commanding officer, who had also rushed forward, was beginning to dig the men out. Nearing his goal, he saw the officer struck and instantly killed by machinegun fire. Undismayed, he set to work swiftly and surely with his hands and the entrenching tool while enemy sniper and machinegun bullets struck all about him. He succeeded in digging one of the men out of the pile of rock and sand. To dig faster he stood up regardless of the greater danger from so exposing himself. He extricated a second man, and then another. As he completed the liberation of the third, he was hit and mortally wounded, but the comrades for whom he so gallantly gave his life were safely evacuated. Pfc. Gonzales' valiant and intrepid conduct exemplifies the highest tradition of the military service.

Epilogue: Gonzales was born and raised in Pacoima, California. Before entering the Army in 1944, he worked as a drill operator. When Gonzales's body was returned to Los Angeles, newspaper articles show that his casket was met at the train station by his mother, Rita, wife, Steffanie, and son, David, Jr., who, later in life, would play a key role in ensuring his father received the recognition he deserved. The city of Pacoima failed to act on an approved resolution to rename a recreational center after Gonzales. The center was eventually renamed after some forty years of efforts by his family, particularly, David Jr. A spokesman for the city council said that the proposal simply fell through the cracks. In another incident, the wrong photo of Gonzales was displayed in the Pentagon's Hall of Heroes, which honors all Medal recipients. With help from the White House and top brass at the Pentagon, David Jr. finally ensured that the correct David Gonzales was on display. Gonzales is buried in Calvary Cemetery, Los Angeles.[137]

GUILLEN, AMBROSIO
US Marine Corps — Korean War
Posthumous Award

Rank and organization: Staff Sergeant, US Marine Corps, Company F, 2nd Battalion, 7th Marines, 1st Marine Division (Rein.). Place and date: Near Songuch-on, Korea, 25 July 1953. Entered service at: El Paso, Tex. Born: 7 December 1929, La Junta, Colo.

Citation: For conspicuous gallantry and intrepidity at the risk of his life above and beyond the call of duty while serving as a platoon sergeant of Company F in action against enemy aggressor forces. Participating in the defense of an outpost forward of the main line of resistance, S/Sgt. Guillen maneuvered his platoon over unfamiliar terrain in the face of hostile fire and placed his men in fighting positions. With his unit pinned down when the outpost was attacked under cover of darkness by an estimated force of 2 enemy battalions supported by mortar and artillery fire, he deliberately exposed himself to the heavy barrage and attacks to direct his men in defending their positions and personally supervise the treatment and evacuation of the wounded. Inspired by his leadership, the platoon quickly rallied and engaged the enemy in fierce hand-to-hand combat. Although critically wounded during the course of the battle, S/Sgt. Guillen refused medical aid and continued to direct his men throughout the remainder of the engagement until the enemy was defeated and thrown into disorderly retreat. Succumbing to his wounds within a few hours, S/Sgt. Guillen, by his outstanding courage and indomitable fighting spirit, was directly responsible for the success of his platoon in repelling a numerically superior enemy force. His personal valor reflects the highest credit upon himself and enhances the finest traditions of the U.S. Naval Service. He gallantly gave his life for his country.

Epilogue: Guillen was born at La Junta, Colorado, but grew up in El Paso, Texas. He enlisted in the Marines at the age of 18, completed boot camp at San Diego, and infantry training at Camp Pendleton. He was assigned to the 1st Marine Division in Korea at the time of his death in 1953. He is buried in Ft. Bliss National Cemetery, Texas.[138]

HERNANDEZ, RODOLFO P.
US Army — Korean War

Rank and organization: Corporal, US Army, Company G, 187th Airborne Regimental Combat Team. Place and date: Near Wontong-ni, Korea, 31 May 1951. Entered service at: Fowler, Calif. Born: 14 April 1931, Colton, Calif. G.O. No.: 40, 21 April 1962.

Citation: Cpl. Hernandez, a member of Company G, distinguished himself by conspicuous gallantry and intrepidity above and beyond the call of duty in action against the enemy. His platoon, in defensive positions on Hill 420, came under ruthless attack by a numerically superior and fanatical hostile force, accompanied by heavy artillery, mortar, and machine gun fire which inflicted numerous casualties on the platoon. His comrades were forced to withdraw due to lack of ammunition but Cpl. Hernandez, although wounded in an exchange of grenades, continued to deliver deadly fire into the ranks of the onrushing assailants until a ruptured cartridge rendered his rifle inoperative. Immediately leaving his position, Cpl. Hernandez rushed the enemy armed only with rifle and bayonet. Fearlessly engaging the foe, he killed 6 of the enemy before falling unconscious from grenade, bayonet, and bullet wounds but his heroic action momentarily halted the enemy advance and enabled his unit to counterattack and retake the lost ground. The indomitable fighting spirit, outstanding courage, and tenacious devotion to duty clearly demonstrated by Cpl. Hernandez reflect the highest credit upon himself, the infantry, and the U.S. Army.

Epilogue: Hernandez was believed dead when his buddies placed him in a body bag. Someone noticed a slight movement and called for medical help. Metal shrapnel had torn into his head, causing brain damage, and he was unable to speak for months. He had to learn to talk all over again, as he recovered from his many wounds from bayonets, bullets, and grenades. Hernandez now lives in Fayetteville, North Carolina, with his wife, Denzil. He wears a beard to hide facial scars, his right arm flails out uncontrollably at times, and he has trouble speaking clearly, for which he frequently apologizes.

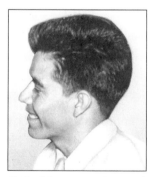

HERRERA, SILVESTRE S.
US Army — World War II
European Theater

Rank and organization: Private First Class, US Army, Company E, 142nd Infantry, 36th Infantry Division. Place and date: Near Mertzwiller, France, 15 March 1945. Entered service at: Phoenix, Ariz. Birth: El Paso, Tex. G.O. No.: 75, 5 September 1945.

Citation: He advanced with a platoon along a wooded road until stopped by heavy enemy machinegun fire. As the rest of the unit took cover, he made a 1-man frontal assault on a strongpoint and captured 8 enemy soldiers. When the platoon resumed its advance and was subjected to fire from a second emplacement beyond an extensive minefield, Pvt. Herrera again moved forward, disregarding the danger of exploding mines, to attack the position. He stepped on a mine and had both feet severed but, despite intense pain and unchecked loss of blood, he pinned down the enemy with accurate rifle fire while a friendly squad captured the enemy gun by skirting the minefield and rushing in from the flank. The magnificent courage, extraordinary heroism, and willing self-sacrifice displayed by Pvt. Herrera resulted in the capture of 2 enemy strongpoints and the taking of 8 prisoners.

Epilogue: Herrea was raised in El Paso by his aunt and uncle. Before being drafted into the Army, he did farm work throughout the southwest. Although he was expecting his fourth child and wasn't a citizen, he felt it his duty to fight for his country. In the action in which he would eventually receive the Medal, he lost both legs to landmines. Despite these injuries, he continued to fight, pinning down the enemy. He was relocated from Europe to Utah to receive medical care and was granted the citizenship he had applied for while in Italy. He received the Medal from President Truman in 1946 and returned to Phoenix to start a leather craft store with his wife, and the number of children grew to seven. A school and road were named in his honor, and he was active in many public service activities and received awards from Los Angeles to Tucson, including the Mexican Medal of Merit, given by the Mexican government.

JIMENEZ, JOSE F.
US Marine Corps — Vietnam War
Posthumous Award

Rank and organization: Lance Corporal, US Marine Corps, Company K, 3rd Battalion, 7th Marines, 1st Marine Division. Place and date: Quang Nam Province, Republic of Vietnam, 28 August 1969. Entered service at: Phoenix, Ariz. Born: 20 March 1946, Mexico City, Mex.

Citation: For conspicuous gallantry and intrepidity at the risk of his life above and beyond the call of duty while serving as a fire team leader with Company K, in operations against the enemy. L/Cpl. Jimenez' unit came under heavy attack by North Vietnamese soldiers concealed in well camouflaged emplacements. L/Cpl. Jimenez reacted by seizing the initiative and plunging forward toward the enemy positions. He personally destroyed several enemy personnel and silenced an antiaircraft weapon. Shouting encouragement to his companions, L/Cpl. Jimenez continued his aggressive forward movement. He slowly maneuvered to within 10 feet of hostile soldiers who were firing automatic weapons from a trench and, in the face of vicious enemy fire, destroyed the position. Although he was by now the target of concentrated fire from hostile gunners intent upon halting his assault, L/Cpl. Jimenez continued to press forward. As he moved to attack another enemy soldier, he was mortally wounded. L/Cpl. Jimenez' indomitable courage, aggressive fighting spirit and unfaltering devotion to duty upheld the highest traditions of the Marine Corps and of the U.S. Naval Service.

Epilogue: Jimenez had been in the Marines only 14 months and 21 days before he died in combat in Vietnam. He was 18 years old and, fearing the draft, had enlisted. Ironically, the fear wasn't necessary because, born in Morelia, Mexico, he wasn't an American citizen. He came to the United States when he was 10 with his mother and settled in the central Arizona town of Eloy. His father died when he was 4. He graduated from Santa Cruz High School, where he was elected president of the Future Farmers of America. After his death in Vietnam, his mother wanted to bury him in Mexico where his other relatives are buried, but Veterans Administration regulations prevent a second shipping of a headstone; it had been sent to his mother in Arizona. A group of local veterans got together and managed to have the headstone shipped the 1300 miles to Mexico. The Medal was presented to Jimenez's mother, Basilia, by President Nixon at a White House ceremony. Jimenez is buried in Panten Municipal Cemetery, Morelia, Mexico.

KEITH, MIGUEL
US Marine Corps — Vietnam War
Posthumous Award

Rank and organization: Lance Corporal, US Marine Corps, Combined Action platoon 1-3-2, 111 Marine Amphibious Force. Place and date: Quang Ngai province, Republic of Vietnam, 8 May 1970. Entered service at: Omaha, Nebr. Born: 2 June 1951, San Antonio, Tex.

Citation: For conspicuous gallantry and intrepidity at the risk of his life above and beyond the call of duty while serving as a machine gunner with Combined Action platoon 1-3-2. During the early morning L/Cpl. Keith was seriously wounded when his platoon was subjected to a heavy ground attack by a greatly outnumbering enemy force. Despite his painful wounds, he ran across the fire-swept terrain to check the security of vital defensive positions and then, while completely exposed to view, proceeded to deliver a hail of devastating machine gun fire against the enemy. Determined to stop 5 of the enemy soldiers approaching the command post, he rushed forward, firing as he advanced. He succeeded in disposing of 3 of the attackers and in dispersing the remaining 2. At this point, a grenade detonated near L/Cpl. Keith, knocking him to the ground and inflicting further severe wounds. Fighting pain and weakness from loss of blood, he again braved the concentrated hostile fire to charge an estimated 25 enemy soldiers who were massing to attack. The vigor of his assault and his well-placed fire eliminated 4 of the enemy soldiers while the remainder fled for cover. During this valiant effort, he was mortally wounded by an enemy soldier. By his courageous and inspiring performance in the face of almost overwhelming odds, L/Cpl. Keith contributed in large measure to the success of his platoon in routing a numerically superior enemy force, and upheld the finest traditions of the Marine Corps and of the U.S. Naval Service.

Epilogue: Born in San Antonio, Texas, Keith enlisted in the Marine Corps Reserves in 1968 and was discharged to reenlist in the Regular Marine Corps in 1969. He completed basic training at the Recruit Depot in San Diego and Individual Combat Training at Camp Pendleton. In 1969, he was ordered to Vietnam, where he was mortally wounded in action at Quang Ngai Province. At the time of his death, Keith was survived by his parents, three brothers, and a sister. He is buried in Forest Lawn Cemetery, Omaha, Nebraska.[139]

LOPEZ, BALDOMERO

US Marine Corps — Korean War

Posthumous Award

Rank and organization: First Lieutenant, US Marine Corps, Company A, 1st Battalion, 5th Marines, 1st Marine Division (Rein.). Place and date: During Inchon invasion in Korea, 15 September 1950. Entered service at: Tampa, Fla. Born: 23 August 1925, Tampa, Fla.

Citation: For conspicuous gallantry and intrepidity at the risk of his life above and beyond the call of duty as a marine platoon commander of Company A, in action against enemy aggressor forces. With his platoon 1st Lt. Lopez was engaged in the reduction of immediate enemy beach defenses after landing with the assault waves. Exposing himself to hostile fire, he moved forward alongside a bunker and prepared to throw a hand grenade into the next pillbox whose fire was pinning down that sector of the beach. Taken under fire by an enemy automatic weapon and hit in the right shoulder and chest as he lifted his arm to throw, he fell backward and dropped the deadly missile. After a moment, he turned and dragged his body forward in an effort to retrieve the grenade and throw it. In critical condition from pain and loss of blood, and unable to grasp the hand grenade firmly enough to hurl it, he chose to sacrifice himself rather than endanger the lives of his men and, with a sweeping motion of his wounded right arm, cradled the grenade under him and absorbed the full impact of the explosion. His exceptional courage, fortitude, and devotion to duty reflect the highest credit upon 1st Lt. Lopez and the U.S. Naval Service. He gallantly gave his life for his country.

Epilogue: No information was available in the CMOHS' archives for Lopez. What is known is that he is buried in Centre Adorim Memorial Park, Tampa, Florida.[140]

LOPEZ, JOSE M.
US Army — World War II
European Theater

Rank and organization: Sergeant, U.S. Army, 23rd Infantry, 2nd Infantry Division. Place and date: Near Krinkelt, Belgium, 17 December 1944. Entered service at: Brownsville, Tex. Birth: Mission, Tex. G.O. No.: 47, 18 June 1945.

Citation: On his own initiative, he carried his heavy machinegun from Company K's right flank to its left, in order to protect that flank which was in danger of being overrun by advancing enemy infantry supported by tanks. Occupying a shallow hole offering no protection above his waist, he cut down a group of 10 Germans. Ignoring enemy fire from an advancing tank, he held his position and cut down 25 more enemy infantry attempting to turn his flank. Glancing to his right, he saw a large number of infantry swarming in from the front. Although dazed and shaken from enemy artillery fire which had crashed into the ground only a few yards away, he realized that his position soon would be outflanked. Again, alone, he carried his machinegun to a position to the right rear of the sector; enemy tanks and infantry were forcing a withdrawal. Blown over backward by the concussion of enemy fire, he immediately reset his gun and continued his fire. Single-handed he held off the German horde until he was satisfied his company had effected its retirement. Again he loaded his gun on his back and in a hail of small arms fire he ran to a point where a few of his comrades were attempting to set up another defense against the onrushing enemy. He fired from this position until his ammunition was exhausted. Still carrying his gun, he fell back with his small group to Krinkelt. Sgt. Lopez's gallantry and intrepidity, on seemingly suicidal missions in which he killed at least 100 of the enemy, were almost solely responsible for allowing Company K to avoid being enveloped, to withdraw successfully and to give other forces coming up in support time to build a line which repelled the enemy drive.

Epilogue: Lopez was born and raised in Mission, Texas, near the Mexican border. He started picking cotton before joining the merchant marine in 1938 to "see the world." One day, when he called home, he discovered he had been drafted into the Army. He remained in the Army and made it a career, eventually retiring with the rank of Sergeant First Class. Lopez died in 2005 at the age of 94 in Houston, Texas, and is buried in Fort Sam Houston National Cemetery, San Antonio, Texas.

LOZADA, CARLOS J.
US Army — Vietnam War
Posthumous Award

Rank and organization: Private First Class, US Army, Company A, 2nd Battalion, 503rd Infantry, 173rd Airborne Brigade. Place and date: Dak To, Republic of Vietnam, 20 November 1967. Entered service at: New York, N.Y. Born: 6 September 1946, Caguas, Puerto Rico.

Citation: For conspicuous gallantry and intrepidity in action at the risk of his life above and beyond the call of duty. Pfc. Lozada, U.S. Army, distinguished himself at the risk of his life above and beyond the call of duty in the battle of Dak To. While serving as a machine gunner with 1st platoon, Company A, Pfc. Lozada was part of a 4-man early warning outpost, located 35 meters from his company's lines. At 1400 hours a North Vietnamese Army company rapidly approached the outpost along a well defined trail. Pfc. Lozada alerted his comrades and commenced firing at the enemy who were within 10 meters of the outpost. His heavy and accurate machine gun fire killed at least 20 North Vietnamese soldiers and completely disrupted their initial attack. Pfc. Lozada remained in an exposed position and continued to pour deadly fire upon the enemy despite the urgent pleas of his comrades to withdraw. The enemy continued their assault, attempting to envelop the outpost. At the same time enemy forces launched a heavy attack on the forward west flank of Company A with the intent to cut them off from their battalion. Company A was given the order to withdraw. Pfc. Lozada apparently realized that if he abandoned his position there would be nothing to hold back the surging North Vietnamese soldiers and that the entire company withdrawal would be jeopardized. He called for his comrades to move back and that he would stay and provide cover for them. He made this decision realizing that the enemy was converging on 3 sides of his position and only meters away, and a delay in withdrawal meant almost certain death. Pfc. Lozada continued to deliver a heavy, accurate volume of suppressive fire against the enemy until he was mortally wounded and had to be carried during the withdrawal. His heroic deed served as an example and an inspiration to his comrades throughout the ensuing 4-day battle. Pfc. Lozada's actions are in the highest traditions of the U.S. Army and reflect great credit upon himself, his unit, and the U.S. Army.

Epilogue: Lozada was born in Puerto Rico, raised in the Bronx, New York, and attended Roosevelt High School in Brooklyn. Severely wounded during a fire fight in Vietnam, he told his fellow soldiers, "I'll hold them off," which allowed others to escape a trap set by the enemy. Using his machine gun, he was able to kill over twenty enemy solders before he was overrun and killed. The Medal was presented to wife, Linda, daughter, Yzette, and parents by Vice-President Agnew at a White House ceremony. Lozada is buried in the Long Island National Cemetery, Farmingdale, New York, at grave site T-2295.

MARTINEZ, BENITO
US Army — Korean War
Posthumous Award

Rank and organization: Corporal, US Army, Company A, 27th Infantry Regiment, 25th Infantry Division. Place and date: Near Satae-ri Korea, 6 September 1952. Entered service at: Fort Hancock, Tex. Born: 21 March 1931, Fort Hancock, Tex. G.O. No.: 96, 29 December 1953.

Citation: Cpl. Martinez, a machine gunner with Company A, distinguished himself by conspicuous gallantry and outstanding courage above and beyond the call of duty in action against the enemy. While manning a listening post forward of the main line of resistance, his position was attacked by a hostile force of reinforced company strength. In the bitter fighting which ensued, the enemy infiltrated the defense perimeter and, realizing that encirclement was imminent, Cpl. Martinez elected to remain at his post in an attempt to stem the onslaught. In a daring defense, he raked the attacking troops with crippling fire, inflicting numerous casualties. Although contacted by sound power phone several times, he insisted that no attempt be made to rescue him because of the danger involved. Soon thereafter, the hostile forces rushed the emplacement, forcing him to make a limited withdrawal with only an automatic rifle and pistol to defend himself. After a courageous 6-hour stand and shortly before dawn, he called in for the last time, stating that the enemy was converging on his position His magnificent stand enabled friendly elements to reorganize, attack, and regain the key terrain. Cpl. Martinez' incredible valor and supreme sacrifice reflect lasting glory upon himself and are in keeping with the honored traditions of the military service.

Epilogue: Little information was available in the CMOHS' archives for Martinez. What is known is that he was born, raised, and entered the Army in Fort Hancock, Texas, served with the 25th Infantry Division in Korea as a machine gunner, and, upon his death, was buried in Fort Bliss National Cemetery, Texas.

MARTINEZ, JOE P.
US Army — World War II
Pacific Theater — Posthumous Award

Rank and organization: Private, US Army, Company K, 32nd Infantry, 7th Infantry Division. Place and date: On Attu, Aleutians, 26 May 1943. Entered service at: Ault, Colo. Birth: Taos, N. Mex. G.O. No.: 71, 27 October 1943.

Citation: For conspicuous gallantry and intrepidity above and beyond the call of duty in action with the enemy. Over a period of several days, repeated efforts to drive the enemy from a key defensive position high in the snow-covered precipitous mountains between East Arm Holtz Bay and Chichagof Harbor had failed. On 26 May 1943, troop dispositions were readjusted and a trial coordinated attack on this position by a reinforced battalion was launched. Initially successful, the attack hesitated. In the face of severe hostile machinegun, rifle, and mortar fire, Pvt. Martinez, an automatic rifleman, rose to his feet and resumed his advance. Occasionally he stopped to urge his comrades on. His example inspired others to follow. After a most difficult climb, Pvt. Martinez eliminated resistance from part of the enemy position by BAR fire and hand grenades, thus assisting the advance of other attacking elements. This success only partially completed the action. The main Holtz-Chichagof Pass rose about 150 feet higher, flanked by steep rocky ridges and reached by a snow-filled defile. Passage was barred by enemy fire from either flank and from tiers of snow trenches in front. Despite these obstacles, and knowing of their existence, Pvt. Martinez again led the troops on and up, personally silencing several trenches with BAR fire and ultimately reaching the pass itself. Here, just below the knifelike rim of the pass, Pvt. Martinez encountered a final enemy-occupied trench and as he was engaged in firing into it he was mortally wounded. The pass, however, was taken, and its capture was an important preliminary to the end of organized hostile resistance on the island.

Epilogue: Martinez fought in what would be the first major combat engagement between Japan and the United States. The battle also marked the first time an enemy force would invade a US territory. The battle occurred in the Aleutian Islands, where savage fighting between the two forces would foreshadow the great Pacific battles. Martinez was born and raised in Taos, New Mexico, the youngest of nine children. In 1927, the Martinez family moved to Ault in northern Colorado where they worked in the fields. Martinez attended Ault High School but left before graduating to join the Army in 1942 along with his brother, Delfino, who would eventually land on Normandy Beach and fight in the Battle of the Bulge. Martinez's company commander told his parents at the Medal ceremony, "When we had been stopped by enemy fire, your son picked up his automatic rifle and led the entire attack." Martinez is buried in Ault Cemetery, Ault, Colorado.

OBREGON, EUGENE A.
US Marine Corps — Korean War
Posthumous Award

Rank and organization: Private First Class, US Marine Corps, Company G, 3rd Battalion, 5th Marines, 1st Marine Division (Rein.). Place and date: Seoul, Korea, 26 September 1950. Entered service at: Los Angeles, Calif. Born: 12 November 1930, Los Angeles, Calif.

Citation: For conspicuous gallantry and intrepidity at the risk of his life above and beyond the call of duty while serving with Company G, in action against enemy aggressor forces. While serving as an ammunition carrier of a machine gun squad in a marine rifle company which was temporarily pinned down by hostile fire, Pfc. Obregon observed a fellow marine fall wounded in the line of fire. Armed only with a pistol, he unhesitating dashed from his covered position to the side of the casualty. Firing his pistol with 1 hand as he ran, he grasped his comrade by the arm with his other hand and, despite the great peril to himself dragged him to the side of the road. Still under enemy fire, he was bandaging the man's wounds when hostile troops of approximately platoon strength began advancing toward his position. Quickly seizing the wounded marine's carbine, he placed his own body as a shield in front of him and lay there firing accurately and effectively into the hostile group until he himself was fatally wounded by enemy machine gun fire. By his courageous fighting spirit, fortitude, and loyal devotion to duty, Pfc. Obregon enabled his fellow marines to rescue the wounded man and aided essentially in repelling the attack, thereby sustaining and enhancing the highest traditions of the U.S. Naval Service. He gallantly gave his life for his country.

Epilogue: Born and raised in Los Angeles, Obregon was 17 when he enlisted in the Marines after graduating from Roosevelt High School and 19 when he died, using his body to shield a fellow Marine from enemy gunfire. To date, a naval ship, freeway, schools, an American Legion chapter, and a monument have been named in his honor. He is buried in Calvary Cemetery, Los Angeles and was survived by his mother and brother.[141]

ORTEGA, JOHN
US Navy — American Civil War

Rank and organization: Seaman, US Navy. Born: 1840, Spain. Accredited to: Pennsylvania. G.O. No.: 45, 31 December 1864.

Citation: Served as seaman on board the U.S.S. Saratoga during actions of that vessel on 2 occasions. Carrying out his duties courageously during these actions, Ortega conducted himself gallantly through both periods. Promoted to acting master's mate.

Epilogue: No information was available in the CMOHS' archives for Ortega. What is known is that for a time he was listed as "deserted" from the Navy in 1865,[142] Ortega is *lost to history.*

PEREZ, MANUEL, JR.
US Army — World War II
Pacific Theater — Posthumous Award

Rank and organization: Private First Class, US Army, Company A, 511th Parachute Infantry, 11th Airborne Division. Place and date: Fort William McKinley, Luzon, Philippine Islands, 13 February 1945. Entered service at: Chicago, Ill. Born: 3 March 1923, Oklahoma City, Okla. G.O. No.: 124, 27 December 1945.

Citation: He was lead scout for Company A, which had destroyed 11 of 12 pillboxes in a strongly fortified sector defending the approach to enemy-held Fort William McKinley on Luzon, Philippine Islands. In the reduction of these pillboxes, he killed 5 Japanese in the open and blasted others in pillboxes with grenades. Realizing the urgent need for taking the last emplacement, which contained 2 twin-mount .50-caliber dual-purpose machineguns, he took a circuitous route to within 20 yards of the position, killing 4 of the enemy in his advance. He threw a grenade into the pillbox, and, as the crew started withdrawing through a tunnel just to the rear of the emplacement, shot and killed 4 before exhausting his clip. He had reloaded and killed 4 more when an escaping Japanese threw his rifle with fixed bayonet at him. In warding off this thrust, his own rifle was knocked to the ground. Seizing the Jap rifle, he continued firing, killing 2 more of the enemy. He rushed the remaining Japanese, killed 3 of them with the butt of the rifle and entered the pillbox, where he bayoneted the 1 surviving hostile soldier. Single-handedly, he killed 18 of the enemy in neutralizing the position that had held up the advance of his entire company. Through his courageous determination and heroic disregard of grave danger, Pfc. Perez made possible the successful advance of his unit toward a valuable objective and provided a lasting inspiration for his comrades.

Epilogue: Perez died from a rifle bullet in his chest while engaged in action against the enemy during the Philippine Campaign. Born and raised in Oklahoma City, he later moved to Chicago and graduated from Crane High School before entering the Army. The Medal was presented to his father, Manuel Perez, of Nuevolaredo, Tamp., Mexico, in 1945. Perez is buried in Fairlawn Cemetery, Oklahoma City.[143]

RASCON, ALFRED V.
US Army — Vietnam War

Rank and organization: Specialist Fourth Class, US Army, Reconnaissance Platoon, Headquarters Company, 1st Battalion (Airborne), 503rd Infantry, 173rd Airborne Brigade (Separate). Place and date: Republic of Vietnam, 16 March 1966. Born: 1945, Chihuahua, Mexico

Citation: Specialist Four Alfred Rascon, distinguished himself by a series of extraordinarily courageous acts on 16 March 1966, while assigned as a medic to the Reconnaissance Platoon, Headquarters Company, 1st Battalion (Airborne), 503rd Infantry, 173d Airborne Brigade (Separate). While moving to reinforce its sister battalion under intense enemy attack, the Reconnaissance Platoon came under heavy fire from a numerically superior enemy force. The intense enemy fire from crew-served weapons and grenades severely wounded several point squad soldiers. Specialist Rascon, ignoring directions to stay behind shelter until covering fire could be provided, made his way forward. He repeatedly tried to reach the severely wounded point machine-gunner laying on an open enemy trail, but was driven back each time by the withering fire. Disregarding his personal safety, he jumped to his feet, ignoring flying bullets and exploding grenades to reach his comrade. To protect him from further wounds, he intentionally placed his body between the soldier and enemy machine guns, sustaining numerous shrapnel injuries and a serious wound to the hip. Disregarding his serious wounds he dragged the larger soldier from the fire-raked trail. Hearing the second machine-gunner yell that he was running out of ammunition, Specialist Rascon, under heavy enemy fire crawled back to the wounded machine-gunner stripping him of his bandoleers of ammunition, giving them to the machine-gunner who continued his suppressive fire. Specialist Rascon fearing the abandoned machine gun, its ammunition and spare barrel could fall into enemy hands made his way to retrieve them. On the way, he was wounded in the face and torso by grenade fragments, but disregarded these wounds to recover the abandoned machine gun, ammunition and spare barrel items, enabling another soldier to provide added suppressive fire to the pinned-down squad. In searching for the wounded, he saw the point grenadier being wounded by small arms fire and grenades being thrown at him. Disregarding his own life and his numerous wounds, Specialist Rascon reached and covered him with his body absorbing the blasts from the exploding grenades, and saving the soldier's life, but sustaining additional wounds to his body. While making his way to the wounded point squad leader, grenades were hurled at the sergeant. Again, in complete disregard for his own life, he reached and covered the sergeant with his body, absorbing the full force of the grenade explosions. Once more Specialist Rascon was critically wounded by shrapnel, but disregarded his own wounds to continue to search and aid the wounded. Severely wounded, he remained on the battlefield, inspiring his fellow soldiers to continue the battle. After the enemy broke contact, he disregarded aid for himself, instead treating the wounded and directing their evacuation. Only after being placed on the evacuation helicopter did he allow aid to be given to him. Specialist Rascon's extraordinary valor in the face of deadly enemy fire, his heroism in rescuing the wounded, and his gallantry by repeatedly risking his own life for his fellow soldiers are in keeping with the highest traditions of military service and reflect great credit upon himself, his unit, and the United States Army.

Epilogue: The first time Rascon, a son of Mexican immigrants, went to Vietnam, he was not an American citizen. After recovering from wounds received during his first tour, when he went back for a second tour, he was a citizen. Within days of the action for which he would eventually receive the Medal, the paper nominating him was submitted but lost. Instead, he was awarded the Silver Star, the third highest award for bravery. Years later, when asked by his former soldiers how it felt to receive the Medal, which they assumed had been awarded, Rascon replied that he didn't know. Efforts to correct the error were taken up by Representative Lane Evans of Illinois, who gave the information about the case to President Clinton. The Pentagon approved the recommendation, and the Medal was finally awarded to Rascon at a White House ceremony in 1996. Rascon initially left the Army in 1966, went to college, and reentered the Army, receiving an officer's commission. A civil servant since 1983, Rascon is Inspector General for the Selective Service System in Arlington, Virginia. He lives in Laurel, Maryland, with his wife and two children.

ROCCO, LOUIS R.
US Army — Vietnam War

Rank and organization: Warrant Officer (then Sergeant First Class), US Army, Advisory Team 162, US Military Assistance Command. Place and date: Northeast of Katum, Republic of Vietnam, 24 May 1970. Entered service at: Los Angeles, Calif. Born: 19 November 1938, Albuquerque, N. Mex.

Citation: WO Rocco distinguished himself when he volunteered to accompany a medical evacuation team on an urgent mission to evacuate 8 critically wounded Army of the Republic of Vietnam personnel. As the helicopter approached the landing zone, it became the target for intense enemy automatic weapons fire. Disregarding his own safety, WO Rocco identified and placed accurate suppressive fire on the enemy positions as the aircraft descended toward the landing zone. Sustaining major damage from the enemy fire, the aircraft was forced to crash land, causing WO Rocco to sustain a fractured wrist and hip and a severely bruised back. Ignoring his injuries, he extracted the survivors from the burning wreckage, sustaining burns to his own body. Despite intense enemy fire, WO Rocco carried each unconscious man across approximately 20 meters of exposed terrain to the Army of the Republic of Vietnam perimeter. On each trip, his severely burned hands and broken wrist caused excruciating pain, but the lives of the unconscious crash survivors were more important than his personal discomfort, and he continued his rescue efforts. Once inside the friendly position, WO Rocco helped administer first aid to his wounded comrades until his wounds and burns caused him to collapse and lose consciousness. His bravery under fire and intense devotion to duty were directly responsible for saving 3 of his fellow soldiers from certain death. His unparalleled bravery in the face of enemy fire, his complete disregard for his own pain and injuries, and his performance were far above and beyond the call of duty and were in keeping with the highest traditions of self-sacrifice and courage of the military service.

Epilogue: Rocco was born and raised in Albuquerque, New Mexico. He entered the Army in 1956 and reenlisted several times, eventually making the military his career, and retiring after 22 years as a Chief Warrant Officer. He is married to Carol and has three children, Roy, Brian, and Theresa. His parents live in Hemet, California. Rocco's Medal was presented to him by President Ford at a White House Ceremony in 1974. He now works as a counselor in Albuquerque.

RODRIGUEZ, CLETO
US Army — World War II
Pacific Theater

Rank and organization: Technical Sergeant (then Private), US Army, Company B, 148th Infantry, 37th Infantry Division. Place and date: Paco Railroad Station, Manila, Philippine Islands, 9 February 1945. Entered service at: San Antonio, Tex. Birth: San Marcos, Tex. G.O. No.: 97, 1 November 1945.

Citation: He was an automatic rifleman when his unit attacked the strongly defended Paco Railroad Station during the battle for Manila, Philippine Islands. While making a frontal assault across an open field, his platoon was halted 100 yards from the station by intense enemy fire. On his own initiative, he left the platoon, accompanied by a comrade, and continued forward to a house 60 yards from the objective. Although under constant enemy observation, the 2 men remained in this position for an hour, firing at targets of opportunity, killing more than 35 hostile soldiers and wounding many more. Moving closer to the station and discovering a group of Japanese replacements attempting to reach pillboxes, they opened heavy fire, killed more than 40 and stopped all subsequent attempts to man the emplacements. Enemy fire became more intense as they advanced to within 20 yards of the station. Then, covered by his companion, Pvt. Rodriguez boldly moved up to the building and threw 5 grenades through a doorway killing 7 Japanese, destroying a 20-mm. gun and wrecking a heavy machinegun. With their ammunition running low, the 2 men started to return to the American lines, alternately providing covering fire for each other's withdrawal. During this movement, Pvt. Rodriguez' companion was killed. In 2 1/2 hours of fierce fighting the intrepid team killed more than 82 Japanese, completely disorganized their defense, and paved the way for the subsequent overwhelming defeat of the enemy at this strongpoint. Two days later, Pvt. Rodriguez again enabled his comrades to advance when he single-handedly killed 6 Japanese and destroyed a well-placed 20-mm. gun by his outstanding skill with his weapons, gallant determination to destroy the enemy, and heroic courage in the face of tremendous odds, Pvt. Rodriguez, on 2 occasions, materially aided the advance of our troops in Manila.

Epilogue: Rodriguez's Medal-winning action was performed with fellow soldier John Reese, who was posthumously awarded the Medal. It was the only time during World War II when two privates fighting side-by-side in the same action were cited for the nation's highest award for military valor. Rodriguez was born in San Marcos, Texas. His parents died before he was nine, and he moved to San Antonio to live with his aunt and uncle. After receiving the Medal from President Truman, he married his longtime sweetheart, Flora Muniz, and remained in the Army, after a brief stint in the Air Force, to make it a career. He retired in 1970 with the rank of Master Sergeant. After returning home to San Antonio the Medal of Honor recipient found a job parking cars. With the aid of his congressman, he became a contract employee for the Veterans Administration for many years. He died in 1991 and was survived by his wife, two sons, Cleto Jr., and Joe, and two daughters, Mary Mayo, and Betty Jean Stewart.[145]

RODRIGUEZ, JOSEPH C.
US Army — Korean War

Rank and organization: Sergeant (then Pfc.), US Army, Company F, 17th Infantry Regiment, 7th Infantry Division. Place and date: Near Munye-ri, Korea, 21 May 1951. Entered service at: California. Born: 14 November 1928, San Bernardino, Calif. G.O.

No.: 22, 5 February 1952.

Citation: Sgt. Rodriguez, distinguished himself by conspicuous gallantry and intrepidity at the risk of his life above and beyond the call of duty in action against an armed enemy of the United Nations. Sgt. Rodriguez, an assistant squad leader of the 2d Platoon, was participating in an attack against a fanatical hostile force occupying well-fortified positions on rugged commanding terrain, when his squad's advance was halted within approximately 60 yards by a withering barrage of automatic weapons and small-arms fire from 5 emplacements directly to the front and right and left flanks, together with grenades which the enemy rolled down the hill toward the advancing troops. Fully aware of the odds against him, Sgt. Rodriguez leaped to his feet, dashed 60 yards up the fire-swept slope, and, after lobbing grenades into the first foxhole with deadly accuracy, ran around the left flank, silenced an automatic weapon with 2 grenades and continued his whirlwind assault to the top of the peak, wiping out 2 more foxholes and then, reaching the right flank, he tossed grenades into the remaining emplacement, destroying the gun and annihilating its crew. Sgt. Rodriguez' intrepid actions exacted a toll of 15 enemy dead and, as a result of his incredible display of valor, the defense of the opposition was broken, and the enemy routed, and the strategic strongpoint secured. His unflinching courage under fire and inspirational devotion to duty reflect highest credit on himself and uphold the honored traditions of the military service.

Epilogue: Rodriguez was born of Mexican parentage and raised in San Bernardino, California. He could hardly have realized the future that lay before him when, as an architecture major, he graduated from San Bernardino Valley College in 1950. Within a few months, he was drafted into the Army and, in the winter, rode in cattle-car conditions from Fort Ord, California, to Camp Carson, Colorado, where he took infantryman's training. Departing from Fort Lawton, Washington, and shipped across the Pacific Ocean, Private Rodriguez found himself in the Korean War, assigned to the 7th Infantry Division, 17th Infantry Regiment, Company F.

Rodriguez soon became a seasoned combat veteran. In May 1951, he distinguished himself in battle near the small, rural community of Munye-ri, some 30 miles north of the 38th parallel in central Korea. A week later, he was hit by enemy small arms fire. After evacuation to a hospital in Japan and three months' rehabilitation, Rodriguez requested to rejoin his unit. Near the end of the year, he was called back stateside for an appointment with President Truman to receive the Medal of Honor for his battlefield accomplishments at Munye-ri. He was next assigned to Reserve Officers Training Corps administration at his alma mater. There, his officers suggested he obtain a commission and explore the opportunities available to a professional Army officer. He became 2nd Lieutenant Rodriguez, Corps of Engineers, with his wife-to-be assisting in pinning on his bars in June 1952.

His first assignment involved engineering support for an Air Force unit that took him from sunny southern California to winter in northern Maine. Subsequent assignments included another tour in Korea assigned to the 802nd Engineer Battalion and as Post Engineer for the Camp Humphries District, and a tour in Vietnam. Duties included Platoon Leader, Company Commander, Battalion Commander, Instructor, Army Advisor, staff member at various levels, and Facilities Engineer. Subsequent assignments brought Rodriguez and his family to Bolivia, Argentina, Puerto Rico, and twice to the Panama Canal Zone. Duties involved working with military missions with further special assignments in Puerto Rico, where he was advisor to the National Guard of Puerto Rico, and in the Panama Canal Zone, where he was Director of the Technology Department at the School of the Americas and where he later served four years with the Inter-American Geodetic Survey Department. His engineering background, diverse military experience, and fluent Spanish made him especially valuable in these positions.

After twelve consecutive years overseas, Rodriguez's last Army assignment was as Facilities Engineer at Fort Bliss. After serving 30 years in the Army, retired Colonel Rodriguez and his wife elected to settle in El Paso. Here, he went on professionally as Director of the Physical Plant at the University of Texas for ten years. Rodriguez attended numerous military schools and universities and with his wife of over 50 years, Rose, raised two sons and a daughter. His eldest son, Charles, a West Point graduate, was an Assistant Vice-President in the University of Texas system, and Lieutenant General Charles Rodriguez is Adjutant General of the Texas National Guard. Lawrence, the second son, is employed by Wells Fargo Bank, and daughter Karen is a Registered Nurse, married to a Lieutenant Colonel in the Army Nurse Corps. Their three children have given the senior Rodriguezes eleven grandchildren. An enthusiastic golfer, retired Colonel Rodriguez officially holds four holes-in-one.[146]

RUBIO, EURIPIDES
US Army — Vietnam War
Posthumous Award

Rank and organization: Captain, US Army, Headquarters and Headquarters Company, 1st Battalion, 28th Infantry, 1st Infantry Division, RVN. Place and date: Tay Ninh Province, Republic of Vietnam, 8 November 1966. Entered service at: Fort Buchanan, Puerto Rico. Born: 1 March 1938, Ponce, Puerto Rico.

Citation: For conspicuous gallantry and intrepidity in action at the risk of his life above and beyond the call of duty. Capt. Rubio, Infantry, was serving as communications officer, 1st Battalion, when a numerically superior enemy force launched a massive attack against the battalion defense position. Intense enemy machinegun fire raked the area while mortar rounds and rifle grenades exploded within the perimeter. Leaving the relative safety of his post, Capt. Rubio received 2 serious wounds as he braved the withering fire to go to the area of most intense action where he distributed ammunition, re-established positions and rendered aid to the wounded. Disregarding the painful wounds, he unhesitatingly assumed command when a rifle company commander was medically evacuated. Capt. Rubio was wounded a third time as he selflessly exposed himself to the devastating enemy fire to move among his men to encourage them to fight with renewed effort. While aiding the evacuation of wounded personnel, he noted that a smoke grenade which was intended to mark the Viet Cong position for air strikes had fallen dangerously close to the friendly lines. Capt. Rubio ran to reposition the grenade but was immediately struck to his knees by enemy fire. Despite his several wounds, Capt. Rubio scooped up the grenade, ran through the deadly hail of fire to within 20 meters of the enemy position and hurled the already smoking grenade into the midst of the enemy before he fell for the final time. Using the repositioned grenade as a marker, friendly air strikes were directed to destroy the hostile positions. Capt. Rubio's singularly heroic act turned the tide of battle, and his extraordinary leadership and valor were a magnificent inspiration to his men. His remarkable bravery and selfless concern for his men are in keeping with the highest traditions of the military service and reflect great credit on Capt. Rubio and the U.S. Army.

Epilogue: Rubio was born and raised in Puerto Rico. He graduated from the University of Puerto Rico before entering the Army, first with the National Guard, and later the Air Force Reserves. He was commissioned and later assigned to the Military Police Corps. Prior to assignment to Vietnam, he served in Germany for three years in the late 1960s. Rubio's Medal was presented by Army Secretary Resor, in the presence of General William Westmoreland, to his wife, Ileana, who wept throughout the Pentagon ceremony, also attended by his son, Edgardo, and daughter, Anaeli.[147] The first Puerto Rican to receive the Medal, Rubio is buried in the Puerto Rico National Cemetery at Bayamon.[148]

RUIZ, ALEJANDRO R.
US Army — World War II
Pacific Theater

Rank and organization: Private First Class, US Army, 165th Infantry, 27th Infantry Division. Place and date: Okinawa, Ryukyu Islands, 28 April 1945. Entered service at: Carlsbad, N. Mex. Birth: Loving, N. Mex. G.O. No.: 60, 26 June 1946.

Citation: When his unit was stopped by a skillfully camouflaged enemy pillbox, he displayed conspicuous gallantry and intrepidity above and beyond the call of duty. His squad, suddenly brought under a hail of machinegun fire and a vicious grenade attack, was pinned down. Jumping to his feet, Pfc. Ruiz seized an automatic rifle and lunged through the flying grenades and rifle and automatic fire for the top of the emplacement. When an enemy soldier charged him, his rifle jammed. Undaunted, Pfc. Ruiz whirled on his assailant and clubbed him down. Then he ran back through bullets and grenades, seized more ammunition and another automatic rifle, and again made for the pillbox. Enemy fire now was concentrated on him, but he charged on, miraculously reaching the position, and in plain view he climbed to the top. Leaping from 1 opening to another, he sent burst after burst into the pillbox, killing 12 of the enemy and completely destroying the position. Pfc. Ruiz's heroic conduct, in the face of overwhelming odds, saved the lives of many comrades and eliminated an obstacle that long would have checked his unit's advance.
Epilogue: Born and raised in New Mexico, it took Ruiz's hometown and state some fifty years to finally recognize him for his achievements. Pat Elkins, a citizen of Carlsbad, Ruiz's hometown, was in the school library one day with her students, when she came across the "Medal of Honor Book." She later said, "Imagine my surprise when I came across a Carlsbad man in the book. I realized when I read him name why I never heard of him. I probably wouldn't have paid attention, except that I knew that we had honored all other WWII veterans. If his name was Russell I have no doubt he would have been recognized." Her efforts led the city to erect a monument to honor his war achievement fifty years after the fact. Ruiz, who survived the war, was living in Visalia, California, when contacted by Elkins and the city of Carlsbad about plans to honor him. Ruiz's Medal was presented to him by President Truman at the White House in 1946.

SANTIAGO, COLON H.

US Army — Vietnam War
Posthumous Award

Rank and organization: Specialist Fourth Class, US Army, Company B, 5th Battalion, 7th Cavalry, 1st Cavalry Division (Airmobile). Place and date: Quang Tri Province, Republic of Vietnam, 28 June 1968. Entered service at: New York, N.Y. Born: 20 December 1942, Salinas, Puerto Rico.

Citation: For conspicuous gallantry and intrepidity in action at the risk of his life above and beyond the call of duty. Sp4c. Santiago-Colon distinguished himself at the cost of his life while serving as a gunner in the mortar platoon of Company B. While serving as a perimeter sentry, Sp4c. Santiago-Colon heard distinct movement in the heavily wooded area to his front and flanks. Immediately he alerted his fellow sentries in the area to move to their foxholes and remain alert for any enemy probing forces. From the wooded area around his position heavy enemy automatic weapons and small-arms fire suddenly broke out, but extreme darkness rendered difficult the precise location and identification of the hostile force. Only the muzzle flashes from enemy weapons indicated their position. Sp4c. Santiago-Colon and the other members of his position immediately began to repel the attackers, utilizing hand grenades, antipersonnel mines and small-arms fire. Due to the heavy volume of enemy fire and exploding grenades around them, a North Vietnamese soldier was able to crawl, undetected, to their position. Suddenly, the enemy soldier lobbed a hand grenade into Sp4c. Santiago-Colon's foxhole. Realizing that there was no time to throw the grenade out of his position, Sp4c. Santiago-Colon retrieved the grenade, tucked it in to his stomach and, turning away from his comrades, absorbed the full impact of the blast. His heroic self-sacrifice saved the lives of those who occupied the foxhole with him, and provided them with the inspiration to continue fighting until they had forced the enemy to retreat from the perimeter. By his gallantry at the cost of his life and in the highest traditions of the military service, Sp4c. Santiago-Colon has reflected great credit upon himself, his unit, and the U.S. Army.

Epilogue: Santiago-Colon was born in Las Mareas, Puerto Rico, educated in the public school system, and graduated from Salinas High School. He was an avid and proficient runner and pole vaulter. While growing up in the sugar cane fields that surround the town, he would walk ten miles to visit his grandmother, sister, and nephew. Upon graduating from high school, he moved to New York in search of job opportunities. He was drafted into the Army during this period and trained as an infantryman. Before departing for Vietnam, he was engaged to Rosita, his girlfriend since the age of 11. Their wedding date was set for October 1968. He was killed in action in June of the same year. Before he was mortally wounded, he sustained wounds that required him to be treated in a military hospital in Japan. There, doctors told him he could return home if he desired. He chose instead to rejoin his unit in Vietnam. Santiago-Colon is buried in Salinas Municipal Cemetery, Puerto Rico.

SILVA, FRANCE
US Marine Corps — Boxer Rebellion

Rank and organization: Private, US Marine Corps. Born: 8 May 1876, Hayward, Calif. Accredited to: California. G.O. No.: 55, 19 July 1901

Citation: In the presence of the enemy during the action at Peking; China, 28 June to 17 August 1900. Throughout this period, Silva distinguished himself by meritorious conduct.

Epilogue: Silva was born in Hayward, California, and joined the Marines in 1899, serving on board the USS Newark in China during the Boxer Rebellion. The last 12 years of his life were spent in Corning as an orchardist. He died in 1951 and is buried at Sunset Hills Cemetery, Corning, California.[149]

VALDEZ, JOSE F.
US Army — World War II
Pacific Theater — Posthumous Award

Rank and organization: Private First Class, US Army, Company B, 7th Infantry, 3rd Infantry Division. Place and date: Near Rosenkrantz, France, 25 January 1945. Entered service at: Pleasant Grove, Utah. Birth: Governador, N. Mex. G. O. No.: 16, 8 February 1946.

Citation: He was on outpost duty with 5 others when the enemy counter-attacked with overwhelming strength. From his position near some woods 500 yards beyond the American lines he observed a hostile tank about 75 yards away, and raked it with automatic rifle fire until it withdrew. Soon afterward he saw 3 Germans stealthily approaching through the woods. Scorning cover as the enemy soldiers opened up with heavy automatic weapons fire from a range of 30 yards, he engaged in a fire fight with the attackers until he had killed all 3. The enemy quickly launched an attack with 2 full companies of infantrymen, blasting the patrol with murderous concentrations of automatic and rifle fire and beginning an encircling movement which forced the patrol leader to order a withdrawal. Despite the terrible odds, Pfc. Valdez immediately volunteered to cover the maneuver, and as the patrol 1 by 1 plunged through a hail of bullets toward the American lines, he fired burst after burst into the swarming enemy. Three of his companions were wounded in their dash for safety and he was struck by a bullet that entered his stomach and, passing through his body, emerged from his back. Overcoming agonizing pain, he regained control of himself and resumed his firing position, delivering a protective screen of bullets until all others of the patrol were safe. By field telephone he called for artillery and mortar fire on the Germans and corrected the range until he had shells falling within 50 yards of his position. For 15 minutes he refused to be dislodged by more than 200 of the enemy; then, seeing that the barrage had broken the counter attack, he dragged himself back to his own lines. He died later as a result of his wounds. Through his valiant, intrepid stand and at the cost of his own life, Pfc. Valdez made it possible for his comrades to escape, and was directly responsible for repulsing an attack by vastly superior enemy forces.

Epilogue: Very little information was available about Valdez's life in the archives of the CMOHS. He was killed in action and his actual burial site is unknown.

VARGAS, SANDO M. JR.
US Marine Corps — Vietnam War

Rank and organization: Major (then Capt.), US Marine Corps, Company G, 2nd Battalion, 4th Marines, 9th Marine Amphibious Brigade. Place and date: Dai Do, Republic of Vietnam, 30 April to 2 May 1968. Entered service at: Winslow, Ariz. Born: 29 July 1940, Winslow, Ariz.

Citation: For conspicuous gallantry and intrepidity at the risk of his life above and beyond the call of duty while serving as commanding officer, Company G, in action against enemy forces from 30 April to 2 May 1968. On 1 May 1968, though suffering from wounds he had incurred while relocating his unit under heavy enemy fire the preceding day, Maj. Vargas combined Company G with two other companies and led his men in an attack on the fortified village of Dai Do. Exercising expert leadership, he maneuvered his marines across 700 meters of open rice paddy while under intense enemy mortar, rocket and artillery fire and obtained a foothold in 2 hedgerows on the enemy perimeter, only to have elements of his company become pinned down by the intense enemy fire. Leading his reserve platoon to the aid of his beleaguered men, Maj. Vargas inspired his men to renew their relentless advance, while destroying a number of enemy bunkers. Again wounded by grenade fragments, he refused aid as he moved about the hazardous area reorganizing his unit into a strong defense perimeter at the edge of the village. Shortly after the objective was secured the enemy commenced a series of counterattacks and probes which lasted throughout the night but were unsuccessful as the gallant defenders of Company G stood firm in their hard-won enclave. Reinforced the following morning, the marines launched a renewed assault through Dai Do on the village of Dinh To, to which the enemy retaliated with a massive counterattack resulting in hand-to-hand combat. Maj. Vargas remained in the open, encouraging and rendering assistance to his marines when he was hit for the third time in the 3-day battle. Observing his battalion commander sustain a serious wound, he disregarded his excruciating pain, crossed the fire-swept area and carried his commander to a covered position, then resumed supervising and encouraging his men while simultaneously assisting in organizing the battalion's perimeter defense. His gallant actions uphold the highest traditions of the Marine Corps and the U.S. Naval Service.

Epilogue: Vargas's father was Hispanic and his mother Italian, and both were immigrants. He was born and raised in Winslow, Arizona, and described by many as an All-American boy. He was a star athlete in high school, graduated from Arizona State University in 1961, from which he immediately entered Officer Candidate School with the Marines, receiving his commission in 1962. Vargas made the Marines a career, with more than 30 years of service. He is one of four sons who served in the armed forces in time of war: Angelo, who served at Iwo Jima; Frank, Okinawa; and Joseph, Korea. Vargas held several public service-related positions after retiring from the Marines. In 1993, he was appointed director of the California Department of Veterans Affairs by Governor Pete Wilson. Vargas's Medal was presented by President Nixon. He is married to the former Dorothy Jean Johnson and has three daughters, Christie, Julie, and Gina.

VILLEGAS, YSMAEL R.
US Army — World War II
Pacific Theater — Posthumous Award

Rank and organization: Staff Sergeant, US Army, Company F, 127th Infantry, 32nd Infantry Division. Place and date: Villa Verde Trail, Luzon, Philippine Islands, 20 March 1945. Entered service at: Casa Blanca, Calif. Birth: Casa Blanca, Calif. G.O. No.: 89, 19 October 1945.

Citation: He was a squad leader when his unit, in a forward position, clashed with an enemy strongly entrenched in connected caves and foxholes on commanding ground. He moved boldly from man to man, in the face of bursting grenades and demolition charges, through heavy machinegun and rifle fire, to bolster the spirit of his comrades. Inspired by his gallantry, his men pressed forward to the crest of the hill. Numerous enemy riflemen, refusing to flee, continued firing from their foxholes. S/Sgt. Villegas, with complete disregard for his own safety and the bullets which kicked up the dirt at his feet, charged an enemy position, and, firing at point-blank range killed the Japanese in a foxhole. He rushed a second foxhole while bullets missed him by inches, and killed 1 more of the enemy. In rapid succession he charged a third, a fourth, a fifth foxhole, each time destroying the enemy within. The fire against him increased in intensity, but he pressed onward to attack a sixth position. As he neared his goal, he was hit and killed by enemy fire. Through his heroism and indomitable fighting spirit, S/Sgt. Villegas, at the cost of his life, inspired his men to a determined attack in which they swept the enemy from the field.

Epilogue: Very little information was available about Villegas' life in the archives of the CMOHS. He was killed in action and is buried at Riverside National Cemetery, Riverside, California.[150]

YABES, MAXIMO
US Army — Vietnam War
Posthumous Award

Rank and organization: First Sergeant, US Army, Company A, 4th Battalion, 9th Infantry, 25th Infantry Division. Place and date: Near Phu Hoa Dong, Republic of Vietnam, 26 February 1967. Entered service at: Eugene, Oreg. Born: 29 January 1932, Lodi, Calif.

Citation: For conspicuous gallantry and intrepidity at the risk of his life above and beyond the call of duty. 1st Sgt. Yabes distinguished himself with Company A, which was providing security for a land clearing operation. Early in the morning the company suddenly came under intense automatic weapons and mortar fire followed by a battalion sized assault from 3 sides. Penetrating the defensive perimeter the enemy advanced on the company command post bunker. The command post received increasingly heavy fire and was in danger of being overwhelmed. When several enemy grenades landed within the command post, 1st Sgt. Yabes shouted a warning and used his body as a shield to protect others in the bunker. Although painfully wounded by numerous grenade fragments, and despite the vicious enemy fire on the bunker, he remained there to provide covering fire and enable the others in the command group to relocate. When the command group had reached a new position, 1st Sgt. Yabes moved through a withering hail of enemy fire to another bunker 50 meters away. There he secured a grenade launcher from a fallen comrade and fired point blank into the attacking Viet Cong stopping further penetration of the perimeter. Noting 2 wounded men helpless in the fire swept area, he moved them to a safer position where they could be given medical treatment. He resumed his accurate and effective fire killing several enemy soldiers and forcing others to withdraw from the vicinity of the command post. As the battle continued, he observed an enemy machinegun within the perimeter which threatened the whole position. On his own, he dashed across the exposed area, assaulted the machinegun, killed the crew, destroyed the weapon, and fell mortally wounded. 1st Sgt. Yabes' valiant and selfless actions saved the lives of many of his fellow soldiers and inspired his comrades to effectively repel the enemy assault. His indomitable fighting spirit, extraordinary courage and intrepidity at the cost of his life are in the highest military traditions and reflect great credit upon himself and the Armed Forces of his country.

Epilogue: A Filipino, Yabes was born and raised in Lodi, California, but made Colorado his home. He first entered the Army in 1951 and saw duty in Korea before Vietnam, where he was killed in action during his second tour of duty. His Medal was presented to his wife, Janis, who herself later enlisted in the Army Reserve, saying, "I just feel like it's a personal obligation.... It been something I've been wanting to do for a long time."

NATIVE AMERICAN RECIPIENTS OF THE MEDAL OF HONOR

ALCHESAY, WILLIAM
US Army — Indian Campaigns

Sergeant, Indian Scouts. Place and date: Winter of 1872-1873. Entry of service date unknown. Entered service at: Camp Verde, Arizona. Born: 1853, Arizona Territory. Date of issue: 12 April 1875.

Citation: Gallant conduct during campaigns and engagements with Apaches.

Epilogue: Alchesay was an Apache, who served in the Army for many years as a scout and was instrumental in the capture of Geronimo. He became chief of the White Mountain Apache tribe until shortly before his death. He died of TB in 1928 and was buried in an unmarked grave site at Whiteriver, Arizona.[151] He was married at the time to Anna.[152] His son, Baha (Baja), became a scout when he was 22. In 1928, Anna applied for an Indian Wars Widow's pension, which was not approved because, under the law, the widow had to have married the soldier before 1917, while Anna did not become Alchesay's legal wife until the death of her sister in 1919. Despite the fact that the federal government did recognize plural marriages, a court of claims adjudication was never secured. Subsequently, the White Mountain Apache community applied to the Bureau of Indian Affairs to give her $20 per month from tribal funds, which was approved.[153]

BANQUET
US Army — Indian Campaigns

Indian Scout. Place and date: Winter of 1872-1873. Entry of service date unknown. Arizona. Date of issue: 12 April 1875.

Citation: Gallant conduct during campaigns and engagements with Apaches.

Epilogue: Very little information was available about Banquet's life in the archives of the CMOHS. He is lost to history.[154]

CHIQUITO
US Army — Indian Campaigns

Indian Scout. Place and date: Winter of 1872-1873. Entry of service date unknown. Birth: Arizona. Date of issue: 12 April 1875.

Citation: Gallant conduct during campaigns and engagements with Apaches.

Epilogue: Chiquito's tribal affiliation is unclear. Various sources, including pension claims, the Smithsonian, and the Medal of Honor History Society (Mesa Arizona Chapter) list him either as a Sierra Blanca Apache, Pinal Coyotero, or Navajo. Archives also reveal that his first wife "ran off with another man," while he was still in the Army. Chiquito died near Crown Point, New Mexico, in 1926. The location of his grave is unknown.[155]

CO-RUX-CHOD-ISH
US Army — Indian Campaigns

Sergeant, Pawnee Scouts, US Army. Place and date: At Republican River, Kansas, 8 July 1869. Entry of service date unknown. Birth: Nebraska. Date of issue: 24 August 1869.

Citation: Ran out from the command in pursuit of a dismounted Indian; was shot down and badly wounded by a bullet from his own command.

Epilogue: Very little information was available about Co-Rux-Chod-Ish's life in the archives of the CMOHS. He is lost to history.[156]

ELSATSOOSU
US Army — Indian Campaigns

Corporal, Indian Scouts. Place and date: Winter of 1872-1873. Entry of service date unknown. Birth: Arizona. Date of issue: 12 April 1875.

Citation: Gallant conduct during campaigns and engagements with Apaches.

Epilogue: Very little information was available about Elsatsoosu's life in the archives of the CMOHS Archives. What is known is that he died in Vinton, Iowa, in 1894 and is buried at Shellsburg Cemetery, Shellsburg, Iowa.[157]

FACTOR, POMPEY
US Army — Indian Campaigns

Rank and organization: Private, Indian Scouts. Place and date: At Pecos River, Tex., 25 April 1875. Entered service at: ------. Birth: Arkansas. Date of issue: 28 May 1875.

Citation: With 3 other men, he participated in a charge against 25 hostiles while on a scouting patrol.

Epilogue: Factor was a Black Seminole Indian Scout for the Army. The action for which received the Medal was performed with fellow scout, John Ward, who also received the Medal. Factor remained in the Army for a number of years after receiving the Medal, but violence and racism in the Army and the community nearby his cavalry unit's base drove him back to Mexico. He died in 1928 and is buried in the Seminole Indian Scout Cemetery in Brackettville, Texas.[158]

JIM
US Army — Indian Campaigns

Sergeant, Indian Scouts. Place and date: Winter of 1872-1873. Entry of service date unknown. Birth: Arizona Territory. Date of issue: 12 April 1875.

Citation: Gallant conduct during campaigns and engagements with Apaches.

Epilogue: Very little information was available about Jim's life in the archives of the CMOHS. An Indian Scout, Jim (aka Koker or Coker) stayed in the Army well after receiving the Medal. He died near Asn Flat, Arizona. His burial site is unknown.[159]

KELSAY
US Army — Indian Campaigns

Indian Scout. Place and date: Winter of 1872-1873. Entry of service date unknown. Birth: Arizona. Date of issue: 12 April 1875.

Citation: Gallant conduct during campaigns and engagements with Apaches.

Epilogue: Very little information was available about Kelsay's life in the archives of the CMOHS. He is *lost to history.*[160]

KOSOHA
US Army — Indian Campaigns

Indian Scout. Place and date: Winter of 1872-1873. Entry of service date unknown. Birth: Arizona. Date of issue: 12 April 1875.

Citation: Gallant conduct during campaigns and engagements with Apaches.

Epilogue: Very little information was available about Kosoha's life in the archives of the CMOHS. He is *lost to history.*

MACHOL
US Army — Indian Campaigns

Private, Indian Scouts. Place and date: Arizona, 1872-1873. Entry of service date unknown. Birth: Arizona. Date of issue: 12 April 1875.

Citation: Gallant conduct during campaign and engagements with Apaches.

Epilogue: Very little information was available about Machol's life in the archives of the CMOHS. He is *lost to history.*[161]

NANNASADDIE
US Army — Indian Campaigns

Indian Scout. Place and date: 1872-1873. Entry of service date unknown. Birth: Arizona. Date of issue: 12 April 1875.

Citation: Gallant conduct during campaigns and engagements with Apaches.

Epilogue: All that is known about Nannasaddie is that he was an Apache. His life before and after receiving the Medal is *lost to history.*[162]

NANTAJE (NANTAHE)
US Army — Indian Campaigns

Indian Scout. Place and date: 1872-1873. Entry of service date unknown. Birth: Arizona. Date of issue: 12 April 1875.

Citation: Gallant conduct during campaigns and engagements with Apaches.

Epilogue: Little is known about Nantaje before and after the actions leading to the Medal. His burial site is also unknown.[163]

PAINE, ADAM
US Army— Indian Campaigns

Rank and organization: Private, Indian Scouts. Place and date: Canyon Blanco tributary of the Red River, Tex., 26-27 September 1874. Entered service at: Fort Duncan, Texas. Birth: Florida. Date of issue: 13 October 1875.

Citation: Rendered invaluable service to Col. R. S. Mackenzie, 4th U.S. Cavalry, during this engagement.

Epilogue: Very little information was available about Paine's life in the archives of the CMOHS. He is *lost to history.*

ROWDY
US Army — Indian Campaigns

Sergeant, Company A, Indian Scouts. Place and date: Arizona, 7 March 1890. Entry of service date unknown. Birth: Arizona. Date of issue: 15 May 1890.

Citation: Bravery in action with Apache Indians.

Epilogue: Rowdy, the only name known for him, is believed to have been Yuma, born during the Civil War. He signed up with an X as an Indian Scout for the Army at 17, serving steadily until his death in 1893. Enlistment papers show he was 5'4" tall with black hair, black eyes, copper complexion, and married to Te-nu-der-vah. Rowdy and his wife probably made their home on the large San Carlos reservation. He began service at a time when the US Army was engaged in major campaigns against the Apaches and continued through that period of minor episodes involving "renegades", such as those that led to Geronimo's surrender in 1886 and Rowdy's Medal of Honor. Three years after that, he was dead. Army papers, including a record of his death and interment, state that Rowdy was shot to death by a civilian in the town of Bonita. Two charges of buckshot were fired from a shotgun, both entering his chest. The death was classified as homicide. The same paper shows Rowdy was buried at Fort Grant. According to unofficial reports, Rowdy went berserk in a local saloon and was shot by the bartender, a man called Lennon. After Fort Grant was closed, Rowdy's remains were removed to Santa Fe National Cemetery and re-interred in Grave 894, Section A.[164]

WARD, JOHN
US Army — Indian Campaigns

Rank and organization: Sergeant, 24th US Infantry Indian Scouts. Place and date: At Pecos River, Tex., 25 April 1875. Entered service at: Fort Duncan, Tex. Birth: Arkansas. Date of issue: 28 May 1875.

Citation. With 3 other men, he participated in

a charge against 25 hostiles while on a scouting patrol.

Epilogue: Ward received his Medal along with fellow Black Seminole Indian Scout Pompey Factor for action against the Indians at the Pecos River. Ward and Factor were probably born and raised in Mexico when their ancestors migrated there from the United States to escape from slavery. Described as 5', 7", with dark hair and dark skin, Ward remained in the Army for 24 years, despite the intense racism he experienced in the west. He was a private for 12 years, a corporal for six years, and a sergeant for six years. One night in January 1887, he lay on the ground to sleep. The next morning he was stiff and sore and unable to saddle his horse. Thereafter, he suffered from rheumatism and finally retired from the Army in 1895. Ward died in 1911, probably in Texas, and is buried in the Seminole Indian Scout Cemetery, Brackettville, Texas.[167] Mrs. Ward received a widow's pension until her death in 1926.

PAYNE, ISAAC
US Army — Indian Campaigns

Rank and organization: Trumpeter, Indian Scouts. Place and date: At Pecos River, Tex., 25 April 1875. Entered service at: ------. Birth: Mexico. Date of issue: 28 May 1875.

Citation: With 3 other men, he participated in a charge against 25 hostiles while on a scouting patrol.

Epilogue: Payne was a Black Seminole Indian, born and raised in Mexico. After his Army service, he returned to Mexico, where he died in 1904. He is buried at the Seminole Indian Scout Cemetery in Brackettville, Texas.[168]

EVANS, ERNEST E.
US Navy — World War II
Pacific Theater — Posthumous Award

Rank and organization: Commander, US Navy. Born: 13 August 1908, Pawnee, Okla. Accredited to: Oklahoma. Other Navy awards: Navy Cross, Bronze Star Medal.

Citation: For conspicuous gallantry and intrepidity at the risk of his life above and beyond the call of duty as commanding officer of the U.S.S. Johnston in action against major units of the enemy Japanese fleet during the battle off Samar on 25 October 1944. The first to lay a smokescreen and to open fire as an enemy task force, vastly superior in number, firepower and armor, rapidly approached. Comdr. Evans gallantly diverted the powerful blasts of hostile guns from the lightly armed and armored carriers under his protection, launching the first torpedo attack when the Johnston came under straddling Japanese shellfire. Undaunted by damage sustained under the terrific volume of fire, he unhesitatingly joined others of his group to provide fire support during subsequent torpedo attacks against the Japanese and, outshooting and out-maneuvering the enemy as he consistently interposed his vessel between the hostile fleet units and our carriers despite the crippling loss of engine power and communications with steering aft, shifted command to the fantail, shouted steering orders through an open hatch to men turning the rudder by hand and battled furiously until the Johnston, burning and shuddering from a mortal blow, lay dead in the water after 3 hours of fierce combat. Seriously wounded early in the engagement, Comdr. Evans, by his indomitable courage and brilliant professional skill, aided materially in turning back the enemy during a critical phase of the action. His valiant fighting spirit throughout this historic battle will venture as an inspiration to all who served with him.

Epilogue: A Cherokee, Evans was born and raised in Pawnee, Oklahoma. He served briefly in the state's National Guard before enlisting in the Navy in 1926. He was subsequently appointed to attend the Naval Academy from which he graduated in 1931. By 1943, he was a full commander and skipper of the USS Johnson, a 2000-ton, Fletcher-class destroyer. Evans was declared missing in the naval action for which he received the Medal. His body was never recovered. At the time of his death, he was survived by his wife, Margaret, and two sons. The Medal was presented to his family by President Truman. [169]

MONTGOMERY, JACK C.
US Army — World War II
European Theater

Rank and organization: First Lieutenant, US Army, 45th Infantry Division. Place and date: Near, Padiglione, Italy, 22 February 1944. Entered service at: Sallisaw, Okla. Birth: Long, Okla. G.O. No.: 5, 15 January 1945.

Citation: For conspicuous gallantry and intrepidity at risk of life above and beyond the call of duty on 22 February 1944, near Padiglione, Italy. Two hours before daybreak a strong force of enemy infantry established themselves in 3 echelons at 50 yards, 100 yards, and 300 yards, respectively, in front of the rifle platoons commanded by 1st Lt. Montgomery. The closest position, consisting of 4 machineguns and 1 mortar, threatened the immediate security of the platoon position. Seizing an Ml rifle and several hand grenades, 1st Lt. Montgomery crawled up a ditch to within hand grenade range of the enemy. Then climbing boldly onto a little mound, he fired his rifle and threw his grenades so accurately that he killed 8 of the enemy and captured the remaining 4. Returning to his platoon, he called for artillery fire on a house, in and around which he suspected that the majority of the enemy had entrenched themselves. Arming himself with a carbine, he proceeded along the shallow ditch, as withering fire from the riflemen and machinegunners in the second position was concentrated on him. He attacked this position with such fury that 7 of the enemy surrendered to him, and both machineguns were silenced. Three German dead were found in the vicinity later that morning. 1st Lt. Montgomery continued boldly toward the house, 300 yards from his platoon position. It was now daylight, and the enemy observation was excellent across the flat open terrain which led to 1st Lt. Montgomery's objective. When the artillery barrage had lifted, 1st Lt. Montgomery ran fearlessly toward the strongly defended position. As the enemy started streaming out of the house, 1st Lt. Montgomery, unafraid of treacherous snipers, exposed himself daringly to assemble the surrendering enemy and send them to the rear. His fearless, aggressive, and intrepid actions that morning, accounted for a total of 11 enemy dead, 32 prisoners, and an unknown number of wounded. That night, while aiding an adjacent unit to repulse a counterattack, he was struck by mortar fragments and seriously wounded. The selflessness and courage exhibited by 1st Lt. Montgomery in alone attacking 3 strong enemy positions inspired his men to a degree beyond estimation.

Epilogue: Montgomery's Medal was presented to him by President Roosevelt at the White House on January 15, 1945.[170] A Cherokee, Montgomery survived the war and returned home to Muskogee, Oklahoma, where he resumed his job at the Veterans Administration. Shy and unassuming, he received many recognitions and honors for his heroic deeds, including a monument to him at his alma mater, Bacone College, in 1991.[171]

CHILDERS, ERNEST
US Army — World War II
European Theater

Rank and organization: Second Lieutenant, US Army, 45th Infantry Division. Place and date: At Oliveto, Italy, 22 September 1943. Entered service at: Tulsa, Okla. Birth: Broken Arrow, Okla. G.O. No.: 30, 8 April 1944.

Citation: For conspicuous gallantry and intrepidity at risk of life above and beyond the call of duty in action on 22 September 1943, at Oliveto, Italy. Although 2d Lt. Childers previously had just suffered a fractured instep he, with 8 enlisted men, advanced up a hill toward enemy machinegun nests. The group advanced to a rock wall overlooking a cornfield and 2d Lt. Childers ordered a base of fire laid across the field so that he could advance. When he was fired upon by 2 enemy snipers from a nearby house he killed both of them. He moved behind the machinegun nests and killed all occupants of the nearer one. He continued toward the second one and threw rocks into it. When the 2 occupants of the nest raised up, he shot 1. The other was killed by 1 of the 8 enlisted men. 2d Lt. Childers continued his advance toward a house farther up the hill, and single-handed, captured an enemy mortar observer. The exceptional leadership, initiative, calmness under fire, and conspicuous gallantry displayed by 2d Lt. Childers were an inspiration to his men.

Epilogue: Childers was Creek from Broken Arrow, Oklahoma. Prior to entering the Army, he worked as an automobile mechanic. Shortly after the action for which he received the Medal, he was given a battlefield commission to Second Lieutenant. He survived the war, remained in the Army, and made it a career, eventually retiring after 29 years with the rank of

BARFOOT, VAN
US Army — World War II
European Theater

Rank and organization: Second Lieutenant, US Army, 157th Infantry, 45th Infantry Division. Place and date: Near Carano, Italy, 23 May 1944. Entered service at: Carthage, Miss. Birth: Edinburg, Miss. G.O. No.: 79, 4 October 1944.

Citation: For conspicuous gallantry and intrepidity at the risk of life above and beyond the call of duty on 23 May 1944, near Carano, Italy. With his platoon heavily engaged during an assault against forces well entrenched on commanding ground, 2d Lt. Barfoot (then Tech. Sgt.) moved off alone upon the enemy left flank. He crawled to the proximity of 1 machinegun nest and made a direct hit on it with a hand grenade, killing 2 and wounding 3 Germans. He continued along the German defense line to another machinegun emplacement, and with his tommygun killed 2 and captured 3 soldiers. Members of another enemy machinegun crew then abandoned their position and gave themselves up to Sgt. Barfoot. Leaving the prisoners for his support squad to pick up, he proceeded to mop up positions in the immediate area, capturing more prisoners and bringing his total count to 17. Later that day, after he had reorganized his men and consolidated the newly captured ground, the enemy launched a fierce armored counterattack directly at his platoon positions. Securing a bazooka, Sgt. Barfoot took up an exposed position directly in front of 3 advancing Mark VI tanks. From a distance of 75 yards his first shot destroyed the track of the leading tank, effectively disabling it, while the other 2 changed direction toward the flank. As the crew of the disabled tank dismounted, Sgt. Barfoot killed 3 of them with his tommygun. He continued onward into enemy terrain and destroyed a recently abandoned German fieldpiece with a demolition charge placed in the breech. While returning to his platoon position, Sgt. Barfoot, though greatly fatigued by his Herculean efforts, assisted 2 of his seriously wounded men 1,700 yards to a position of safety. Sgt. Barfoot's extraordinary heroism, demonstration of magnificent valor, and aggressive determination in the face of pointblank fire are a perpetual inspiration to his fellow soldiers.

Epilogue: Barfoot never knew he was Chactaw. His mother never registered him in Carthage, Mississippi, where his family owned and operated a cotton farm, and he attended public school. He served three years in the Civilian Conservation Corps at Lexington, Mississippi, and Salem, Oregon, before enlisting in the Army in 1940. Barfoot received a battlefield commission after the action that earned him the Medal, made the Army his career, and retired with the rank of Colonel.

GEORGE, CHARLES
US Army — Korean War
Posthumous Award

Rank and organization: Private First Class, US Army, Company C, 179th Infantry Regiment, 45th Infantry Division. Place and date: Near Songnae-dong, Korea, 30 November 1952. Entered service at: Whittier, N.C. Born: 23 August 1932, Cherokee, N.C. G.O. NO.: 19, 18 March 1954.

Citation: Pfc. George, a member of Company C, distinguished himself by conspicuous gallantry and outstanding courage above and beyond the call of duty in action against the enemy on the night of 30 November 1952. He was a member of a raiding party committed to engage the enemy and capture a prisoner for interrogation. Forging up the rugged slope of the key terrain feature, the group was subjected to intense mortar and machine gun fire and suffered several casualties. Throughout the advance, he fought valiantly and, upon reaching the crest of the hill, leaped into the trenches and closed with the enemy in hand-to-hand combat. When friendly troops were ordered to move back upon completion of the assignment, he and 2 comrades remained to cover the withdrawal. While in the process of leaving the trenches a hostile soldier hurled a grenade into their midst. Pfc. George shouted a warning to 1 comrade, pushed the other soldier out of danger, and, with full knowledge of the consequences, unhesitatingly threw himself upon the grenade, absorbing the full blast of the explosion. Although seriously wounded in this display of valor, he refrained from any outcry which would divulge the position of his companions. The 2 soldiers evacuated him to the forward aid station and shortly thereafter he succumbed to his wound. Pfc. George's indomitable courage, consummate devotion to duty, and willing self-sacrifice reflect the highest credit upon himself and uphold the finest traditions of the military service.

Epilogue: Archives reveal only that George was an Eastern Cherokee Indian, single, a Baptist, and a farmer at the time he entered the Army. At the time of his death, he was survived by his father, Jacob. George is buried at Yellow Hill Cemetery, Cherokee, North Carolina.[172]

HARVEY, RAYMOND
US Army — Korean War

Rank and organization: Captain, US Army, Company C, 17th Infantry Regiment. Place and date: Vicinity of Taemi-Dong, Korea, 9 March 1951. Entered service at: Pasadena, Calif. Born: 1 March 1920, Ford City, Pa. G.O. No.: 67, 2 August 1951.

Citation: Capt. Harvey Company C, distinguished himself by conspicuous gallantry and intrepidity above and beyond the call of duty in action. When his company was pinned down by a barrage of automatic weapons fire from numerous well-entrenched emplacements, imperiling accomplishment of its mission, Capt. Harvey braved a hail of fire and exploding grenades to advance to the first enemy machine gun nest, killing its crew with grenades. Rushing to the edge of the next emplacement, he killed its crew with carbine fire. He then moved the 1st Platoon forward until it was again halted by a curtain of automatic fire from well fortified hostile positions. Disregarding the hail of fire, he personally charged and neutralized a third emplacement. Miraculously escaping death from intense crossfire, Capt. Harvey continued to lead the assault. Spotting an enemy pillbox well camouflaged by logs, he moved close enough to sweep the emplacement with carbine fire and throw grenades through the openings, annihilating its 5 occupants. Though wounded he then turned to order the company forward, and, suffering agonizing pain, he continued to direct the reduction of the remaining hostile positions, refusing evacuation until assured that the mission would be accomplished. Capt. Harvey's valorous and intrepid actions served as an inspiration to his company, reflecting the utmost glory upon himself and upholding the heroic traditions of the military service.

Epilogue: One-quarter Chickasaw, Harvey was career Army, serving from 1939 to 1962, including combat tours during World War II that earned him the Distinguished Service Cross, three Silver Stars, three Bronze Stars, and many other decorations. After retiring from the Army, Harvey worked for the Northrop Corporation in California for five years before starting an investment banking firm based in Kansas. He then became the Director of Indian Affairs for the state of Arizona before retiring due to poor health. Harvey died in 1996 and is buried in Arlington National Cemetery. He was survived by his wife, Pamela, four children, and eight grandchildren.[173] Harvey's father, who was half Chickasaw, was murdered while crossing a stream by a man named "Black James." Harvey's relatives avenged his death at a baseball game.[174]

RED CLOUD, MITCHELL, JR.
US Marine Corps — Korean War
Posthumous Award

Rank and organization: Corporal, US Army, Company E, 19th Infantry Regiment, 24th Infantry Division. Place and date: Near Chonghyon, Korea, 5 November 1950. Entered service at: Merrilan, Wis. Born: 2 July 1924, Hatfield, Wis. G.O. No.: 26, 25 April 1951.

Citation: Cpl. Red Cloud, Company E, distinguished himself by conspicuous gallantry and intrepidity above and beyond the call of duty in action against the enemy. From his position on the point of a ridge immediately in front of the company command post he was the first to detect the approach of the Chinese Communist forces and give the alarm as the enemy charged from a brush-covered area less than 100 feet from him. Springing up he delivered devastating pointblank automatic rifle fire into the advancing enemy. His accurate and intense fire checked this assault and gained time for the company to consolidate its defense. With utter fearlessness he maintained his firing position until severely wounded by enemy fire. Refusing assistance he pulled himself to his feet and wrapping his arm around a tree continued his deadly fire again, until he was fatally wounded. This heroic act stopped the enemy from overrunning his company's position and gained time for reorganization and evacuation of the wounded. Cpl. Red Cloud's dauntless courage and gallant self-sacrifice reflects the highest credit upon himself and upholds the esteemed traditions of the

U.S. Army.

Epilogue: A Winnebago, Red Cloud was a veteran of two wars, having served in World War II as a Marine with Carlson's Raiders. He saw extensive combat against the Japanese, especially at Guadalcanal. He described how, after 16 days of fighting, he fell asleep, exhausted, and woke the next day to learn that he had slept between two dead Japanese bodies. He contracted malaria in the Pacific and, at one point, weighed 115 pounds, down from his normal weight of 195 pounds. Red Cloud reenlisted in the Army in 1948 and was sent to Korea in 1950.[175] At the time of his death, he was survived by his mother, Nellie, and brother, Merlin. Numerous honors and recognitions were given him, including the naming of a Navy ship and an Army base in Korea. The Medal was presented to his mother by General Omar Bradley at the Pentagon. Red Cloud is buried in Decorah Cemetery, Komensky, Wisconsin.[176]

REESE, JOHN N., JR.
US Army — World War II
Pacific Theater — Posthumous Award

Rank and organization: Private First Class, US Army, Company B, 148th Infantry, 37th Infantry Division. Place and date: Paco Railroad Station, Manila, Philippine Islands. 9 February 1945. Entered service at: Pryor, Okla. Birth. Muskogee, Okla. G.O. No.: 89, 19 October 1945.

Citation: He was engaged in the attack on the Paco Railroad Station, which was strongly defended by 300 determined enemy soldiers with machineguns and rifles, supported by several pillboxes, 3 20mm. guns, 1 37-mm. gun and heavy mortars. While making a frontal assault across an open field, his platoon was halted 100 yards from the station by intense enemy fire. On his own initiative he left the platoon. accompanied by a comrade, and continued forward to a house 60 yards from the objective. Although under constant enemy observation. the 2 men remained in this position for an hour, firing at targets of opportunity, killing more than 35 Japanese and wounding many more. Moving closer to the station and discovering a group of Japanese replacements attempting to reach pillboxes, they opened heavy fire, killed more than 40 and stopped all subsequent attempts to man the emplacements. Enemy fire became more intense as they advanced to within 20 yards of the station. From that point Pfc. Reese provided effective covering fire and courageously drew enemy fire to himself while his companion killed 7 Japanese and destroyed a 20-mm. gun and heavy machinegun with handgrenades. With their ammunition running low, the 2 men started to return to the American lines, alternately providing covering fire for each other as they withdrew. During this movement, Pfc. Reese was killed by enemy fire as he reloaded his rifle. The intrepid team, in 21/2 hours of fierce fighting, killed more than 82 Japanese, completely disorganized their defense and paved the way for subsequent complete defeat of the enemy at this strong point. By his gallant determination in the face of tremendous odds, aggressive fighting spirit, and extreme heroism at the cost of his life, Pfc. Reese materially aided the advance of our troops in Manila and providing a lasting inspiration to all those with whom he served.

Epilogue: A Cherokee, Reese was awarded the Medal with another soldier (see RODRIGUEZ, CLETO) for the same military action. Reese is buried in Fort Gibson National Cemetery, Oklahoma.[177]

1945.

HARMON, ROY
US Army — World War II
European Theater — Posthumous Award

Rank and organization: Sergeant, US Army, Company C, 362nd Infantry, 91st Infantry Division. Place and date: Near Casaglia, Italy, 12 July 1944. Entered service at: Pixley, Calif. Birth: Talala, Okla. G.O. No.: 83, 2 October

Citation: He was an acting squad leader when heavy machinegun fire from enemy positions, well dug in on commanding ground and camouflaged by haystacks, stopped his company's advance and pinned down 1 platoon where it was exposed to almost certain annihilation. Ordered to rescue the beleaguered platoon by neutralizing the German automatic fire, he led his squad forward along a draw to the right of the trapped unit against 3 key positions which poured murderous fire into his helpless comrades. When within range, his squad fired tracer bullets in an attempt to set fire to the 3 haystacks which were strung out in a loose line directly to the front, 75, 150, and 250 yards away. Realizing that this attack was ineffective, Sgt. Harmon ordered his squad to hold their position and voluntarily began a 1-man assault. Carrying white phosphorus grenades and a submachine gun, he skillfully took advantage of what little cover the terrain afforded and crept to within 25 yards of the first position. He set the haystack afire with a grenade, and when 2 of the enemy attempted to flee from the inferno, he killed them with his submachine gun. Crawling toward the second machinegun emplacement, he attracted fire and was wounded; but he continued to advance and destroyed the position with hand grenades, killing the occupants. He then attacked the third machinegun, running to a small knoll, then crawling over ground which offered no concealment or cover. About halfway to his objective, he was again wounded. But he struggled ahead until within 20 yards of the machinegun nest, where he raised himself to his knees to throw a grenade. He was knocked down by direct enemy fire. With a final, magnificent effort, he again arose, hurled the grenade and fell dead, riddled by bullets. His missile fired the third position, destroying it. Sgt. Harmon's extraordinary heroism, gallantry, and self-sacrifice saved a platoon from being wiped out, and made it possible for his company to advance against powerful enemy resistance.

Epilogue: The archives contained little or no information about Harmon. What is known from records is that Harmon was born in Talala, Oklahoma, was killed in action, and is buried in Florence, Italy, in the ABMC Florence Cemetery. The Medal was presented to his father.

JEWISH AMERICAN RECIPIENTS OF THE MEDAL OF HONOR

COHN, ABRAHAM
US Army — American Civil War

Rank and organization: Sergeant Major, 6th New Hampshire Infantry. Place and date: At Wilderness, Va., 6 May 1864; At the mine, Petersburg, Va., 30 July 1864. Entered service at: Campton, N.H. Birth: Guttentag, Silesia, Prussia. Date of issue: 24 August 1865.

Citation: During Battle of the Wilderness rallied and formed, under heavy fire, disorganized and fleeing troops of different regiments. At Petersburg, Va., 30 July 1864, bravely and coolly carried orders to the advanced line under severe fire.

Epilogue: Cohn was born and raised in Prussia and attended the University of Berlin, where he received military training before emigrating with his parents to the United States. He enlisted in the Army as a Sergeant Major and was later promoted to Captain while serving with the New Hampshire Volunteers. After the Civil War, Cohn worked as a merchant in New York. He was married to Fanny Geller and had six children: Moritz, Eugene, Johanna, Sigmund, Emma, and Bella. He died at his residence at 36 East 84th Street at the age of sixty-five and is buried in Cypress Hills Cemetery in New York.[179]

GAUSE, ISAAC
US Army — American Civil War

Rank and organization: Corporal, Company E, 2nd Ohio Cavalry. Place and date: Near Berryville, Va., 13 September 1864. Entered service at: ------. Birth: Trumbull County, Ohio. Date of issue: 19 September 1864.

Citation: Capture of the colors of the 8th South Carolina Infantry while engaged in a reconnaissance along the Berryville and Winchester Pike.

Epilogue: The archives had very little information on Gause. He was probably born and raised in Ohio and returned to that state after the Civil War.

GUMPERTZ, SYDNEY G.
US Army — World War I

Rank and organization: First Sergeant, US Army, Company E, 132nd Infantry, 33rd Division. Place and date: In the Bois-de-Forges, France, 29 September 1918. Entered service at: Chicago, Ill. Born: 24 October 1879, San Raphael, Calif. G.O. No.: 16, W.D., 1919.

Citation: When the advancing line was held up by machinegun fire, 1st Sgt. Gumpertz left the platoon of which he was in command and started with 2 other soldiers through a heavy barrage toward the machinegun nest. His 2 companions soon became casualties from bursting shells, but 1st Sgt. Gumpertz continued on alone in the face of direct fire from the machinegun, jumped into the nest and silenced the gun, capturing 9 of the crew.

Epilogue: Gumpertz was born in 1880 in San Raphael, California. He enlisted in the Army in Chicago, Illinois, at the beginning of World War I and was assigned to the Illinois National Guard. Little is known about Gumpertz's life after his military service. He resided in New York City, where he worked in advertising and theatrical bookings. In 1920, he became leader of the Jewish Valor Legion, a group dedicated to countering slanders against the patriotism of American Jews then being circulated by Henry Ford. He wrote the heralded "Jewish Legion of Valor," a series of stories about Jews who fought for the United Sates from the Revolutionary War. It is believed that Gumpertz never married. He died on February 16, 1971 at the age of 91, while a patient at the VA Hospital in New York City. He is buried in Arlington National Cemetery.[180]

HELLER, HENRY

US Army — American Civil War

Rank and organization: Sergeant, Company A, 66th Ohio Infantry. Place and date: At Chancellorsville, Va., 2 May 1863. Entered service at: Urbana, Ohio. Birth: ------. Date of issue: 29 July 1892.

Citation: One of a party of 4 who, under heavy fire, voluntarily brought into the Union lines a wounded Confederate officer from whom was obtained valuable information concerning the position of the enemy.

Epilogue: Heller is believed to have been born in Ohio. He was once married to Mariam Conover. He died in 1895 and is buried in King's Creek Baptist Church Cemetery in Campaign County, Ohio.[181]

GEIGER, GEORGE

US Army — Indian Campaigns

Rank and organization: Sergeant, Company H, 7th US Cavalry. Place and date: At Little Big Horn River, Mont., 25 June 1876. Entered service at: -----. Birth: Cincinnati, Ohio. Date of issue: S October 1878.

Citation: With 3 comrades during the entire engagement courageously held a position that secured water for the command.

Epilogue: Geiger was a sergeant with the famed US 7th Cavalry that engaged Chief Sitting Bull with Custer at the battle of Little Big Horn. Very little is known about him except that a descendent, Larry Geiger, currently resides in Nebraska. When contacted, he indicated that he knew very little about Geiger the Medal recipient but had heard he fought at Little Big Horn.[182] George Geiger died in 1904 and is buried in Dayton National Cemetery, Dayton, Ohio.[183]

LEVY, BENJAMIN
US Army — American Civil War

Rank and organization: Private, Company B, 1st New York Infantry. Place and date: At Glendale, Va., 30 June 1862. Entered service at: ------. Birth: New York, N.Y. Date of issue: 1 March 1865.

Citation: This soldier, a drummer boy, took the gun of a sick comrade, went into the fight, and when the color bearers were shot down, carried the colors and saved them from capture.

Epilogue: Born and raised in New York City, a drummer boy during the Civil War with the 1st New York Volunteers, Levy was only sixteen when he engaged in the action cited to receive the Medal. Little is known about him after his service. He returned to New York, living at 641 Washington Street for many years. The records indicate he was married and had children and grandchildren, but no names are provided. He died at the age of 72 in 1921 and is buried in Cypress Hills Cemetery in Brooklyn, New York.[184]

ORBANSKY, DAVID
US Army — American Civil War

Rank and organization: Private, Company B, 58th Ohio Infantry. Place and date: At Shiloh, Tenn.; Vicksburg, Miss., etc., 1862 and 1863. Entered service at: Columbus, Ohio. Birth: Lautenburg, Prussia. Date of issue: 2 August 1879.

Citation: Gallantry in actions.

Epilogue: Also known as David Arrin Urbransky, Orbransky was born and raised in Lautenberg, Prussia, and came to this country with his parents at the age of fifteen. Locating in New York City, he entered the same trade as his father and became a cabinetmaker. Later, he moved to Columbus, Ohio, where he became a shopkeeper. He entered the Army in 1861 and was assigned to the 58th Ohio Volunteers. Medical and pension application records found in the National Archives indicate Orbransky suffered from various serious medical problems, including ailments of the kidney and lungs. He died in 1897 but attempts to locate his gravesite were complicated because after the Civil War, he shortened his name to Urban. After an extensive search of Jewish cemeteries, his grave was located in Walnut Hills Cemetery in Cincinnati, Ohio, next to those of his wife and children.[185]

GROSS, SAMUEL
US Marine Corps — Haiti

Rank and organization: Private, US Marine Corps, 23rd Co. (Real name is Marguiles, Samuel.) Born: 9 May 1891, Philadelphia, Pa. Accredited to: Pennsylvania.

Citation: In company with members of the 5th, 13th, 23d Companies and the marine and sailor detachment from the U.S.S. Connecticut, Gross participated in the attack on Fort Riviere, Haiti, 17 November 1915. Following a concentrated drive, several different detachments of marines gradually closed in on the old French bastion fort in an effort to cut off all avenues of retreat for the Caco bandits. Approaching a breach in the wall which was the only entrance to the fort, Gross was the second man to pass through the breach in the face of constant fire from the Cacos and, thereafter, for a 10-minute period, engaged the enemy in desperate hand-to-hand combat until the bastion was captured and Caco resistance neutralized.

Epilogue: Gross, whose real name was Samuel Marguiles, was one of a trio of men who received the Medal in the same action during the first campaign in Haiti. He was born and raised in Philadelphia and ran away from home to join the Marines in 1913. At the time of his enlistment, he gave May 9, 1891 as his birthday, but sources say it is probably closer to 1897. Initially, Gross's primary job in the Marines was to serve as an orderly for General Smedley Butler and to care for the General's children, which he did with great dedication and care. After the action cited above, Gross returned to the United States in 1917 and was honorably discharged. He subsequently reenlisted in the Marines, but there is no record of his activities. Gross suffered from various war wounds and epilepsy. He died in 1934 at the VA Hospital in Philadelphia. By the time of his death, although everyone knew his true name, he was officially buried as Samuel Gross in Har-Nebo Jewish Cemetery, Philadelphia.[186]

ZUSSMAN, RAYMOND
US Army — World War II
European Theater — Posthumous Award

Rank and organization: Second Lieutenant, US Army, 756th Tank Battalion. Place and date: Noroy le Bourg, France, 12 September 1944. Entered service at: Detroit, Mich. Birth: Hamtramck, Mich. G.O. No.: 42, 24 May 1945.

Citation: On 12 September 1944, 2d Lt. Zussman was in command of 2 tanks operating with an infantry company in the attack on enemy forces occupying the town of Noroy le Bourg, France. At 7 p.m., his command tank bogged down. Throughout the ensuing action, armed only with a carbine, he reconnoitered alone on foot far in advance of his remaining tank and the infantry. Returning only from time to time to designate targets, he directed the action of the tank and turned over to the infantry the numerous German soldiers he had caused to surrender. He located a road block and directed his tanks to destroy it. Fully exposed to fire from enemy positions only 50 yards distant, he stood by his tank directing its fire. Three Germans were killed and 8 surrendered. Again he walked before his tank, leading it against an enemy-held group of houses, machinegun and small arms fire kicking up dust at his feet. The tank fire broke the resistance and 20 enemy surrendered. Going forward again alone he passed an enemy-occupied house from which Germans fired on him and threw grenades in his path. After a brief fire fight, he signaled his tank to come up and fire on the house. Eleven German soldiers were killed and 15 surrendered. Going on alone, he disappeared around a street corner. The fire of his carbine could be heard and in a few minutes he reappeared driving 30 prisoners before him. Under 2d Lt. Zussman's heroic and inspiring leadership, 18 enemy soldiers were killed and 92 captured.

Epilogue: Zussman was born in Hamtramck, Michigan, in 1917. His father was Nathan Zussman, and they lived at 2918 Sturtevant Street in

Detroit.[187] Zussman entered the Army in 1941 and was subsequently commissioned as a Second Lieutenant in 1943. After the action for which he received the Medal, he was killed in combat on September 21, 1944. He is buried at Machpelah Cemetery, Ferndale, Michigan.[188]

JACHMAN, ISADORE
US Army — World War II
European Theater — Posthumous Award

Rank and organization: Staff Sergeant, US Army, Company B, 513th Parachute Infantry Regiment. Place and date: Flamierge, Belgium, 4 January 1945. Entered service at: Baltimore, Md. Birth: Berlin, Germany. G.O. No.: 25, 9 June 1950.

Citation: For conspicuous gallantry and intrepidity above and beyond the call of duty at Flamierge, Belgium, on 4 January 1945, when his company was pinned down by enemy artillery, mortar, and small arms fire, 2 hostile tanks attacked the unit, inflicting heavy casualties, S/Sgt. Jachman, seeing the desperate plight of his comrades, left his place of cover and with total disregard for his own safety dashed across open ground through a hail of fire and seizing a bazooka from a fallen comrade advanced on the tanks, which concentrated their fire on him. Firing the weapon alone, he damaged one and forced both to retire. S/Sgt. Jachman's heroic action, in which he suffered fatal wounds, disrupted the entire enemy attack, reflecting the highest credit upon himself and the parachute infantry.

Epilogue: Jachman was born in Berlin, Germany, the first son of Leo and Lea Jachman. The family immigrated to the United States and settled in Baltimore, Maryland, in 1923. Jachman attended Yeshiva Baltimore Hebrew Parochial School, Public School #40, Baltimore City College High School, and the University of Baltimore before enlisting in the Army in 1943.[189] His parents operated a grocery store. After the action for which he received the Medal, it was believed he was missing in action until his body was identified almost two months later. Jachman was buried in Foy, Belgium until he was returned to Baltimore in 1946 and buried again at Adath Israel Anshe Sfard Cemetery. His Medal was presented to his parents in a ceremony in 1950.[190]

SHULER, SIMON (alias Charles Gardner)
US Army — Indian Campaigns

Rank and Organization: Private, Company B, 8th US Cavalry. Place and Date: Arizona, August to October 1868. Birth: Bavaria. Date of Issue: 24 July 1869.

Citation: Bravery in scouts and actions against Indians.

Epilogue: The only known Jewish Medal recipient from the Indian Campaigns, Shuler had a colorful and controversial military history. He was born in Bavaria in 1884 and emigrated to the United States around 1860. He originally enlisted in the Army under his true name (Shuler) and later deserted only to reenlist under an assumed name (Charles Gardner). After a heroic military action against the Indians, he was recommended for promotion to Lieutenant but it never took place, perhaps because evidence of the desertion was soon discovered. He was given a dishonorable discharge, which was later changed to honorable. When Shuler left the Army and applied for a pension under his true name, his application was disapproved because he could not prove he was, in fact, Shuler. He died in 1895 and is buried in San Antonio National Cemetery, Section I, Grave 1610.[191]

SAWELSON, WILLIAM
US Army — World War I
Posthumous Award

Rank and organization: Sergeant, US Army, Company M, 312th Infantry, 78th Division. Place and date: At Grand-Pre, France, 26 October, 1918. Entered service at: Harrison, N.J. Born: S August 1895, Newark, N.J. G.O. No.: 16, W.D., 1919.

Citation: Hearing a wounded man in a shell hole some distance away calling for water, Sgt. Sawelson, upon his own initiative, left shelter and crawled through heavy machinegun fire to where the man lay, giving him what water he had in his canteen. He then went back to his own shell hole, obtained more water, and was returning to the wounded man when he was killed by a machinegun bullet.

Epilogue: Sawelson was the youngest (23) of the three Jews to receive the Medal during World War I. Born and raised in Newark, New Jersey, he attended the Public School of East Newark and Kearney High School before enlisting in the Army in 1918.[192] At the time of his death, he was survived by his parents, three brothers, and sisters. He is buried in the Meuse-Argonne Military Cemetery in France.[193]

KAUFMAN, BENJAMIN
US Army — World War I

Rank and organization: First Sergeant, US Army, Company K, 308th Infantry, 77th Division. Place and date: In the forest of Argonne, France, 4 October 1918. Entered service at: Brooklyn, N.Y. Born: 10 March 1894, Buffalo, N.Y. G.O. No.: 50, W.D., 1919.

Citation: He took out a patrol for the purpose of attacking an enemy machinegun which had checked the advance of his company. Before reaching the gun he became separated from his patrol and a machinegun bullet shattered his right arm. Without hesitation he advanced on the gun alone, throwing grenades with his left hand and charging with an empty pistol, taking one prisoner and scattering the crew, bringing the gun and prisoner back to the first-aid station.

Epilogue: Born in 1894 in Buffalo, New York, Kaufman attended public school in New York City and graduated from Syracuse University before enlisting in the Army a the beginning of World War I. He was shortly afterward made a First Sergeant. He refused a commission because it would have required him to leave his buddies in the unit to which he was assigned. At one point in France, Kaufman went AWOL (absent without authorization). When he was returned, a reduction in rank was recommended but never carried out by his company commander.[195] Upon his return to civilian life, he was appointed director of the New Jersey Employment Service Bureau in Trenton. He helped organized the Jewish War Veteran's Post 156 in 1937. He was also active in the American

Legion's Junior Baseball Program. Ill for most of his life after World War I, he never had the opportunity to participate in many of the activities of the Congressional Medal of Honor Society. He died in 1981 and is buried in Fountain Lawn Memorial Park, Trenton, New Jersey, survived by his wife, Dorothy, daughter Rita, and a sister.[196]

SALOMON, BEN L.
US Army — World War II
Pacific Theater — Posthumous Award

Citation: Captain Ben L. Salomon was serving at Saipan, in the Marianas Islands on July 7, 1944, as the Surgeon for the 2d Battalion, 105th Infantry Regiment, 27th Infantry Division. The Regiment's 1st and 2d Battalions were attacked by an overwhelming force estimated between 3,000 and 5,000 Japanese soldiers. It was one of the largest attacks attempted in the Pacific Theater during World War II. Although both units fought furiously, the enemy soon penetrated the Battalions' combined perimeter and inflicted overwhelming casualties. In the first minutes of the attack, approximately 30 wounded soldiers walked, crawled, or were carried into Captain Salomon's aid station, and the small tent soon filled with wounded men. As the perimeter began to be overrun, it became increasingly difficult for Captain Salomon to work on the wounded. He then saw a Japanese soldier bayoneting one of the wounded soldiers lying near the tent. Firing from a squatting position, Captain Salomon quickly killed the enemy soldier. Then, as he turned his attention back to the wounded, two more Japanese soldiers appeared in the front entrance of the tent. As these enemy soldiers were killed, four more crawled under the tent walls. Rushing them, Captain Salomon kicked the knife out of the hand of one, shot another, and bayoneted a third. Captain Salomon butted the fourth enemy soldier in the stomach and a wounded comrade then shot and killed the enemy soldier. Realizing the gravity of the situation, Captain Salomon ordered the wounded to make their way as best they could back to the regimental aid station, while he attempted to hold off the enemy until they were clear. Captain Salomon then grabbed a rifle from one of the wounded and rushed out of the tent. After four men were killed while manning a machine gun, Captain Salomon took control of it. When his body was later found, 98 dead enemy soldiers were piled in front of his position. Captain Salomon's extraordinary heroism and devotion to duty are in keeping with the highest traditions of military service and reflect great credit upon himself, his unit, and the United States Army.

Epilogue: Saloman received the Medal 58 years after his death. He was shot more than 70 times, "but he never even received the Purple Heart," said his father.[197] Saloman was a dentist who served as a surgeon during the war, which may be why his recommendation for the Medal was not processed. According to the Geneva Conventions, which provide guidelines for how wars are to be conducted, medical personnel are prohibited from bearing arms against an enemy. It may be that somewhere in the long Medal review process, someone thought that, because of this provision, Saloman should not receive the Medal. Saloman's case was taken up by Dr. Robert West, also a World War II veteran who served as a dentist and attended the same dental school as Saloman—the University of California. Dr. West advocated on behalf of Saloman and discovered a sub-clause in the Geneva Convention rule, which states that medical personnel can bear arms if they are defending their patients. On May 1, 2002, since Saloman did not have any living relatives, Dr. West accepted the Medal for Saloman and presented it to Major General Patrick Sculley, the Army's chief dentist. The Medal is now on display at the Army Medical Department Museum in San Antonio, Texas.[198] Upon his death, Saloman's remains were brought back to the United States and buried in Forest Lawn Memorial Park in Glendale, California.[199]

JACOBS, JACK H.
US Army — Vietnam War

Rank and organization: Captain, US Army, US Army Element, US Military Assistance Command, Republic of Vietnam. Place and date: Kien Phong Province, Republic of Vietnam, 9 March 1968. Entered service at: Trenton, N.J. Born: 2 August 1945, Brooklyn, N.Y.

Citation: For conspicuous gallantry and intrepidity in action at the risk of his life above and beyond the call of duty. Capt. Jacobs (then 1st Lt.),

Infantry, distinguished himself while serving as assistant battalion advisor, 2d Battalion, 16th Infantry, 9th Infantry Division, Army of the Republic of Vietnam. The 2d Battalion was advancing to contact when it came under intense heavy machine gun and mortar fire from a Viet Cong battalion positioned in well fortified bunkers. As the 2d Battalion deployed into attack formation its advance was halted by devastating fire. Capt. Jacobs, with the command element of the lead company, called for and directed air strikes on the enemy positions to facilitate a renewed attack. Due to the intensity of the enemy fire and heavy casualties to the command group, including the company commander, the attack stopped and the friendly troops became disorganized. Although wounded by mortar fragments, Capt. Jacobs assumed command of the allied company, ordered a withdrawal from the exposed position and established a defensive perimeter. Despite profuse bleeding from head wounds which impaired his vision, Capt. Jacobs, with complete disregard for his safety, returned under intense fire to evacuate a seriously wounded advisor to the safety of a wooded area where he administered lifesaving first aid. He then returned through heavy automatic weapons fire to evacuate the wounded company commander. Capt. Jacobs made repeated trips across the fire-swept open rice paddies evacuating wounded and their weapons. On 3 separate occasions, Capt. Jacobs contacted and drove off Viet Cong squads who were searching for allied wounded and weapons, single-handedly killing 3 and wounding several others. His gallant actions and extraordinary heroism saved the lives of 1 U.S. advisor and 13 allied soldiers. Through his effort the allied company was restored to an effective fighting unit and prevented defeat of the friendly forces by a strong and determined enemy. Capt. Jacobs, by his gallantry and bravery in action in the highest traditions of the military service, has reflected great credit upon himself, his unit, and the U.S. Army.

Epilogue: A career military officer and the first American Jew to receive the Medal during the Vietnam War, Jacobs was born and raised in Brooklyn as well as New Jersey, where his family later moved. He attended public school in Woodbridge and graduated from Rutgers University in 1966. He was commissioned a Second Lieutenant (ROTC) and entered active duty the same year. Based on numerous news articles and interviews, Jacobs seems reflective about his time in uniform, especially the Vietnam War and being a Medal recipient. He indicated that the 1960s were a period of growing pains in America, and the soldier's role was disconcerting and difficult. He talked of having many moments of frustration while serving as an advisor to Vietnamese units but felt that, mostly, the Vietnamese solders fought bravely and attempted to defend their country against a foreign enemy with valor and vigor. The major problem with the Vietnam War was America's failure to find the way to achieve our objectives. The Vietnamese government wanted more of a commitment from America and actions like bombing Hanoi. When America disagreed, it signaled we had lost our will to win.[200] He also said, "Being in the Army was a thankless job." Jacobs describes martial strains caused by the Army, poor pay, and not having the opportunity to relax or enjoy life.[201] However, if given the opportunity to do it over again, he said he would change nothing. "If people have the choice of doing something onerous but important, how can they choose?" Jacob today resides in Millington, New Jersey, where numerous schools and playgrounds are named after him. He serves on various corporate board and spends a great deal of time in community service.

LEVITOW, JOHN L.
US Army — Vietnam War

Rank and organization: Sergeant, US Air Force, 3rd Special Operations Squadron. Place and date: Long Binh Army post, Republic of Vietnam, 24 February 1969. Entered service at: New Haven, Conn. Born: 1 November 1945, Hartford, Conn.

Citation: For conspicuous gallantry and intrepidity in action at the risk of his life above and beyond the call of duty. Sgt. Levitow (then A1c.), U.S. Air Force, distinguished himself by exceptional heroism while assigned as a loadmaster aboard an AC-47 aircraft flying a night mission in support of Long Binh Army post. Sgt. Levitow's aircraft was struck by a hostile mortar round. The resulting explosion ripped a hole 2 feet in diameter through the wing and fragments made over 3,500 holes in the fuselage. All occupants of the cargo compartment were wounded and helplessly slammed against the floor and fuselage. The explosion tore an activated flare from the grasp of a crewmember who had been launching flares to provide illumination for Army ground troops engaged in combat. Sgt. Levitow, though stunned by the concussion of the blast and suffering from over 40 fragment wounds in the back and legs, staggered to his feet and turned to assist the man nearest to him who had been knocked down and was bleeding heavily. As he was moving his wounded comrade forward and away from the opened cargo compartment door, he saw the smoking flare ahead of him in the aisle. Realizing the danger involved and completely disregarding his own wounds, Sgt. Levitow started toward the burning flare. The aircraft was partially out of control and the flare was rolling wildly from side to side. Sgt. Levitow struggled forward despite the loss of blood from his many wounds and the partial loss of feeling in his right leg. Unable to grasp the rolling flare with his hands, he threw himself bodily upon the burning flare. Hugging the deadly device to his body, he dragged himself back to the rear of the aircraft and hurled the flare through the open cargo door. At that instant the flare separated and ignited in the air, but clear of the aircraft. Sgt. Levitow, by his selfless and heroic actions, saved the aircraft and its entire crew from certain death and destruction. Sgt. Levitow's gallantry, his profound concern for his fellowmen, at the risk of his life above and beyond the call of duty are in keeping with the highest traditions of the U.S. Air Force and reflect great credit upon himself and the Armed Forces of his country.

Epilogue: Levitow was the youngest and the only enlisted US Air Force personnel to receive the Medal. He died in 2000 after a long battle with cancer. On the night of February 24, 1969, Levitow was serving as loadmaster of an AC-47 gunship circling over the besieged United States Army base at Long Binh. The plane was firing thousands of rounds of ammunition at enemy forces and dropping magnesium flares to illuminate their positions for the American ground troops. Levitow, on his 181st combat sortie, was responsible for removing the flares from a rack, setting their controls, and passing them to a gunner, who would pull the safety pins, then throw the flares out a cargo door. The flares, attached to parachutes, ignited in midair 20 seconds later. In the fifth hour of the mission, a Vietcong mortar hit the plane's right wing and exploded, opening a hole two feet in diameter and sending shrapnel through the aircraft's skin. Levitow was hit by 40 pieces of shrapnel in his back and legs and was stunned from the blast's concussion. "It felt like a large piece of wood struck my side," he would recall. The other four crewmen in the cargo compartment were also wounded, as the pilot struggled to keep the plane under control. The gunner, Airman Ellis Owen, was about to toss a flare out the cargo door when he was wounded. The flare, fully armed and capable of burning through the plane's metal skin if it ignited, fell from his grasp. Levitow was moving another wounded crewman away from the open cargo door, when he saw the smoking flare rolling wildly from side to side among thousands of rounds of ammunition. An explosion seemed imminent. He reached three times for the 3-foot-long, 27-pound metal tube holding the flare, but it slipped from his grasp each time. Finally, he threw himself on it, hugged it to his body and dragged it to the open door, trailing blood from his wounds and having lost partial feeling in his right leg. He heaved the flare outside the door. A second or so later it ignited, but it was clear of the aircraft. The pilot, Major Kenneth Carpenter, made a safe landing at the Bien Hoa airbase with more than 3,500 shrapnel holes in the fuselage. "I had the aircraft in a 30-degree bank, and how Levitow ever managed to get to the flare and throw it out, I'll never know," Major Carpenter said. After being treated for his injuries, Airman Levitow flew an additional 20 combat missions. He was discharged from the Air Force in August 1969 as a sergeant and received the Medal of Honor from President Richard M. Nixon at the White House on May 14, 1970. The citation stated that he "saved the aircraft and its entire crew from certain death and destruction." Levitow, a native of Hartford, worked for federal and state veterans' agencies for more than two decades after leaving the Air Force. He was the legislative liaison and director of planning for the Connecticut Department of Veterans Affairs at the time of his death. He is survived by a son, John Jr., of Charlotte, N.C.; a daughter, Corrie Wilson, of Cromwell, Conn.; his mother, Marion Levitow, of South Windsor, Conn.; a sister, Mary-Lee Constatino, of East Hartford, Conn., and a grandson. In January 1998, in a ceremony at Long Beach, Calif., the Air Force named a C-17 Globemaster plane for him. The legend on the fuselage read: "The Spirit of Sgt. John L. Levitow."[202]

KARPELES, LEOPOLD
US Army — American Civil War

Rank and organization: Sergeant, Company E, 57th Massachusetts Infantry. Place and date: At Wilderness, Va., 6 May 1864. Entered service at: Springfield, Mass. Birth: Hungary. Date of issue: 30 April 1870.

Citation: While color bearer, rallied the retreating troops and induced them to check the enemy's advance.

Epilogue: Karpeles was born and raised in Prague and immigrated to the United States in 1840, when he was eleven. He lived initially in Galveston, Texas, with his older brother. Having served with, and mustered out of, the

46th Massachusetts Volunteers, Karpeles reenlisted with the 57th Massachusetts Volunteers, the unit he was assigned to at the time he engaged in the action for which he received the Medal.[203] Not much is known about Karpeles's life after leaving the Army. He lived in Washington, DC, for many years, was married to a woman named Henerietta, and died at the age of seventy at Garfield Hospital, Washington, DC, after undergoing surgery for obstructed bowels.[204] He is buried in the Washington Hebrew Cemetery.

TIBOR, RUBIN
US Army — Korean War

Citation: For conspicuous gallantry and intrepidity at the risk of his life above and beyond the call of duty: Corporal Tibor Rubin distinguished himself by extraordinary heroism during the period from July 23, 1950, to April 20, 1953, while serving as a rifleman with Company I, 8th Cavalry Regiment, 1st Cavalry Division in the Republic of Korea. While his unit was retreating to the Pusan Perimeter, Corporal Rubin was assigned to stay behind to keep open the vital Taegu-Pusan Road link used by his withdrawing unit. During the ensuing battle, overwhelming numbers of North Korean troops assaulted a hill defended solely by Corporal Rubin. He inflicted a staggering number of casualties on the attacking force during his personal 24-hour battle, single-handedly slowing the enemy advance and allowing the 8th Cavalry Regiment to complete its withdrawal successfully. Following the breakout from the Pusan Perimeter, the 8th Cavalry Regiment proceeded northward and advanced into North Korea. During the advance, he helped capture several hundred North Korean soldiers. On October 30, 1950, Chinese forces attacked his unit at Unsan, North Korea, during a massive nighttime assault. That night and throughout the next day, he manned a .30 caliber machine gun at the south end of the unit's line after three previous gunners became casualties. He continued to man his machine gun until his ammunition was exhausted. His determined stand slowed the pace of the enemy advance in his sector, permitting the remnants of his unit to retreat southward. As the battle raged, Corporal Rubin was severely wounded and captured by the Chinese. Choosing to remain in the prison camp despite offers from the Chinese to return him to his native Hungary, Corporal Rubin disregarded his own personal safety and immediately began sneaking out of the camp at night in search of food for his comrades. Breaking into enemy food storehouses and gardens, he risked certain torture or death if caught. Corporal Rubin provided not only food to the starving Soldiers, but also desperately needed medical care and moral support for the sick and wounded of the POW camp. His brave, selfless efforts were directly attributed to saving the lives of as many as forty of his fellow prisoners.

Epilogue: Sixty years ago, elements of the 11th Armored Division from Patton's own 3rd Army liberated the Mauthausen concentration camp in Austria. Among the prisoners freed was Tibor "Ted" Rubin, a 15-year-old Hungarian Jew, who had lost his father, mother, and sister to the camps. Five years later, Rubin joined the US Army and showed his appreciation for his newly adopted country by serving in the Korean War as a rifleman with Company I, 8th Cavalry Regiment, 1st Cavalry Division. On October 30, 1950, after an intense nighttime battle, in which Rubin manned a .30 caliber machine gun where three previous gunners had been killed, he was wounded and captured by the Chinese. He spent 30 months in a prisoner-of-war camp in North Korea. All these years later, Rubin has received recognition for his service and the valiant actions that set him apart from his comrades. He was awarded the Medal of Honor, September 23, 2007 at the White House and subsequently inducted into the Pentagon Hall of Heroes. Prior to entering the Army, Rubin worked as a butcher and later a liquor store manager. The Medal was presented to him by President George Bush at a White House ceremony.

APPENDIX A:

Sample Enlistment Record from Civil War Era

APPENDIX B:

Medal of Honor Recommendation Form:
Captain Jack Jacobs, Vietnam War

GENERAL ORDERS

No. 63

HEADQUARTERS
DEPARTMENT OF THE ARMY
WASHINGTON, DC, *27 October 1969*

AWARD OF THE MEDAL OF HONOR

By direction of the President, under the Joint Resolution of Congress approved 12 July 1862 (amended by act of 3 March 1863, act of 9 July 1918 and act of 25 July 1963), the Medal of Honor for conspicuous gallantry and intrepidity at the risk of life above and beyond the call of duty is awarded by the Department of the Army in the name of Congress to:

Captain *Jack H. Jacobs*, 142–36–7539 (then First Lieutenant), Infantry, United States Army, who distinguished himself on 9 March 1968 while serving as Assistant Battalion Advisor, 2d Battalion, 16th Infantry, 9th Infantry Division, Army of the Republic of Vietnam, during an operation in Kien Phong Province, Republic of Viet nam. The 2d Battalion was advancing to contact when it came under intense heavy machinegun and mortar fire from a Viet Cong battalion positioned in well-fortified bunkers. As the 2d Battalion deployed into attack formation its advance was halted by devastating fire. Captain *Jacobs*, with the command element of the lead company, called for and directed air strikes on the enemy positions to facilitate a renewed attack. Due to the intensity of the enemy fire and heavy casualties to the command group, including the company commander, the attack stopped and the friendly troops became disorganized. Although wounded by mortar fragments, Captain *Jacobs* assumed command of the allied company, ordered a withdrawal from the exposed position and established a defensive perimeter. Despite profuse bleeding from head wounds which impaired his vision, Captain *Jacobs*, with complete disregard for his own safety, returned under intense fire to evacuate a seriously wounded advisor to the safety of a wooded area where he administered life-saving first aid. He then returned through heavy automatic weapons fire to evacuate the wounded company commander. Captain *Jacobs* made repeated trips across the fire-swept open rice paddies evacuating wounded and their weapons. On three separate occasions, Captain *Jacobs* contacted and drove off Viet Cong squads who were searching for allied wounded and weapons, singlehandedly killing three and wounding several others. His gallant actions and extraordinary heroism saved the lives of one United States advisor and thirteen allied soldiers. Through his effort the allied company was restored to an effective fighting unit and prevented defeat of the friendly forces by a strong and determined enemy. Captain *Jacobs*, by his conspicuous gallantry and intrepidity in action in the highest traditions of the military service, has reflected great credit upon himself, his unit and the United States Army.

GO 63

By Order of the Secretary of the Army:

W. C. WESTMORELAND,
General, United States Army,
Chief of Staff.

Official:
KENNETH G. WICKHAM,
Major General, United States Army,
The Adjutant General.

Distribution:
To be distributed in accordance with DA Form 12–4 requirements.

FOR OFFICIAL USE ONLY

043
Ser: 5054
09 DEC 1968

EIGHTH ENDORSEMENT on DA Form 638 of 7 August 1968

From: Commander in Chief Pacific
To: Secretary of the Army
Via: Chairman, Joint Chiefs of Staff

Subj: Medal of Honor; recommendation for award of, case of Captain Jack H. JACOBS, OF108672, USA

1. Readdressed and forwarded concurring in COMUSMACV's recommendation that the Medal of Honor be awarded to Captain JACOBS.

JOHN S. McCAIN, Jr.

Copy to:
COMUSMACV. ←

MACAG-PD JACOBS, Jack H.   7th Ind
OF108672 (7 Aug 68)
SUBJECT: Recommendation for Award

HEADQUARTERS, UNITED STATES MILITARY ASSISTANCE COMMAND,
VIETNAM, APO 96222   24 NOV 1968

TO: Commander in Chief, Pacific, FPO 96610

1. Recommend approval of the Medal of Honor.

2. Request this headquarters (ATTN: MACAG-PD) be advised when final
action has been taken.

CREIGHTON W. ABRAMS
General, United States Army
Commanding

10 Incl
1. Witness Statement (MSG
    Berry)
2. Witness Statement (SSG
    Ramirez)
3. Witness Statement (SSG
    Waiwaiole)
4. Sketch of Battle Area
5. Overlays (6)
6. Msg from Co 2/16
7. Biographic Sketch (CPT Jacobs)
8. Summary of Recommendation
9. Proposed Citation
10. Certificate (MAJ Nolen)

12

FOR OFFICIAL USE ONLY

24 NOV 1968

MACAG-PD

SUBJECT: Recommendation for Award of the Medal of Honor

Commander in Chief
United States Army, Pacific
APO 96558

Forwarded in accordance with Department of the Army Message UNCLAS 794106 from AGPB-AC.

FOR THE COMMANDER:

1 Incl
Recm for Awd
(CPT J.H.JACOBS)

R. W. VINTON
Major, USA
Asst AG

FOR OFFICIAL USE ONLY

MACAG-PD JACOBS, Jack H. 7th Ind
OF103674 (7 Aug 68)
SUBJECT: Recommendation for Award

HEADQUARTERS, UNITED STATES MILITARY ASSISTANCE COMMAND,
VIETNAM, APO 96222 24 NOV 1968

TO: Commander in Chief, Pacific, FPO 96610

1. Recommend approval of the Medal of Honor.

2. Request this headquarters (ATTN: MACAG-PD) be advised when final
action has been taken.

Signed

CREIGHTON W. ABRAMS
General, United States Army
Commanding

10 Incl
1. Witness Statement (MSG
   Berry)
2. Witness Statement (SSG
   Ramirez)
3. Witness Statement (SSG
   Waiwaiole)
4. Sketch of Battle Area
5. Overlays (6)
6. Msg from Co 2/16
7. Biographic Sketch (CPT Jacobs)
8. Summary of Recommendation
9. Proposed Citation
10. Certificate (MAJ Nolen)

12

A7

GPAG-PA Jacobs, Jack H. 1st Ind
OF108672 (24 Nov 68)
SUBJECT: Recommendation for Award of the Medal of Honor

HQ, US Army, Pacific, APO San Francisco 96558   1 2 DEC 1968

TO: The Adjutant General, ATTN: AGPB-AB, Department of the Army,
     Washington, D. C. 20310

Recommend approval of award of the Medal of Honor.

FOR THE COMMANDER IN CHIEF:

1 Incl   MICHAEL S. DAVISON
nc   Lieutenant General, USA
                                Deputy Commander in Chief

Copy furnished:
COMUSMACV
ATTN: MACAG-PD
APO 96222

2

RECOMMENDATION FOR AWARD		PREPARE TO REACH APPROV- ING AUTHORITY IN DUPLICATE.	DATE
☐ HEROISM ☐ MERITORIOUS ACHIEVEMENT OR SERVICE (AR 672-5-1)			7 August 1968

THRU: Senior Advisor IV Corps USAAG APO 96215	TO: Department of the Army Washington, D.C. 20315	FROM: (Unit) Senior Advisor 2nd Bn, 16th Inf (ARVN) APO 96357

PART I – STATUS AT TIME OF RECOMMENDATION

1. LAST NAME – FIRST NAME – MIDDLE NAME	2. SERVICE NO.	3. GRADE	4. BRANCH (Or MOS II WO)
JACOBS, JACK H.	OF 108 672	Captain	Infantry

5. ORGANIZATION	6. RESIDENCE (Number, Street, City, and State)
Advisory Team 60, APO 96357	MACV

7. RECOMMENDED AWARD	8. POSTHUMOUS AWARD	9. NAME, RELATIONSHIP, AND ADDRESS OF NEXT OF KIN
Medal of Honor	☐ YES ☒ NO	Mrs. Karen Jacobs – Wife 106 Blandford Ave., Avenel, New Jersey

PART II – STATUS AT TIME OF ACT OR SERVICE

10. SERVICE NUMBER	11. GRADE	12. BRANCH (Or MOS II WO)	13. ORGANIZATION
OF 108 672	1LT	Infantry	Advisory Team 60, APO 96357.

14. HAS ALL SERVICE BEEN HONORABLE SUBSEQUENT TO THIS ACT OR SERVICE (If not, summarize on reverse side.)

☒ YES ☐ NO

15. IF PREVIOUS RECOMMENDATIONS WERE SUBMITTED FOR THIS ACT OR SERVICE, INDICATE TYPE OF AWARD RECOMMENDED, BY WHOM, WHEN, ACTION TAKEN, AND HEADQUARTERS

16. OTHER U.S. DECORATIONS RECEIVED (Include date and authority) (Do not list service medals; list foreign decorations only when same period as this recommendation.)

None

17. DID YOU HAVE PERSONAL KNOWLEDGE OF THE ACT OR SERVICE ☒ YES ☐ NO

PART III – RECOMMENDATION FOR AWARD FOR HEROISM

18. WERE YOU AN EYE WITNESS TO THE ACT	19. IF CERTIFICATES OR AFFIDAVITS OR EYE WITNESSES OR PERSONS HAVING PERSONAL KNOWLEDGE OF FACTS ARE NOT INCLOSED, GIVE REASONS
☒ YES ☐ NO	N/A

20. PERSONS IN IMMEDIATE PROXIMITY OR WHO ASSISTED IN ACT OR SHARED IN SAME HAZARD

a. FULL NAME	b. SERVICE NO.	c. GRADE	d. UNIT
NOLEN, James T.	086 578	MAJ	Adv Tm 60
WAIWAIOLE, Ainsley K.	RA 29041599	SSG	Adv Tm 60
RAMIREZ, Ramiro G.	RA 25845594	SSG	Adv Tm 60
BERRY, Robert J.	RA 13279199	MSG	Adv Tm 84 57N

21. IF ANY OF ABOVE PERSONS HAVE BEEN AWARDED OR RECOMMENDED FOR AN AWARD FOR HEROISM FOR PARTICIPATION IN THIS ACT, GIVE NAME AND TYPE OF AWARD

22. CONDITIONS UNDER WHICH ACT WAS PERFORMED

a. LOCATION	b. INCLUSIVE DATES	c. TIME OF DAY
Kien Phong Province, RVN	9 March 1968	1330

d. CHARACTER AND CONDITIONS OF TERRAIN AND WEATHER

Dry rice paddies, tree line along canals, weather clear and hot.

23. DESCRIBE ENEMY CONDITIONS (Morale, Proximity, Fire, Observation, Casualties, and Action; what the enemy was doing and what it did as the result of the act.)

Morale: High; Proximity: 100 - 250 meters; Observation: excellent; Fire: extremely accurate ASA, Automatic weapons and 82mm mortar.

Morale: high; Casualties: 2 US WIA, 5 ARVN KIA, 14 WIA. Unit was engaged in assault phase of search and destroy operation against heavily fortified positions.

25. WHAT WERE COMRADES WHO WERE IN IMMEDIATE PROXIMITY DOING — HOW DID THEY PARTICIPATE IN THE ACT

SSG Ramirez was in the same location with Captain Jacobs. Major Nolen, MSG Berry, and SSG Waiwaiole were with the other lead company engaged in the assault.

PART IV – RECOMMENDATION FOR AWARD FOR ACHIEVEMENT OR SERVICE

26. UNIT, HEADQUARTERS, OR SECTION IN WHICH DUTY WAS PERFORMED

27. INCLUSIVE DATES FOR WHICH RECOMMENDED

29. NOW IN SAME OR RELATED ASSIGNMENT

☐ NO   ☐ TO BE REASSIGNED ON OR ABOUT

☐ TO BE RETIRED ON OR ABOUT

28. SERVICE COMPLETED   ☐ YES

☐ TO BE COMPLETED ON OR ABOUT

☐ TO BE RELIEVED FROM AD ON OR ABOUT

PART V - TO BE USED FOR ALL RECOMMENDATIONS

30. NARRATIVE DESCRIPTION OF [X] DEED OR ACT ☐ ACHIEVEMENT PERFORMED OR SERVICE RENDERED

FOR AWARD FOR HEROISM: WAS ACT VOLUNTARY? DESCRIBE WHY ACT WAS OUTSTANDING AND IF IT WAS MORE THAN WAS NORMALLY EXPECTED, EXPLAIN HOW. IF IN AERIAL FLIGHT, DESCRIBE TYPE AND POSITION OF AIRPLANE, CREW POSITION OF INDIVIDUAL, AND ALL UNUSUAL CIRCUMSTANCES.

FOR AWARD FOR ACHIEVEMENT OR SERVICE: TITLE AND DUTIES OF ASSIGNMENT, INCLUDING CHARACTER OF SERVICE DURING PERIOD FOR WHICH RECOMMENDED (Give complete description of technical or specialized positions, including duties of assignment and relief) WHAT DID THE INDIVIDUAL DO THAT MERITS THE AWARD? WHY WAS THIS OUTSTANDING WHEN COMPARED TO OTHERS OF LIKE RANK AND EXPERIENCE IN SIMILAR POSITIONS?

Captain (then 1LT) Jack H. Jacobs, OF 108 672, United States Army, Distinguished himself by heroic action above and beyond the call of duty on 9 March 1968, while serving as Assistant Advisor, 2nd Battalion, 16th Infantry, 9th Division, Army of the Republic of Vietnam during Operations Dan Thang 34/KP. On this date, at approximately 1330 hours, Captain Jacobs and SSG Ramirez, NCO Advisor, were accompaning the battalion along a prescribed route of advance, (overlay #1) when it received heavy automatic weapons and mortar fire from a well-entrenched and bunkered Viet Cong Battalion. The Battalion Commander immediately deployed his unit, (overlay #2) for an attack with two companies abreast. Captain Jacobs and SSG Ramirez were with the company on the left. The attack commenced, but after moving only 50 meters, it came under extremely intense and accurate enemy automatic weapons, small arms and mortar fire, (overlay #3). During the ensuing moments, the company on the left suffered numerous casualties. Captain Jacobs then directed airstrikes against the enemy positions and the battalion was prepared to continue the attack. As the air-strikes were completed, the attack resumed only to be met again by extremely accurate and intense enemy fire. During this attack, Captain Jacobs received   (cont'd)

31. DESCRIBE EFFECTS OR RESULTS

Successful evacuation of dead and wounded from battlefield and boosted fighting spirit of ARVN unit.

32. RELATED POSITION OF PERSON INITIATING RECOMMENDATION TO PERSON BEING RECOMMENDED

Senior Advisor, 2nd Bn, 16th Inf (ARVN)

33. IF APPROVED, FORWARD AWARD FOR PRESENTATION TO

34. INCLOSURES (Include proposed citation, sketches, and eye witness statements when required.)

See attached sheet.

35. TYPED NAME, GRADE, BRANCH, AND TITLE OF PERSON INITIATING RECOMMENDATION

JAMES T. NOLEN, Major, Infantry

36. SIGNATURE

*OR DRAFT OR PROPOSED CITATION, AND CONTINUANCE OF ABOVE ITEMS, IF NECESSARY.

* U.S. GOVERNMENT PRINTING OFFICE : 1961 O—584283

multiple head wounds from an exploding enemy mortar round, and SSG Ramirez received multiple wounds in the legs, stomach, chest and head. Captain Jacobs's radio bearer received multiple leg wounds, and his counterpart was mortally wounded. Realizing that the unit was in a perilous position and precarious state of mind, he ordered the surviving soldiers to move to a wooded area and organize a defensive position. In the meantime, he took the radio from his bearer and dispite the pains of his own wounds and blurred vision caused by an eye wound, Captain Jacobs dragged and carried SSG Ramirez, now unconscious, out of the open battle area (overlay #4) under intense enemy automatic and small arms fire, to a wooded area, (overlay #4) and administered lifesaving first aid. He reported the situation to the Battalion Senior Advisor and was instructed to remain in position until help arrived.

The surviving troops were seized by terror and loss of confidence at the sudden crippling of key officers. Captain Jacobs realizing the danger, rapidly moved to the area where his radio bearer and counterpart were located and carried both of them, with their weapons, to the safe area, (overlay #4) hoping to inspire the Vietnamese soldiers to assist in the evacuation of all of the wounded or dead. Observing that the soldiers were still gripped by fear, Captain Jacobs crawled back to the open area searching for more wounded to extract. Upon arriving in the area, a squad of Viet Cong were also searching for weapons while at the same time killing the wounded soldiers. With complete disregard of his own life, Captain Jacobs singly assaulted the VC squad killing one, wounding several and causing them to scatter and take refuge in their well fortified positions. He then searched the area for weapons, finding ten. He then hid them in a near-by canal. Returning to the most seriously wounded comrades, he carried two (2) more back to the safe area, (overlay #4).

Though weakened by his wounds, Captain Jacobs, ignoring his wounds, again started back to the rest of the wounded soldiers. As he approached the open area, he received small arms fire by a squad of Viet Cong from the vicinity where the wounded lay. Captain Jacobs moved, while concealed by a heavy brush, to a position that provided him flanking fire on the enemy. From this position, he placed effective grazing fire on the enemy, killing two more VC and wounding one, again causing them to scatter and leave the area. Captain Jacob, exhausted and further weakened, doggedly moved the wounded and dead, two at a time, to the nearest woodline, (overlay #5) while the area was being covered with withering volumes of enemy mortar, cal. 50 machine gun, automatic and small arms fire. Captain Jacobs personally removed ten (10) more wounded and five (5) dead ARVN soldiers.

Once evacuated from the open area, he encouraged the wounded to remain silent, reassuring them that he would take them to a safe area. Captain Jacobs unassisted, proceeded to evacuate the wounded and dead to the area where the rest of the unit was located, (overlay #5). When he returned to carry the last of the dead, a Viet Cong squad, occupied a position that cut him off from the rest of the unit and proceeded to place violent smallarms fire on his position. Unhesitantly, Captain Jacobs called for gunship support and skillfully directed the strikes extremely close (15 meters) to his position with pinpoint accuracy to eliminate the obstacle and clear his escape route. Once the route was cleared, he completed the evacuation.

On two occasions while moving the ARVN soldiers to the safe area, Captain Jacobs blacked out because of the pains his wounds and the loss of blood. Nevertheless, by sheer determination and devotion to duty, he continued to evacuate the wounded, maintain his professional manner, encourage the remainder of the unit to place effective fire on the well bunkered enemy, coordinate gunship strikes, while continuously keeping the Battalion Senior Advisor abreast of the situation. When Senior Advisor and Battalion Commander arrived at the area of the affected unit, Captain Jacobs was caring for the wounded and refused evacuation for himself until he was certain all wounded had received medical attention. Finally, he was evacuated at approximately 1630 hours. His actions of unsurpassed valor above and beyond the call of duty were directly responsible for saving the lives of one (1) US Advisor and fourteen (14) fellow soldiers and prevented the defeat of friendly forces by a strong and determined enemy force.

Captain Jacobs conspicuous gallantry and intrepidity at the risk of his own life above and beyond the call of duty were in the highest traditions of the United States Army.

9 Incls
nc
  1. - Witness Statement (SGT Berry)
  2. - Witness Statement (SGT Ramirey)
  3. - Witness Statement (SGT Waiwaiole)
  4. - Sketch of Battle Area
  5. - Overlays 1 - 6
  6. - Msg from Co 2/16
  7. - Biographic Sketch
  8. - Summary of Recommendation
  9. - Proposed Citation

MACV-9TH-SA JACOBS, Jack H.   1st Ind
OF 108 672 (27 Apr 68)
SUBJECT: Recommendation for Decoration for Valor.

HEADQUARTERS, 9th Infantry Division Advisory Detachment, Advisory Team 60,
APO 96357, 11 June 1968.

TO: Senior Advisor, IV Corps Advisory Group, Advisory Team 96, APO 96215

1. This recommendation has been delayed for the reason that the unit concerned has been under the operational control of the 44th Special Tactical Zone
for the past six months. This detachment had been under the impression that
the recommendation was originated with the Headquarters, 44th Special Tactical
Zone.

2. Recommend approval.

10 Incls   HARRY C. SMYTHE JR.
    1. Witness Statement   Colonel, Armor
    2. Witness Statement   Senior Advisor
    3. Witness Statement
    4. Witness Statement
    5. Message
    6. Legend
    7. Biographical Sketch
    8. Summary of Recommendation
    9. Proposed Citation
   10. Overlay

A14

MACV-9TH-AD JACOBS, Jack H.   3d Ind
OF108672 (27 Apr 68)
SUBJECT: Recommendation for Award

HEADQUARTERS, 9TH INFANTRY DIVISION ADVISORY DETACHMENT, Advisory Team 60,
APO 96357, 14 August 1968.

Senior Advisor, USAAG, IV CTZ, Advisory Team 96, APO 96215

Preceding indorsement complied with.

FOR THE SENIOR ADVISOR:

9 Incls   ROBERT H. CROWELL
nc   Captain, Infantry
                                 Administrative Officer

A15

MACCZ-IV-1 JACOBS, Jack H. 4th Ind
OF108672 (27 Apr 68)
SUBJECT: Recommendation for Decoration for Valor

HEADQUARTERS, US ARMY ADVISORY GROUP, IV CTZ, ADVISORY TEAM 96, APO 96215
10 Oct 68

TO: Senior Advisor, 9th Infantry Division Advisory Detachment, Advisory
     Team 60, APO 96357

1. The recommendation for CPT Jack H. Jacobs is returned for the following reasons:

     a. Discrepancies of statements. The basic recommendation indicates
that CPT Jacobs dragged 1 US Advisor (WIA), 14 ARVN soldiers (WIA) and 5
ARVN soldiers (KIA) to safety. The statements of MSG Robert J. Berry indicates that CPT Jacobs removed 23 WIA and 6 KIA to safety and the statement of SSG Ainsley K. Waiwaiole indicates that CPT Jacobs removed 14 WIA
and 5 KIA to safety.

     b. There is a lack of eyewitness statements. Although the statements
of SSG Ramiro G. Ramirez is listed as an eyewitness statement he was re-
portedly unconscious during most of this time. The eyewitness statements
do not include all of the action which CPT Jacobs was involved.

2. It is requested that the discrepancies be explained or corrected and
that more eyewitness statements be obtained. If there are no US personnel
who saw the action, translated Vietnamese statements are acceptable.

3. The Senior Advisor has indicated that the foregoing is required prior
to recommending approval of this award.

FOR THE SENIOR ADVISOR:

9 Incl
nc
KENNETH E. FEE
MAJ, AGC
Adjutant General

FOR OFFICIAL USE ONLY

MACCZ-IV-60-AD JACOBS, Jack H. 5th Ind
OF108672 (27 Apr 68)
SUBJECT: Recommendation for Decoration for Valor

HEADQUARTERS, 9TH INFANTRY DIVISION ADVISORY DETACHMENT, Advisory Team 60, APO 96357, 21 Oct 68.

TO: Senior Advisor, US Army Advisory Group, IVCTZ, Advisory Team 96, APO 96215.

1. Resubmitted for approval.

2. Discrepancies listed in 4th Indorsement have been explained or corrected.

3. Certificate of Major James T. Nolen is attached explaining the discrepancies. There are no other US or Vietnamese personnel that can make an eyewitness statement.

FOR THE SENIOR ADVISOR:

JACKIE G. JONES
Captain, Infantry
Administrative Officer

10 Incl
Added 1 incl
10. Certificate

FOR OFFICIAL USE ONLY

MACCZ-IV-AGA JACOBS, Jack H. 6th Ind
OF108672 (27 Apr 68)
SUBJECT: Recommendation for Decoration for Valor

HEADQUARTERS, UNITED STATES ARMY ADVISORY GROUP, IV CTZ, ADVISORY TEAM 96,
APO 96215   1 NOV 1968

TO: Commander, United States Military Assistance Command, Vietnam, ATTN:
MACAG-PD, APO 96222

1. Recommend approval of the Distinguished Service Cross.

2. Although CPT Jacobs displayed extraordinary heroism on 9 Mar 68 with clear
disregard for his personal safety, his actions do not appear to meet the criteria of conspicuous gallantry and intrepidity established for award of the
Medal of Honor in Annex A to MACV Directive 672-1.

10 Incl   G. S. ECKHARDT
nc   Major General, USA
                                           Senior Advisor

A18

STATEMENT

On 9 March 1968 while helping to operate an forward command post for a combat operation named Dan Thang 34 Kien Phong Province Vietnam I, MSG Robert J. Berry, was manning the command radio for the operation. At approximately 1330 hrs 2/16 Bn came under heavy 82mm fire and automatic weapons fire in the vicinity of WS 77/5/7 Lt Jacobs' Battalion had the mission of attacking across an open field where an well entrenched and bunkered VC Battalion opened fire on the lead company of the Battalion, of which SSG Ramriez and LT Jacobs were advisors. The initial firing by the VC Battalion cut down either wounding or killing most of the lead company of the battalion who at this time were exposed in the open field. Although LT Jacobs was wounded by enemy mortar fire, and suffered a head wound, which effected his sight, he found SGT Ramierz who was also wounded by mortar fire in the head, chest, stomach and arm, and could not walk because of unconsciousness. LT Jacobs managed to drag him out of the open field back to a wooded area. Upon reaching the wooded area he lost his sight, knowing that his only chance for any help that might be forthcomming he had to crawl back to the area where the Sergeant was initially wounded and probe around until he found the radio. Upon securing the radio he was instrumental in marking the positions for an airstrike while the Airstrike was going on and while the VC's were still firing at the exposed troops LT Jacobs continued to crawl around the field pulling the dead and wounded back to the wooded area. At one point his Battalion Senior Advisor Maj Nolen who at this time was pinned down by mortar fire told LT Jacobs that he was trying to move the rest of the Battalion into a position of where he could come to his aid, told him (LT Jacobs) to stay put in the wooded area; but LT Jacobs explained that he, although wounded, and his sight would come and go that he was one of the few men left that was capable at this time of helping the men of the lead company who were wounded and needed help, so with complete disregard for his own life LT Jacobs continued to recover the dead and wound while under constant mortar and automatic small arms fire. When Maj Nolen was able to reach LT Jacobs and now the almost annihilated company with help, he had to personally evacuate LT Jacobs because LT Jacobs did not want to leave the area as long as some of his men were still there. LT Jacobs was personally responsible for dragging 23 WIA's and six KIA back to this wooded area under intense fire. This determination is indicative of LT Jacobs' courageous actions throughout the seige of the 2 Bn 16th Inf Regt, which is considered, by the undersigned, as conpicuous gallantry and intrepidity at the risk of his own life above and beyond the call of duty.

ROBERT J. BERRY
RA13279199
MSG E-8

A19

EYE WITNESS STATEMENT

On 9 March 1968 we went out on an operation. Went from Cao Lanh Ferry to the Line of Departure by boats. 1LT Jacobs and myself were with the lead company and as we landed we searched the area and found nothing but a couple of old folks that said one platoon of VC were waiting to ambush us at checkpoint 6. We went ahead as we came up on 6 we saw some men run across the field into the woodline. We opened up on them and got fire back. Counterpart and 1LT Jacobs got together and sent out flank security and not a minute too soon cause we got hit from the side too. We made contact about 1000 hours in the morning and we were still pinned down at 1400 hours. By this time there was not a platoon of VC but about a battalion of VC. We were getting hit by 60s, 82MM Mortar, and many machine guns. At this time 1LT Jacobs got up to see what was going on and as we started to move a mortar round hnded between all of us. 1LT Jacobs was hit in the head and could hardly see and he saw his counterpart lying in the water and nobody would help him so 1LT Jacobs jump in and got him out and to the rear for first aid. At this time 1LT Jacobs got on the radio and call in for MEDEVAC. All this time he could hardly see what he was doing all the time running back and forth to keep the troops from falling back river. Then XO was hit when he got the MEDEVAC. He helped move all the wounded men back so that they would be picked up. All this helped the troops. "THIS IS A TRUE STATE-MENT."

A TRUE COPY

RAMIRO G. RAMIREZ

JAMES T. NOLEN
Major, Infantry

rcl 2

A20

EYE WITNESS STATEMENT

On 9 March 1968, the 2d Battalion, 16th Infantry Regiment, 9th (ARVN) Infantry Division, was participating in Operation Dan Thang 34/KP. At 0800 hours the battalion departed Cao Lanh by vehicle convoy to the Tan Thich ferry site. From this point the battalion embarked on LST's enroute to the line of departure. The battalion crossed the line of departure at approximately 0945 hours. The battalion advanced along its assigned route with no contact until approximately 1330 hours, at coordinate WS 771517. Contact was made with an estimated Viet Cong Battalion. 1LT Jack H. Jacobs and SSG Ramiro G. Ramirez were with the lead company. MAJ James T. Nolon and myself, SSG Ainsley Waiwaiole, were with the battalion command group. The battalion received the order to attack across an open field approximately 150 to 200 meters wide. The battalion advanced approximately 50 meters when it came under intense enemy automatic weapons, small arms, and 82MM Mortar fire. The battalion was unable to advance and the company on the left was pinned down. At this time an airstrike was requested and three (3) were received. At approximately 1500 hours the first airstrike came in and Lieutenant Jacobs was coordinating the airstrikes from his position. After the airstrikes ended the battalion attempted another assault. The battalion once again was stopped by intense enemy fire and Lieutenant Jacobs, SSG Ramirez, and 13 Vietnamese were wounded and five (5) killed. Lieutenant Jacobs received multiple fragment wounds in the head and SSG Ramirez received wounds in the leg, stomach, chest, left arm, and head. Lieutenant Jacobs completely ignored his wounds and began to run and crawl across the open field administering first aid to the wounded and dragging them back to the safety of a woodline approximately 50 meters to the South. All this time Lieutenant Jacobs was taking heavy fire from two (2) 50 Caliber Machine Guns, small arms, hand grenades, and 82 MM Mortar. Lieutenant Jacobs completely disregarded his own safety as he repeatedly ran back into the open field to retrieve the dead and wounded. Lieutenant Jacobs pulled back fourteen (14) wounded and five (5) dead; returning them from the open field to the evacuation area. Only after he was sure that all the dead and wounded had been taken care of did he allow himself to be evacuated. The evacuation was completed at approximately 1630 hours by SEA HCIM 35 in an insecure area. When the MEDEVAC was completed the battalion pulled back into a tight defensive perimeter and requested resupply of ammunition. At 1800 hours the battalion received the order to return to Cao Lanh. The battalion closed into base camp at approximately 2030 hours.

Ainsley K. Waiwaiole
AINSLEY K. WAIWAIOLE

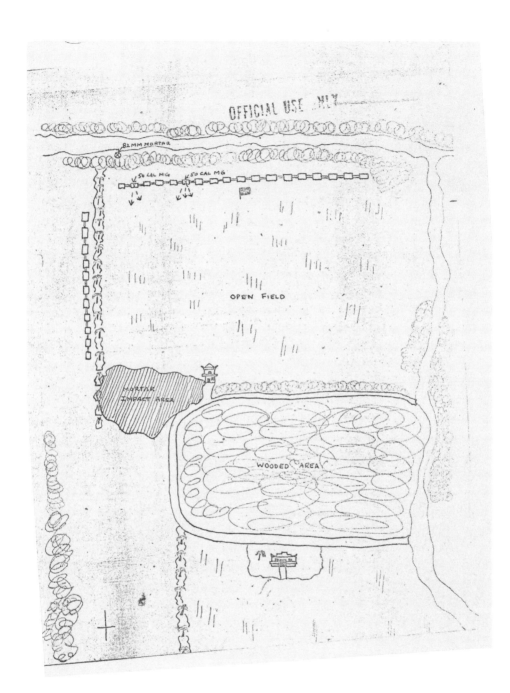

81MM MORTAR

50 CAL MG   50 CAL MG

OPEN FIELD

MORTAR
IMPACT AREA

WOODED AREA

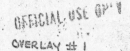

OVERLAY # 1

Battalion moving on prescribed
route of advance.

A23

FOR OFFICIAL USE ONLY

OVERLAY #2

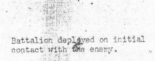

Battalion deployed on initial
contact with the enemy.

OVERLAY #3

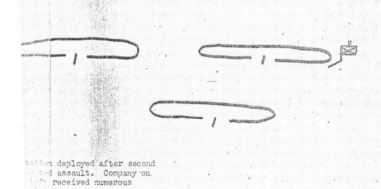

...tion deployed after second
...d assault. Company on.
...t received numerous
...ualties.

OVERLAY # 4

Route CPT Jacobs used to evacuate
fellow Advisor, counterpart,
radio bearer and two of the most
seriously wounded. Total:
1 US, 4 ARVN.

OVERLAY #5

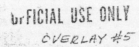

Route CPT Jacobs used to evacuate 10 more
wounded & 5 dead. Moving all of them to
the woodline, then to safe area, taking
two at a time.

A27

OVERLAY # 56

FOR OFFICIAL USE ONLY

FROM: BATTALION 2/16/HQ

TO . : 44TH SPECIAL ZONE HQS/G - 1

INFO: REGIMENT 16/1/HQ AND SENIOR 16TH REGIMENT ADVISOR

MSG NO. 749/TD2/16/1/HQ.

FIRST LIEUTENANT JACK H. JACOBS, 108672, DEPUTY ADVISOR OF 2/16 BATTALION IS HEREWITH CITED FOR EXTRAORDINARY HEROISM AND GALLANTRY ABOVE AND BEYOND THE CALL OF DUTY DURING OPERATION DAN THANG 33/KP 9 MARCH 1968, APPROXIMATELY EIGHT (8) KILOMETERS SOUTH EAST OF CAO LANH, KIEN PHONG PROVINCE, VIETNAM. (EXACT LOCATION WS771517)

DESPITE BEING SERIOUSLY WOUNDED BY VC 82MM MORTAR FRAGMENTS, FIRST LIEUTENANT JACOBS SUCCESSFULY EVACUATED THIRTEEN (13) WOUNDED AND FIVE (5) DEAD VIETNAMESE SOLDIERS ACROSS A ONE HUNDRED METERS OF OPEN FIELD, UNDER HEAVY FIRE FROM TWO (2) FIFTY CALIBER MACHINE GUNS, GRENADE LAUNCHERS, 82MM MORTAR, AND MISCELANEOUS SMALL ARMS.

ALTHOUGH SUFFERING FROM A HEAD WOUND, LIEUTENANT JACOBS MAIN- TAINED COMMUNICATIONS WITH SUPPORTING ELEMENTS THROUGHOUT THE ENGAGEMENT WITH THE VIET CONG BATTALION, AND REFUSED TO BE EVACUATED UNTIL ALL ELEMENTS OF THE 2/16 WERE EXTRICATED FROM THE AMBUSH.

LIEUTENANT JACOBS CALM COURAGE, INTREPID ACTIONS, AND OUTSTANDING GALLANTRY DURING THIS ACTION ARE A CREDIT TO THE ARMED FORCES OF THE UNITED STATES, AND IT IS RESPECTFULLY REQUESTED THAT HE BE RECOMMENDED FOR THE MEDAL OF HONOR OF THE U.S. ARMED FORCES.

(XⓄ ÔNG - ✕Ⓞ) ĐIÊN

- &&& -

NOI   GOI : TIEU DOAN 2/16/HQ

NOI   NHAN : CO-VAN-TRUONG TRD16/BB.

THONG BAO : TRUNG DOAN 16/1/HQ

FROM: BATTALION 2/16 BANR VEAN SCOS : ___8/TD2/16/1/HQ #

T.T.K.T. # TRONG CUOOCV HANHL QAAN ZAAN THEANIS 33/KP NGHYL 09-3-68 #

TIEEUR DOANL DAX CHAMV MANHV V.C. TAIV VS 771517 LUCS C916000/3/68 #

THWS 1 : TR/UY JACK H. JACOBS OF 100672 # COOS VAANS FOS TIEEUR DOANL

2/16 # DI VOUIS DAIV DOOIV DAAUL BEEN CAEHS TRAIS # TIEENS CHIEEMS NUCY

TIEEU QA MOOTV KHOANGR DAATS TROONGS LOOIS 200 TH'OCS # ZWOIS LANL NWA

DANV CUAR V.C. # TR/UY JACOBS TOR RA TICHS CWCV TRONG MOIV HOATV DOONGV#

DAX XIN THWCV THLANG VAL FANR LWCV YEEMR TRONV # DOOMGL THOMIL H'WONGS ZAANV

OANH KICHS VIV TRIS DICHV RAATS CHINHS XACS # GAAY CHO DICHV MOOTV SCOS

CHEETS VAL BIV THWONG DANGS KEER # HOWN THEES NHAX # AUL DAY BIV TH'ONG

OWR DAAUL BOWIR MANHR DANV 82 LY CUAR V.C. # TR/UY JACOBS VAANX DIEEML

TINHX TANGR THWONG JUPS CHO 13 BINH SIX BIV TH'ONG VAL 05 BINH SIX TW

TRAANV RA KHU VWCV TWONG DOOIS AN MINH ZWOIS HOAR LWCV HUNGL RAAUV CUAR

DICHV GOS CAR 02 KHAAUR DAIV LIEEN 50 VAL SUNGG COOIS 82 LY GUNGL FONGS

LWUV # NGOAIL RA # TR/UY JACOBS CONL LAL MOOTV COONGV SW VIEEN DEACS

LWCV CHO TIEEUR DOANL TRONG THOWIL JAN QA # DAX XIN TIEEPS TEES DANV

ZWOCV # TANGR THWONG VAL YEEMR TROWV CHO TIEEUR DOANL RAAYS NWUX NIEEUV #

THWS 2 : DEER TWONGR THWONGR X'NGS DANGS COONG LAO VAL TINH THAANL QAR CANR

TAANV TUYV VOWIS NHIEEMV VUV TREEN # KINRS XIN THIEEUS TAS COOS VAANS

TRWONGR TD16/BB AAN THWONGR HUY CHWONG BANH ZWV CUAR QAAN DOOIV HOA KYL

CHO TR/UY JACOBS # HEETS #

BIOGRAPHICAL SKETCH

NAME: Jack Howard Jacobs RANK: 1LT BASIC BRANCH: INF CONTROL BRANCH: INF
SN: OF 108 672 DOR: 6 Jun 67 DOB: 2 Aug 45 POB: Brooklyn, N.Y.
HOME ADDRESS: 106 Blandford Ave, Avenel, N.J. UNIT: Advisory Team 60
       07001   APO San Francisco 96357
FATHER: David Jacobs (AGE: 49) FATHER'S OCCUPATION: Electrical Engineer
       6 Marie Rd, Fords, N.J.   Western Electric Co.
       08863   222 Broadway, NY., N.Y.
MOTHER: Mildred Rosenblatt Jacobs (AGE: 47) WIFE: Karen Markulin Jacobs (AGE: 24)
       Address same as above   106 Blandford Ave, Avenel, N.J.
                                                      07001
CHILDREN: David Mark Jacobs (Son, AGE: 1)   RELIGION: Jewish
          Heather Renee Jacobs (Daughter, AGE: 3½)
HEIGHT: 5'4" WEIGHT: 125 lbs. CLEARANCE: Secret

Attended public schools in Jackson Heights, N.Y., Long Island City, N.Y., and
Fords, N.J. Attended Woodbridge High School, Woodbridge, N.J. Graduated June 1962.
Entered Rutgers University in September, 1962. Bachelor of Arts Degree in Political
Science from Rutgers University. Commissioned 2LT, United States Army Reserve on
1 June 1966. Commissioned 2LT, Infantry, Regular Army on 6 June 1966. Through
Senior ROTC program at Rutgers University, New Brunswick, N.J., attained grade of
Cadet LTC. Assigned to Company "C", 2d Battalion (ABN), 505th Infantry, 82d Airborne
Division, Fort Bragg, North Carolina, for duty as Platoon Leader. Attended Airborne
School; Infantry Officer Basic Course; Jumpmaster School; Air Transportation Planning
Course (Fort Eustis, Va.); Combat Operations Specialist Course (Elgin AFB, Fla.) -
received additional MOS 72163); Basic Forward Air Controller School (Elgin AFB, Fla.);
MATA Course (Fort Bragg, N.C.); Vietnamese Language School (Fort Bliss, Texas) -
Honor Graduate.
     Served as Platoon Leader with Company "C", 2/505, until approximately January
1967. Served as S-3 Air, 2/505, from January 1967 until May 1967. Arrived Republic
of Vietnam 6 September 1967. Assigned duty as Battalion Advisor, 2d Battalion, 16th
Infantry Regiment, 9th Infantry Division (ARVN). Acted as Senior Advisor from
approximately 28 October 1967 until late February 1968. Participated in over 120
Combat operations. Wounded on 9 March 1968. Sent to 3d Surgical Hospital, Dong Tam,
RVN; 9th Medical Bn, Dong Tam, RVN; 24th Evacuation Hospital, Long Binh, RVN. Returned
to duty 16 March 1968 as Assistant G-3 Advisor, 9th Infantry Division (ARVN), where
presently assigned.

A31

NAME: Jack H. Jacobs

STATUS: Assistant Battalion Advisor

ORGANIZATION: Advisory Team 60, APO 96215

NEXT OF KIN: Mrs. Karen Jacobs (Wife)
106 Blandford Ave, Avenel, New Jersey

PERSON WHO ASSISTED: N/A

CONDITIONS UNDER WHICH ACT PERFORMED

LOCATION: Kien Phong Province, RVN

DATE: 9 March 1968

TERRAIN: Dry rice paddies, tree line along canals

WEATHER: Clear and hot

ENEMY CONDITION: Morale high; Proximately 100-250 meters; Observation excellent;
Fire extremely accurate; Weapons consisted of ASA, automatic
weapons, 82mm mortar.

FRIENDLY CONDITIONS: Morale high. Unit was engaged in assault of search and
destroy operation against heavily fortified positions.
(2 US WIA, 5 ARVN KIA, 14 ARVN WIA)

NARRATIVE DESCRIPTION OF GALLANT CONDUCT

At 1330, 9 March 1968, the 2d Battalion, 16th Infantry (ARVN) was moving along
a prescribed route of march during a search and destroy operation when it suddenly came under heavy automatic weapons and mortar fire from a well entrenched
and bunkered Viet Cong Battalion. When the Battalions assault was halted,
because of extremely intense and accurate enemy assorted small arms, automatic
and mortar fire, it received numerous casualties to key personnel, including
CPT Jacobs and his enlisted advisor. CPT Jacobs received multiple head wounds,
which caused immediate vision damage, while his assistant received multiple
wounds in the legs, stomach, chest and head. He reorganized the stricken unit
into defensive positions, carried his enlisted assistant to a covered area
and administered life saving first aid. To prevent panic, he rushed to the open
area to extract his counterpart and radio bearer and carried them to a safe area,
hoping to inspire the Vietnamese to assist in the evacuation of the wounded and
dead. When this failed, he decided to evacuate as many as he could. Returning
to the devestated area, he assaulted a VC squad who were searching for weapons
and killing the wounded, killing one and wounding several. He cleared the
area of friendly weapons and equipment and proceeded to evacuate the most

seriously wounded, dragging and carrying two at a time to the safe area. When his efforts were hampered by another VC squad, he placed effective fire on the enemy killing two more VC and wounding one. CPT Jacobs then evacuated ten (10) more friendly wounded and five (5) dead ARVN soldiers to a covered area in a nearby treeline. He then proceeded to move them two at a time, to where the rest of the unit was located. During this evacuation a VC squad cut him off from the rest of the unit and placed violent small arms fire on his position. CPT Jacobs called for gunship support and skillfully directed the strikes extremely close to his position to eliminate the obstacle and clear his escape route. On two occasions during the evacuation, CPT Jacobs blacked out because of his wounds and by sheer determination and devotion to duty he continued to evacuate the wounded, maintained his professional manner, encouraging his comrads, coordinated gunship strikes, while continuously keeping higher headquarters abreast of the situation. Only after being assured that all casualties had been cared for and that evacuation had been planned, did he allow himself to be evacuated from the battle field.

PROPOSED CITATION

FOR CONSPICUOUS GALLANTRY AND INTREPIDITY AT THE RISK OF LIFE ABOVE AND
BEYOND THE CALL OF DUTY: CAPTAIN (THEN FIRST LIEUTENANT) JACK H. JACOBS,
OF 108 672, UNITED STATES ARMY, DISTINGUISHED HIMSELF BY ACTION ABOVE
AND BEYOND THE CALL OF DUTY ON 9 MARCH 1968 WHILE SERVING AS ASSISTANT
BATTALION ADVISOR, 2D BATTALION, 16TH REGIMENT, 9TH INFANTRY DIVISION,
ARMY OF THE REPUBLIC OF VIETNAM DURING A SEARCH AND DESTROY OPERATION
IN KIEN PHONG PROVINCE, REPUBLIC OF VIETNAM. ON THIS DATE, THE BATTALION
WAS ON A SEARCH AND DESTROY MISSION, MOVING ALONG A PRESCRIBED ROUTE OF
ADVANCE WHEN IT CAME UNDER HEAVY AUTOMATIC WEAPONS AND MORTAR FIRE FROM
AN ESTIMATED VIET CONG BATTALION IN HEAVILY BUNKERED POSITIONS. THE
BATTALION DEPLOYED FOR AN ATTACK BUT WAS HALTED BY THE INTENSITY AND
EXTREME ACCURACY OF ENEMY FIRE. CAPTAIN JACOBS CALLED FOR AND DIRECTED
AIR STRIKES ON THE ENEMY POSITIONS WHILE THE BATTALION PREPARED TO CON-
TINUE THE ATTACK. AS THE ATTACK CONTINUED, THE INTENSITY OF ENEMY FIRE
INCREASED, HALTING THE ADVANCE AND CAUSING NUMEROUS CASUALTIES TO THE
COMMAND ELEMENT. ALTHOUGH PAINFULLY WOUNDED BY AN EXPLODING MORTAR ROUND,
CAPTAIN JACOBS, IGNORING HIS WOUNDS, ASSUMED CONTROL OF THE UNIT AND OR-
GANIZED THE TROOPS INTO A DEFENSIVE POSTURE. WITH COMPLETE DISREGARD FOR
HIS OWN PERSONAL SAFETY AND DESPITE MULTIPLE HEADWOUNDS, WHICH IMPAIRED
HIS VISION, CAPTAIN JACOBS DRAGGED AND CARRIED A SERIOUSLY WOUNDED FELLOW
ADVISOR 100 METERS ACROSS OPEN RICE PADDIES TO A SECURE WOODED AREA AND
ADMINISTERED LIFE SAVING FIRST AID, THE ENTIRE TIME BEING EXPOSED TO THE
INTENSE ENEMY FIRE. REALIZING THE TROOPS WERE SEIZED BY TERROR AND LOSS
OF CONFIDENCE AT THE SUDDEN CRIPPLING OF KEY OFFICERS, CAPTAIN JACOBS,

CERTIFICATE

Although it is not indicated anywhere on the recommendation, the narrative description is the eye witness statement of myself, Major James T. Nolen, I was the Battalion Senior Advisor and I was an eye witness to the actions of Captain Jacobs. I am the recommending official on the recommendation.

The discrepancies of statements has been corrected on the basic recommendation The correct number of casualties Captain Jacobs recovered are: One (1) US MIA (SSG Ramirez), thirteen (13) ARVN WIA, and five (5) ARVN KIA. The reason for the discrepancy in MSG Berry's statement is that he included the entire number of casualties suffered by both battalions involved in the operation. The 41st Ranger Battalion (ARVN) was also involved in the operation, however, they were moving on a different axis. MSG Berry was not an eye witness, however, he is qualified to make a statement because he was monitoring the command radio at the field command post.

SSG Waiwaiole's eye witness statement states "Lieutenant Jacobs pulled back fourteen (14) wounded and five (5) dead;" The 14 wounded included SSG Ramirez.

SSG Ramirez is qualified to make an eyewitness statement. Although he did lose consciousness on two occasions, he regained his consciousness and called me several times during the action explaining what Captain Jacobs was doing and asking for a medical evacuation helicopter. SSG Ramirez made his eye witness statement while in a hospital somewhere in Saigon.

The eye witness statements of the two enlisted men do not include all of the action in which Captain Jacobs was involved because of their limited education and inability to express themselves thoroughly in writing.

A Vietnamese message is included with the recommendation. Even though it is not classified as an eye witness statement, it is made by the Battalion Commander who was present and was an eye witness to the entire action. This is substantiated by his signature and official seal on the Vietnamese message.

There is no one else, Vietnamese or American, who can make an eyewitness statement other than Captain Jacobs.

JAMES T. NOLEN
Major, Infantry

DISPOSITION FORM

FOR OFFICIAL USE ONLY

(AR 340-15)

REFERENCE OR OFFICE SYMBOL	SUBJECT		
MACAG-PD	Recommendation for Award		

THRU ACofS, J1	FROM AG	DATE 22 NOV 1968	CMT 1
TO CofS		MAJ Vinton/gmm/2274	

1. PURPOSE. To obtain the signature of COMUSMACV on the forwarding indorsement at Tab A to the recommendation for award at Tab B.

2. DISCUSSION.

    a. At Tab B is a recommendation for award of the Medal of Honor to Captain Jack H. Jacobs, OF108672, United States Army.

    b. The recommendation has been reviewed by the Awards and Decorations Board, this headquarters. Notwithstanding the recommendation of the SA, IV CTZ, the board recommends approval of the Medal of Honor. This recommendation was concurred in by the ACofS, J1 (Tab C). Captain Jacobs, although seriously wounded, and hampered in the performance of his duty by blurred vision, found the strength and determination to successfully extract 18 wounded and deceased soldiers from the battlefield. His conspicuous gallantry in action and intrepidity fulfills the criteria for award of the Medal of Honor.

    c. The recommendations of intervening headquarters are as follows:

    SA, 9th Inf Div Adv Det, Adv Tm 60   MH
    SA, IV CTZ, Adv Tm 96   DSC

3. RECOMMENDATION. That indorsement at Tab A be signed by COMUSMACV and correspondence returned to this office for dispatch.

3 Incl
as

SIDNEY GRITZ
Colonel, USA
Adjutant General

Signed/Approved by COMUSMACV
Dispatched 24 NOV 1968

FOR OFFICIAL USE ONLY

DA FORM 2496
1 FEB 62

REPLACES DD FORM 96, EXISTING SUPPLIES OF WHICH WILL BE ISSUED AND USED UNTIL 1 FEB 63 UNLESS SOONER EXHAUSTED.

PPC-Japan

DISPOSITION FORM

(AR 340-15)

REFERENCE OR OFFICE SYMBOL	SUBJECT
MACAG-PD	Recommendation of the Board Session #135A

TO ACofS, J1	FROM MACV Awds & Dec Bd	DATE 17 November 1968	CMT 1
		MAJ Pfaff/bgw/4138	

1. The Awards and Decorations Board, MACV, met at 1500 hours, 16 November 1968 to consider the recommendation at Tab B. The following members were present:

COL Gritz, MACAG, Acting President
COL Frauenheim, MACT, Member
COL Lincoln, MACJ6, Member
MAJ Pfaff, MACAG, Recorder

2. The recommendation of the Board is as indicated at Tab A.

3. Recommend approval of the Board's recommendation.

2 Incl
as

SIDNEY GRITZ
Colonel, USA
Acting President

TO AG ATTN: MACAG-PD	FROM ACofS, J1	DATE 19 NOV 1968	CMT 2

Approved.

2 Incl
nc

FRANK B. CLAY
Brigadier General, USA
Assistant Chief of Staff, J1

DA FORM 2496
1 FEB 62

REPLACES DD FORM 96, EXISTING SUPPLIES OF WHICH WILL BE
ISSUED AND USED UNTIL 1 FEB 63 UNLESS SOONER EXHAUSTED.

FPC-Japan

A37

$\mathbf{b}$ O A R D   A C T I O N   L I S T

TAB	NAME	GRADE	MIL SVC	AWARD RECM	BOARD RECM
B	JACOBS, JACK H.	CPT	USA	MH	*MH*

REMARKS:

A38

RATIONALE

After careful review of basic recommendation and accompanying eyewitness
statement, the Senior MACV Awards Board agreed that the criteria for award
of the Medal of Honor has been fulfilled. Although seriously wounded and
additionally hampered with blurred vision, Captain Jacobs somehow found
physical strength to extract numerous wounded and dead from a battlefield
alive with devasting fire. His gallant feats were accomplished single-
handedly and without fear or concern for his own well being. The Awards
Board contends that this officer earned, is deserving of, and should be
awarded the Medal of Honor.

APPENDIX C:

Claim for Compensation for Ex-Slave: Brent Woods

CLAIM FOR COMPENSATION FOR ENLISTED SLAVE.

No.

I, *Edward Riden jr.* a loyal citizen, and a resident of *Baltimore*, County of , State of *Maryland*, hereby claim compensation, under the provisions of Section 24, Act approved February 24, 1864, and Section 2, Act approved July 28, 1866, for my slave *Cato or Decatur Dorsey*, enlisted 186 , at , by Regiment U. S. Colored Tro. ; Co. ; certificate of which enlistment and a descriptive list, as required, accompany this application.

In proof of my loyalty to the Constitution and Government of the United States, I present the accompanying oath, which I have taken, signed and acknowledged; to be filed with this application, in accordance with requirement of General Orders, No. 329, 1863, War Department, Adjutant General's Office.

Edward Riden Jr

January 31, 186 7

test

Gideon Herbert)

OATH OF ALLEGIANCE.

I, *Edward Riden jr*, the owner and claimant, do solemnly swear that the foregoing claim is a just and true claim due to me as master and owner of the said slave, and that the facts alleged in said claim in respect to the draft or enlistment (*as the case may be*) of said slave into the military service of the United States are true. And I do further swear that I have never joined, *or been concerned in, any insurrection* or rebellion; *that I have never borne arms against the United States; that I have never given any aid, countenance, counsel or encouragement* to any person or persons engaged, or whom I had reason to believe were about to engage, in insurrection, rebellion or armed hostility *against the United States;* that I have neither sought, nor accepted, nor attempted to exercise the functions of any office, civil or military, nor to perform any service whatever, under any authority or pretended authority in hostility to the United States; that I have not yielded a voluntary support to any insurrection, rebellion or pretended government, authority, power or constitution within the United States hostile thereto. And I do further swear that, to the best of my knowledge and ability, I have supported and defended, and will continue to support and defend, the United States *against all enemies, foreign and domestic; and that I have supported, defended and obeyed, and will continue to support, defend and obey, the Constitution and laws of the United States;* that I will bear true faith and allegiance to the same; and that I take this oath freely, without any mental reservation or purpose of evasion: So help me God.

Edward Riden Jr

Sworn to and subscribed before me, at *Crownsville*, this *31st* day of *January*, 186 7

Gideon Herbert

A40

APPENDIX D:

Denied Medal of Honor Recommendation: Freddie Stowers

Headquarters 371st Infantry, U.S.
Secteur Postal 239, France.
December 28thh 1918.

The following named man of this regiment is recommended for the Medal of Honor,

Corporal Freddie Stowers, C Co., 1872491. (Deceased)

For extraordinary heroism in an attack on Hill 188, Champagne Sector, Sept. 28th, 1918. Corporal Stowers showed remarkable bravery under terrific machine gun and shell fire, disregarding personal danger. He helped to kill the enemy in a machine gun nest and after being mortally wounded kept crawling ahead in the face of terrific machine gun fire and urging the members of his squad to go forward until he died. Nearest relative : Pearl Stowers (Wife) Sandy Springs, South Carolina, U.S.

Certificate.
I certify that I have personal knowledge as an eye witness of the facts stated above in the recommendation for medal of honor of Corporal Freddie Stowers, C Co., 371st Infantry, and that the above statement is true.

Name   ,   Rank   Organization.

NO WHERE CAN IT BE FOUND THAT ANY ACTION WAS TAKEN ON THIS.

Filed 4-0-30. A. G. 314. 73-371 Inf. 4-0-30,

A41

Headquarters 371st Infantry, U.S.
Secteur Postal 229, France.
December 28th, 1918.

The following named man of this regiment is recommended for the Medal of Honor:

Private Burton Holmes, Co. C, 1872566 (Deceased)

For extraordinary heroism in an attack in the Champagne sector, Hill 188 Sept. 28th, 1918. Pvt. Holmes after his automatic rifle was out of commission and he himself badly wounded, returned to the company's headquarters of his own volition, got a reserve automatic rifle, went back and fired with it on the enemy until he was killed. This happened under heavy machine gun and shell fire. Nearest relative Bill Holmes, (Uncle) Clemson College, South Carolina, U.S.A.

Certificate.

I certify that I have personal knowledge as an eye witness of the facts stated above in the recommendation for medal of honor of Pvt. Burton Holmes, Co. C, 371st Infantry, and that the above statement is true.

PAGE 668

APPROVED AS DSC

Name Rank Organization

Filed ~~1-9-~~30. A. G. 3[illegible].73-371 Inf. ~~1-9-30~~

The following named officers and men of this regiment are recommended for
the Distinguished Service Cross.

1st Lt. James A. Boswell, Co. D. (Deceased)

Commanding Co. D. For extraordinary heroism displayed in the presence of deadly
artillery and machine gun fire on Hill 188, Sept. 28th, 1918. Lt. Boswell's
company was ordered to execute a flank attack on an enemy machine gun nest in
order to relieve Co. C which had attacked the enemy in front. Before taking his
company into position, Lt. Boswell crawled out to make a personal reconnaissance
of the enemy's position and in so doing fell mortally wounded from machine gun
fire. He was a splendid leader and never failed to inspire courage in his
officers and men by his personal disregard of danger. Nearest relative—Dr. F.A.
Boswell, (Father) Elmore, Alabama, U.S.A.

1st Lt. Marcus H. Boulware, Co. D.

Commanding Co. D. For exceptional heroism and high sense of duty displayed
while his company was in action between Hill 188 and Alim Creek, from Sept.
28th, 1918 to Oct. 6th, 1918, inclusive. The commander of Company D fell
mortally wounded during the afternoon of Sept. 28th, 1918 while the company
was about to execute a flanking movement. Lt. Boulware immediately took command
and succeeded in driving the enemy out of a strong position and capturing a
battery of five trench mortars and two machine guns. During the afternoon of
Sept. 29th, 1918, Co. D was subjected to a terrible artillery bombardment for
two hours during which time the company lost one officer and more than twenty
men. The company moved forward again during the morning of Sept. 30th, 1918
through a heavy artillery and machine gunbarrage over a flooded area during
which time it suffered heavily. From Oct. 1 to Oct. 6th, 1918 the regiment was
in reserve and Co. D was held in shell holes in an exposed position and frequently subjected to effective artillery fire. During this entire period Lt.
Boulware commanded his company so skillfully and treated the element of personal
danger with such utter disregard that he inspired the members of his command
with much the same spirit of courage and so maintained a high degree of morale
during this long period of continuous danger and hardship, although he was sick fro
exposure and had a high fever for three days. He refused to be evacuated until his
company was relieved. Nearest relative—Mrs. M. H. Boulware, (Mother) Winnsboro,
South Carolina, U.S.A.

Captain Robert L. Brunson, Comdg AB.

For exceptional courage and endurance displayed while in action between Hill
188 and Alim Creek from Sept. 28th to Oct. 6th, 1918, inclusive. On Sept. 28th,
1918, Co. B was ordered to relieve Co. C after the latter company had suffered so
heavily in men and officers that it was almost completely disorganized. Captain
Brunson showed such a fine spirit of courage, good judgement and absolute disregar
of personal danger that he was able to outflank a very powerful machine gun nest
and either kill or capture the defenders with their guns. During the afternoon of
Sept. 29th, 1918, Co. D was subjected to a terrific bombardment of hostile artillery for two hours during which time it lost more than twenty-five men; but so well
had this company been held together that it was able to move forward immediately

A43

in approach formation when ordered to take up a new position. On the morning
of Sept. 30th, 1918, the battalion moved forward again through a terrific
artillery and machine gun barrage during which Co. B suffered heavily in men
and lost two officers. In spite of this the company reached its objective well
organized. From Octo. 1st to Oct. 6th, 1918, the regiment was in support.
During this period Co. B was frequently subjected to effective artillery fire
but due to Captain Brunson's fine spirit he so encouraged his men that they
came out of the action in a high state of morale despite the fact that the company had lost half its strength. Nearest relative-Mrs. Robert L. Brunson (wife)
Florence,South Carolina, U.S.A.

2nd Lieutenant Robert H. Riggs, Co. C. (Deceased)

For extraordinary heroism in action on Hill 188, Sept. 28th, 1918. Lt. Riggs
led his platoon with remarkable coolness and disregard of personal danger against
a very strong enemy position under terrific machine and shell fire. The following
day he led his platoon with the same coolness through a terrific artillery bombardment until mortally wounded. Nearest relative-Mrs. Ida L. Riggs, Dobson, N.

1st Lieutenant Carlos C. Harris, Co. C.

For extraordinary heroism in action on Hill 188 Sept. 28th, 1918. Lt. Harris
led his platoon with remarkable coolness and disregard of personal danger against
a very strong enemy position under a terrific machine gun and shell fire. The
following day he led his platoon with the same coolness through a
terrific artillery bombardment until seriously wounded. Nearest relative-Mrs.
J.W. Harris, Route 3, Spartanburg, South Carolina, U.S.A. (Mother)

2nd Lieutenant Benjamin F. Simmons, Co. B.

This officer led his platoon into action at Hill 188 on the morning of Sept.
28th, 1918. Though his platoon suffered very heavy losses he led them forward to
the enemy lines. He led his platoon through very heavy artillery fire on the
afternoon of Sept. 29th in meadow north of Bussy Farm. He kept his platoon in
hand at all times and showed a cheerful disregard of danger that was most inspir
to his men. He was seriously wounded on the morning of Sept. 30th in the
advance on Monthois and while lying in a wounded condition where shells were con
tinually falling showed wonderful coolness and fortitude. Nearest relative-
Mrs. C. E. Smith (Mother) Reevesville, South Carolina, U.S.A.

1st Lieutenant Thomas D. Lake, Jr. Co. B (Deceased)

This officer, second in command, was in battle with his company at Hill 188
Sept. 28th, 1918. He showed great courage and ability. He was again under very
heavy artillery fire in the meadow near Bussy Farm on the afternoon of Sept. 29
That night he led a patrol to the enemy's lines with wonderful coolness and dis
regard of personal danger and was an inspiration to the entire company. This
officer was killed in action on the morning of Sept. 30th, 1918 in the meadow
near Askin Creek near the village of Mininmoya while advancing with the compan
Nearest relative-Mr. T. D. Lake, Lawrens, South Carolina, U.S.A.

1st Lieutenant Sam D. Turtletaub, Machine Gun Co. (Deceased)

For extraordinary heroism displayed in the face of deadly artillery and machi
gun fire at Hill 188 Sept. 28th, 1918. After repeated efforts had been made to
place a machine gun so as to be able to return the fire of the enemy machine
guns and all had failed, Lt. Turtletaub requested permission to make another
effort to get a gun into position, and while doing so he fell mortally wounded.

Lt. Turtletaub had frequently showed a fine spirit of courage and daring and was a great inspiration to the members of his platoon. Nearest relative- Jacob Turtletaub, 86 Vanderhoist St., Charleston, South Carolina, U.S.A.

1st Lieutenant Monette C. Ford, Co. B.

Lt. Ford led his platoon into action at Hill 168, Champagne Sector, France, on the morning of Sept. 28th, 1918 and went forward to the enemy line thru heavy machine gun and artillery fire. Though in this advance the platoon suffered many casualties, Lt. Ford set an example of bravery that inspired his men to follow him. On the afternoon of Sept. 29th, 1918, Lt. Ford and his platoon were again under heavy fire and again on Sept. 30th, 1918 along the Aine Creek, when he again displayed great courage and under the most trying circumstances. Oct. 2nd to Oct. 6th, 1918 while the company was in support though still under fire, Lt. Ford became sick and could scarcely speak above a whisper but he refused to go to the rear and remained with his platoon until relieved. Nearest relative- Mr. H. B. Ford, Centerville, Mississippi, U.S.A.

2nd Lieutenant Cherry Steele, Co. B

This officer led his platoon into action at Hill 188 on the morning of Sept. 28th, 1918 and again on the afternoon of Sept. 29th, 1918 across the meadow near Bussy Farm when he was subjected to terrific artillery fire. On Sept. 30th, 1918, in the advance on Monthois, this officer showed unusual bravery and efficiency in keeping his platoon together while under heavy fire. He also displayed excellent judgement in marching his platoon on the morning of Sept. 30th, 1918 and placing it so as to suffer a minimum loss from shell fire. While the company was in support Lt. Nat Steele became sick with cold and fever and refused to be evacuated. Nearest relative-Mr. G. M. Steele, (Father) Obrion, Tenn. U.S.A.

Private Harton Holmes, Co. C, 1872566, (Deceased)

~~For extraordinary heroism in an attack in the Champagne Sector Hill 188 Sept. 28th, 1918, Pvt. Holmes after his automatic rifle was out of commission and he himself badly wounded, returned to the company's headquarters of his own volition got a reserve automatic rifle, went back and fired with it on the enemy until he was killed. This happened under heavy machine gun and shell fire. Nearest relative Bill Holmes, (Uncle) Anderson, South Carolina, U.S.A.~~
~~Clemson College.~~

~~Corporal Franklin Stomers, C Co, 1872472, (Deceased)~~

~~For extraordinary heroism in an attack on Hill 168 Sept. 20th, 1918, Corporal Stomers showed remarkable bravery under terrific machine gun and shell fire, disregarding personal danger. He helped to kill the enemy in a machine gun nest, and after being mortally wounded kept crawling ahead in the very face of terrific machine gun fire and urging the members of his squad to go forward until he died. Nearest relative-Pearl Stomers (wife) Sandy Springs, South Carolina, U.S.A.~~

Private Monroe Jones, C Co. 1872578.

During the attack of Sept. 28th, 1918, on Hill 188 Pvt. Monroe Jones crawled forward from his position together with three other enlisted men of the 372nd Inf., and flanked a position that was held by eight enemy machine gunners, killed three and captured the remaining five of the occupants together with their guns. Nearest relative-William Jones (Brother) R.F.D.1, Troy, South Carolina, U.

CORP. SANDY E. JONES. Co C, 371 INF

...Co. 1872473.

...and initiative displayed in the ...reorganizing
...its officers and most of the noncommissioned officers had
...on Hill 188, Champagne Sector, Sept. 28th and 29th, 1918.
...very heavy losses suffered by Co. C it had become badly broken
...Corporal Jones collected the scattered elements of his
...reorganized them under extremely difficult circumstances due to the
...effective hostile artillery fire. Corporal Jones was company clerk and had
...left in the rear in charge of company records and as soon as he learned that
...his company officers had been killed or wounded he came forward of his own
volition and joined the company; from Sept. 30th, to Oct. 6th, 1918, he made
numerous trips over shell swept areas collecting the scattered elements of his
company. Nearest relative-J.F.Jones, (Father) Sumter, South Carolina, U.S.A.

Private Reuben Burrell, Machine Gun Co. 1794075

Disregarded personal danger by carrying numerous messages across areas swept by
the enemy's machine guns and artillery fire on Hill 188 Sept. 28th, 1918 and by his
fine spirit of courage served as an example to other members of the group. He was
painfully wounded in the knee by a bursting shell on Sept. 30th, 1918 but refused
to be evacuated, as he said there would not be enough men left in the group if
he went to the rear. Nearest relative-Nathan Burrell (Father) Sundena, Virginia,
U.S.A.

Private Robert Tilghman, Machine Gun Co. 1794410.

Disregarded personal danger and carried numerous messages to company commanders
across shell swept areas on Hill 188 Sept. 28th, 1918. He was seriously wounded
in the leg by a bursting shell on Sept. 29th, 1918 and had to be evacuated although
he begged to be allowed to continue with the group. Nearest relative-Carrie Tilghman,
Mother) 135 N 35th Street, Philadelphia, Pa. U.S.A.

Sergeant Chris J. Blasingame, B Co. 1872247.

At Hill 188 Sept. 28th, to 30th, 1918.Though sick and having a high fever he
stayed with his platoon for four days under heavy fire until relieved. Nearest
relative-Emma Blasingame (Wife) Liberty, South Carolina, U.S.A.

Sergeant Raymond Collins, B Co. 1872246.

At Hill 188, Bussy Farm and Alin Creek, Sept. 28th to 30th, 1918. Though sick
and having a high fever he remained on duty with his platoon, thereby setting a
fine example to his men. Nearest relative-Hannah Collins, (Mother) R.F.D. 3,
Manley, South Carolina, U.S.A.

1st Class Private Jerome Young, B Co. 1872422.

At Hill 188, Bussy Farm and along Alin Creek Sept. 30th to Oct. 6th, 1918. Though
his feet were so sore swollen he could scarcely walk, this man refused to go to the
rear and remained with his company, thereby setting a fine example of bravery and

Headquarters 371st Infantry, U.S.
Secteur Postal 227, France.

November 25th, 1918.

From: Commanding Officer, 371st Infantry, U.S.

To: The Adjutant General, American E. F.

Subject: Recommendations for award of Distinguished Service Crosses.

1. Attached in duplicate are recommendations from this regiment for award of Distinguished Service Crosses for officers and men. Recommendations are also submitted for award of Distinguished Service Crosses to French Personnel attached to the regiment and for one deserving case of a Y.M.C.A. Secretary who is on duty with the regiment.

P. L. MILES,
Colonel, 371st Infantry, U.S.

Origin of the attached
M.C.O. resp.
F.F. 210 S 2 P 7.
(11-27-18)

A47

SELECT BIBLIOGRAPHY/
RECOMMENDED READING

Beyer, W. F. & O. F. Keydel. *Deeds of Valor.* New York: Longmeadow Books, 1994.

Gumpertz, Sydney G. *The Jewish Legion of Valor: The Story of Jewish Heroes in the Wars of the Republic.* Self-published, 1934.

Hardy, Gordon (ed.) *Above and Beyond: A History of the Medal of Honor from the Civil war to Vietnam.* Boston: Boston Publishing Co., 1985

Lemon, Peter C. *Beyond the Medal: A Journey from Their Hearts to Yours.* Golden, CO: Fulcrum, 1997.

McChristian, Douglas. *The U. S. Army in the West, 1870 – 1880.* Norman: University of Oklahoma Press, 1995.

O'Neil, Bill. *Fighting Men of the Indian Wars.* Western Publications, 1992.

Proft, R. J. (ed.) *United States of America's Congressional Medal of Honor Recipients.* Columbia Heights, MN: Highland House, 1998.

Ward, Geoffrey C. *The Civil War.* New York: Alfred A. Knopf, 1990.

Lee, Irvin H. Negro Medal of Honor Men New York: Dodd, Mead, 1967

Smith, Larry. *Beyond Glory: Extraordinary Stories of Courage from World War 2 to Vietnam War.*

Wallace, Mike. *Medal of Honor: Profiles of American Military Heroes from the Civil War to the Present.* New York: Artisan Press.

Jordan, Kenneth N. *Yesterday's Heroes: 433 Men of world War II Awarded the Medal of Honor 1941-1945.*

Del Calzo, Nick & Collier, Peter. *Medal of Honor: portraits of Valor Beyond the call of Duty.* New York: Artisan.

Wesley, Charles H & Patricia W. Romero. *Afro-Americans in the Civil War, from Slavery to Citizenship.* Pennsylvania: The Publishers Agency, Inc., 1978.

INDEX OF RECIPIENTS

Muranaga, Kiyoshi K
Nakae, Masato
Jimenez, Jose F
Keith, Miguel
Lopez, Baldomero
Lopez, Jose M
Lozada, Carlos J
Martinez, Benito
Martinez, Joe P
Obregon, Eugene A
Ortega, John
Perez, Manuel
Rascon, Alfred V
Rocco, Louis
Rodriguez, Cleto
Rodriguez, Joseph C
Rubio, Euripides
Ruiz, Alejandro R
Santiago-Colon, Hector
Silva, France
Valdez, Jose F
Vargas, Sando M
Villegas, Ysmael R
Yabes, Maximo

JEWISH RECIPIENTS

Cohn, Abraham
Gardner, Charles
Gause, Isaac
Geiger, George
Gross, Samuel
Gumpertz, Sydney G
Heller, Henry
Jachman, Isadore S
Jacobs, Jack H
Karpeles, Leopold
Kaufman, Benjamin
Levitow, John L
Levy, Benjamin
Orbansky, David

Holland, Milton M
James, Miles
James, Willy F
Jenkins, Robert H
Joel, Lawrence
John, John
Johnson, Dwight H
Johnson, Henry
Johnson, Ralph H
Johnson, William
Jordan, George
Kelly, Alexander
Langhorn, Garfield M
Lawson, John
Lee, Fitz
Leonard, Matthew
Long, Donald R
Mays, Isaiah
McBryar, William
Mifflin, James
Noil, Joseph
Olive, Milton L
Paine, Adam
Payne, Isaac
Pease, Joachim
Penn, Robert
Pinn, Robert
Pitts, Riley L
Ratcliff, Edward
Rivers, Ruben
Rogers, Charles C
Sanderson, Aaron
Sargent, Rupert L
Sasser, Clarence E
Shaw, Thomas
Sims, Clifford C
Nakamine, Shinyei
Nakamura, William K
Nishimoto, Joe M
nisperos, jose

Ohata, Allan M
Okubo, James K
Okutsu, Yukio
Otani, Kazuo
PILILAAU,
Sakato, George T
Tanouye, Ted T
Trinidad, Telesforo
Wai, Francis B
YANO,

FEMALE RECIPIENT
Walker, Mary

HISPANIC/LATINO RECIPIENTS
Adams, Lucian
Baca, John P
Barkeley, David B
Bazaar, Philip
Benavidez, Roy P
De Castro, Joseph H
De La Garza, Emilio A
Dias, Ralph E
Fernandez, Daniel
Garcia, Fernando
Garcia, Marcario
Gomez, Edward
Gonsalves, Harold
Gonzales, David M
Gonzalez, Alfredo
Guillen, Ambrosio
Hernandez, Rodolfo P
Herrera, Silvestre S
Salomon, Ben L
Sawelson, William
Shuler, Simon
Tibor, Rubin
Zussman, Raymond

NATIVE AMERICAN RECIPIENTS
Alchesay, William
Banquet,
Barefoot, Van T
Childers, Ernest
Chiquito,
Co-Rux-Chod-Ish,
Elsatsoosu,
Evans, Ernest
George, Charles
Harmon, Roy
Harvey, Raymond
Jim,
Kosoha,
Machol,
Montgomery, Jack C
Nannasaddie,
Nantaje,
Red Cloud, Mitchell
Reese, John
Rowdy,

ABOUT THE AUTHOR

An army brat, John Johnson was born in Seoul, South Korea, where his father was stationed with the US. Army. Currently residing in Atlanta, John is a retired educator, small businessman, and writer.

REFERENCES & ENDNOTES

1. African American recipient Robert Sweeney received two Medals of Honor.

2. Some sources list 22 Natives Americans as having received the Medal of Honor, while others list 18. The discrepancy is related to Medal of Honor recipients Factor, Paine, Ward, and Payne, men whose ethnicity was most probably African American, but were members of the Seminole Indian tribe when they were recruited by the army as scouts. Due to the ambiguous nature of their ethnicity, the Congressional Medal of Honor Society in conjunction with the Department of Defense have placed their names under two ethnic categories: African American and Native American.

3. The actual number of Jewish recipient is 17 as opposed to 18. The discrepancy is related to recipient Simon Shuler who entered and deserted the army, only to reenlist under an assumed name (Charles Gardner). During his term of enlistment as Charles Gardner, he received the Medal of Honor. When the deception was discovered by the army, they decided to list the award under both names (Shuler and Gardner). Sources: U.S. Department of Defense, Congressional Medal of Honor Society, U.S. Army, U.S. Navy, U.S. Air Force, U.S. Marine Corps.

4. This source of this information was the Department of Defense, which prepared and published the data.

5. All citations were prepared and published by the Department of Defense and is part of the official record.

6. Courtesy of St. Lawrence County, NY Branch, AAUW researched and published Women of Courage, Ten North Country Pioneers in Profile

7. Recipient data file, CMOHS Archives.

8. Letter dated 5 May 1995 from Raymond Collins of the Medal of Honor Historical Society.

9. Handwritten notes in the CMOHS files .

10. Preston Amos, *The Facts About the Birthplace of Robert Blake.*

11. Lee, Irvin H. *Negro Medal of Honor Men New York:* Dodd, Mead, 1967

12. Notes found in the CMOHS archives.

13. Handwritten notes in the CMOHS files.

14. Company muster and pay book of the 5th US Colored Troops.

15. Handwritten notes in the CMOHS files.

16. Handwritten notes in the CMOHS files.

17. Letter of 1968 from Rudolf Friederich to Natchez Cemetery superintendent David Corson. Corson confirmed Brown was a "negro."

18 Rick Reaves, *The Old Flag Never Touched the Ground* (publication data unavailable)

19 Recipient data file, CMOHS Archives.

20 Unknown author, *Union County Dispatch*, 21 May 1984.

21 Preston Amos, "A Short Biography of Christian Fleetwood," undated manuscript.

22 Recipient data file, CMOHS Archives.

23 Ibid.

24 Ibid.

25 Unknown newspaper article in CMOHS Archives.

26 Recipient data file, CMOHS Archives.

27 Ibid.

28 Handwritten notes in CMOHS files.

29 Recipient data file, CMOHS Archives.

30 Ibid.

31 Ibid.

32 Ibid.

33 *Lafayette Journal and Courier,* Staff Reports, 17 January 2001.

34 55th Massachusetts Regiment Enlistment Record.

35 Handwritten notes in CMOHS files.

36 Ibid.

37 Ibid.

38 Ibid.

39 Recipient data file, CMOHS Archives.

40 Excerpts from Raymond J. Albert, research paper, n.d., n.p., CMOHS Archives.

41 Recipient data file, CMOHS Archives.

42 Handwritten notes in CMOHS files.

43 Recipient data file, CMOHS Archives.

44 Ibid.

45 Ibid.

46 Jim Reis, Untitled, undated news clipping, CMOHS Archives.

47 Letter dated 1973 from Dr. Charles M. Neal, state director of the Medal of Honor Roundtable.

48 Handwritten notes in CMOHS files.

49 Blog (1997) about deceased Buffalo soldiers from the Baltimore area.

50 Recipient data file, CMOHS Archives.

51 Ward, W.C. 782-965: Letter from Department of Interior, US Indian Service, Pueblo and Jicarilla Agency, 27 March 1897.

52 Recipient data file, CMOHS Archives.

53 Ibid.

54 Lee, Irvin H. *Negro Medal of Honor Men New York:* Dodd, Mead, 1967

55 Medal citation provided by the Department of Defense.

56 Recipient data file, CMOHS Archives.
57 *Herald-Mail*, 7 December 1997.
58 Ibid.
59 Recipient data file and handwritten notes, CMOHS Archives.
60 Ibid.
61 Ibid.
62 Ibid.
63 Ibid.
64 Ibid.
65 Ibid.
66 Ibid.
67 Ibid.
68 Ibid.
69 Ibid.
70 Ibid.
71 Letter, 25 September 1979, from a Veterans Administration official in response to an inquiry.
72 Frank Schubert, *Black Valor*. (publication data available).
73 Recipient data file, CMOHS Archives.
74 SFC Darrell Cochran, Soldier Magazine, n.d.
75 Department of the Army, press conference transcripts, n.d.
76 Press Release, The White House, (date issued available)
77 *Post and Courier*, 12 January 1997.
78 Newspaper article of unknown origin, CMOHS Archives.
79 Recipient data file, CMOHS Archives.
80 *Stars and Stripes*, 6 November 2001.
81 Recipient data file, CMOHS Archives.
82 Ibid.
83 Lee, Irvin H.. *Negro Medal of Honor Men* New York: Dodd, Mead, 1967
84 Bill Archer, untitled article, CMOHS Archives.
85 Recipient data file, CMOHS Archives.
86 Handwritten notes, CMOHS Archives, possibly from Al Rutledge, *A Splendid Soldier* (pub data?).
87 Ibid.
88 Recipient data file, CMOHS Archives.
89 *Navy Times*, 4 September 1968
90 *The State*, 2 June 1985
91 Home of Heroes website, http://www.homeofheroes.com/.
92 Recipient data file, CMOHS Archives.
93 DoD Press Release, n.d.
94 News release, HQMC, 20 April 1970.
95 Recipient data file, CMOHS Archives.
96 Ibid.

[97] Ibid.

[98] *The Times,* 11 November 1996.

[99] Untitled article, CMOHS Archives.

[100] Ibid.

[101] John Nordheimer, "Death of a Troubled Soldier," *New York Times,* 25 May 1971.

[102] Recipient data file, CMOHS Archives.

[103] Ibid.

[104] Ibid.

[105] Undated, unidentified news clipping.

[106] Ibid.

[107] John McDonald, *Newsday,* 18 May 1983.

[108] Recipient data file, CMOHS Archives.

[109] Ibid.

[110] Ibid

[111] *National Enquirer,* 12 September 1970.

[112] Recipient data file, CMOHS Archives.

[113] *Philadelphia New Observer,* 8 May 1996, Helen Blue; *Philadelphia Inquirer,* n.d., Wayne Dawkins

[114] Recipient data file, CMOHS Archives.

[115] Army Times, 22 July 1970.

[116] Recipient data file, CMOHS Archives.

[117] 11 March 1969, unidentified news clipping.

[118] Department of the Army, Statement of Military Record, undated.

[119] Ibid.

[120] Recipient data file, CMOHS Archives.

[121] Ibid.

[122] Ibid.

[123] Ibid.

[124] Ibid.

[125] Unreferenced newspaper article.

[126] Scott Sunde, article, *Seattle Post-Intelligencer Reporter,* 2001.

[127] Ibid.

[128] Recipient data file, CMOHS Archives.

[129] Excerpts from *DROP*, Spring 1999, publication of the Special Forces Association

[130] USMC News Release, July 1974, CMOHS Archives.

[131] Untitled newspaper article.

[132] Recipient data file, CMOHS Archives.

[133] Ibid.

[134] Ibid.

[135] Untitled newspaper article.

[136] Recipient data file, CMOHS Archives.

[137] Ibid.

[138] Ibid.

[139] Biographical data sheet, July 1971, HQMC.

[140] CMOHS Archives.

[141] Ibid.

[142] Ibid.

[143] Ibid.

[144] Ibid.

[145] Untitled newspaper article.

[146] Excerpts from the Korean War Veterans Association obituary,

[147] Untitled newspaper article.

[148] Recipient data file, CMOHS Archives.

[149] Untitled newspaper article.

[150] Recipient data file, CMOHS Archives of the.

[151] *Mesa Tribune,* 19 July 19, 1973.

[152] Copy of death certificate, CMOHS Archives.

[153] Excerpts of a draft article about Alchesay by Frank Tyndall.

[154] Recipient data file, CMOHS Archives.

[155] Letter and research notes of Frank Tyndall of the Medal of Honor History Roundtable, Arizona Chapter.

[156] Recipient data sheet, CMOHS Archives.

[157] Ibid.

[158] Ibid.

[159] Ibid.

[160] Ibid.

[161] Ibid.

[162] Ibid.

[163] Ibid.

[164] Biographical sketch, CMOHS Archives, author unknown.

[165] Recipient data file, CMOHS Archives.

[166] Ward, W.C. 782-965: Letter from Department of Interior, US Indian Service, Pueblo and Jicarilla Agency, 27 March 1897.

[167] Recipient data file, CMOHS Archives.

[168] Ibid.

[169] *Retired Officers Magazine,* October 1994.

[170] Recipient data file, CMOHS Archives.

[171] *Muskogee Daily Phoenix,* 2 November 1991.

[172] Recipient data file, CMOHS Archives.

[173] 7th Infantry Division press release, n.d.

[174] Letter from Pam, Harvey's wife, updating his biography in the CMOHS Archives.

[175] Excerpts from an article in the *Banner-Journal,* 4 April 1951.

[176] Recipient data file, CMOHS Archives.

[177] Ibid.

[178] Gumpertz, Sydney G. The Jewish Legion of Valor: The Story of Jewish Heroes in the Wars of the Republic. (SELF-PUBLISHED, 1934).

[179] Obituary in unidentified newspaper, 5 June 1897.

[180] Handwritten founds notes in archives, authors unknown.

[181] Handwritten archival notes, author unknown.

[182] Handwritten notes and letters from Larry Geiger.

[183] Recipient data file, CMOHS Archives.

[184] Ibid.

[185] Undated report prepared by Roxanne Albert and Raymond Albert of the Medical of Honor Society.

[186] Handwritten archival notes, author unknown.

[187] War Department Press release, 10 May 1945.

[188] Gumpertz, Sydney G. The Jewish Legion of Valor: The Story of Jewish Heroes in the Wars of the Republic. (SELF-PUBLISHED, 1934).

[189] Notes of the Jewish Historical Society of Baltimore.

[190] Notes of the Medal of Honor Society.

[191] Handwritten notes, CMOHS Archives.

[192] Gumpertz, Sydney G. The Jewish Legion of Valor: The Story of Jewish Heroes in the Wars of the Republic. (SELF-PUBLISHED, 1934).

[193] Recipient data file, CMOHS Archives.

[194] *Jewish Veteran*, April-May-June 1981.

[195] Gumpertz, Sydney G. The Jewish Legion of Valor: The Story of Jewish Heroes in the Wars of the Republic. (SELF-PUBLISHED, 1934).

[196] Obituary, *Trentonian* 6 February 1981.

[197] *Washington Times*, 4 July 2002.

[198] Ibid.

[199] *LA Times*, 27 May 2002.

[200] *Jewish Veteran*, July-August 1983.

[201] Ibid.

[202] Richard Goldstein, *New York Times*, 24 November 2000.

[203] Unit enlistment records, War Department.

[204] Death Certificate, City Health Department, Washington, DC.